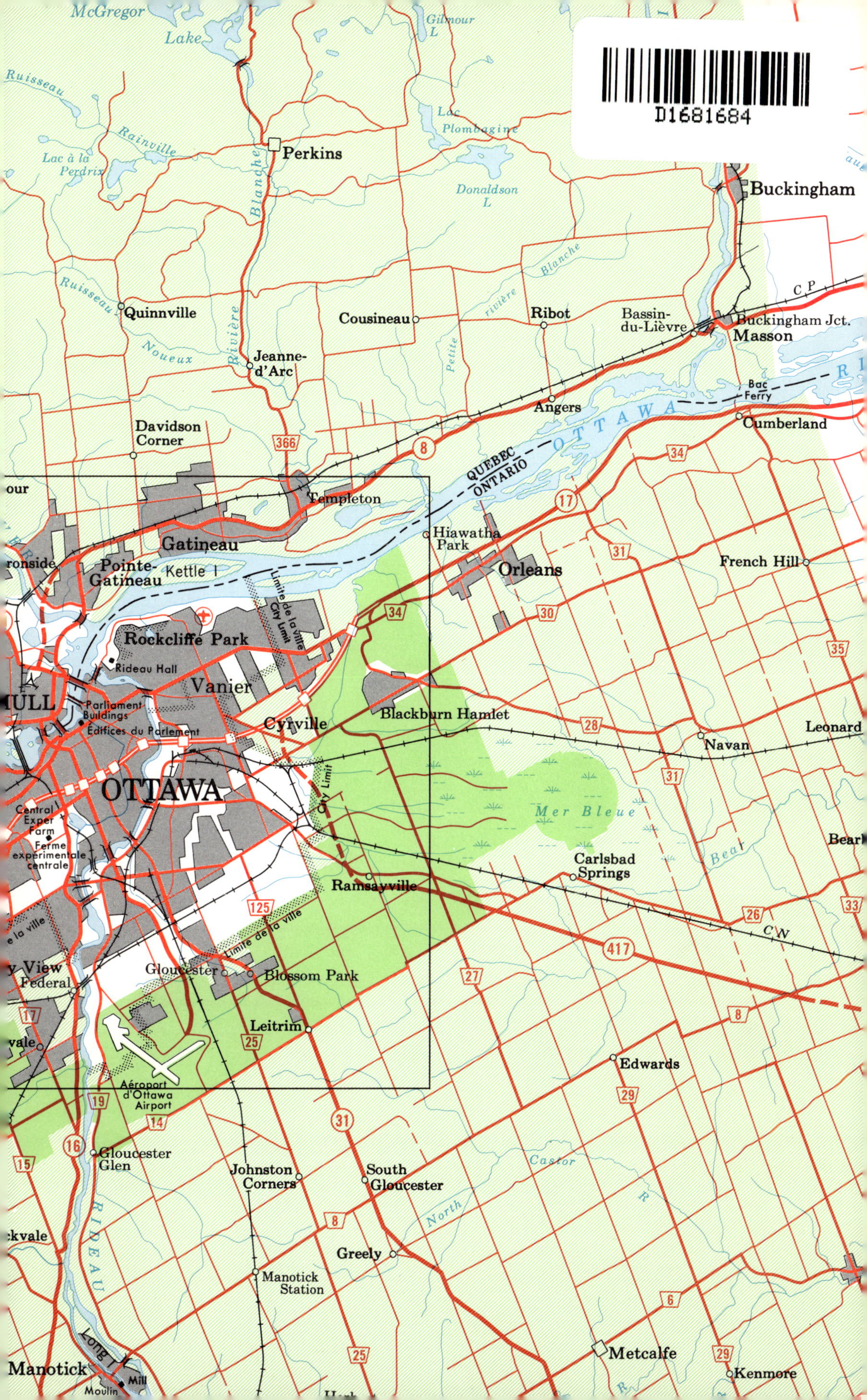

McGregor
Lake
Gilmour L
Ruisseau
Rainville
Lac à la Perdrix
Perkins
Lac Plombagine
Donaldson L
Buckingham
Blanche
Rivière Blanche
Ruisseau Noueux
Quinnville
Cousineau
Petite rivière Blanche
Ribot
Bassin-du-Lièvre
Buckingham Jct.
Masson
CP
Jeanne-d'Arc
Angers
Bac Ferry
Cumberland
Davidson Corner
366
8
QUEBEC
ONTARIO
OTTAWA
34
Templeton
17
Gatineau
Hiawatha Park
Pointe-Gatineau
Kettle I
Orleans
31
French Hill
Limite de la ville
City Limit
34
30
Rockcliffe Park
35
Rideau Hall
Vanier
HULL
Parliament Buildings
Édifices du Parlement
Cyrville
Blackburn Hamlet
28
Navan
Leonard
OTTAWA
City Limit
31
Central Exper Farm
Ferme expérimentale centrale
Mer Bleue
Carlsbad Springs
Bear
Ramsayville
125
26
33
CN
Limite de la ville
417
Federal
Gloucester
Blossom Park
27
17
8
Leitrim
25
Edwards
Aéroport d'Ottawa Airport
29
19
14
31
16
Gloucester Glen
15
Johnston Corners
South Gloucester
Castor
RIDEAU
North
8
Greely
Manotick Station
6
25
Metcalfe
29
Manotick
Long I
Mill
Moulin
Kenmore

THE CAPITAL OF CANADA: HOW SHOULD IT BE GOVERNED?

A Special Study on the National Capital

by

Douglas H. Fullerton

VOLUME I

Ottawa, Canada
May, 1974

Available by mail from Information Canada, Ottawa, K1A 0S9
and at the following Information Canada bookshops:

HALIFAX
1683 Barrington Street

MONTREAL
640 St. Catherine Street West

OTTAWA
171 Slater Street

TORONTO
221 Yonge Street

WINNIPEG
393 Portage Avenue

VANCOUVER
800 Granville Street

or through your bookseller

Price: $5.00 Catalogue No. CP22-874/1

Price subject to change without notice

Information Canada
Ottawa, 1974

Letter Advising Completion of the Study

May 16, 1974.

The Right Honourable P. E. Trudeau,
Prime Minister,
Parliament Buildings,
Ottawa.

Mr. Prime Minister:

I am happy to inform you that my study on the governing of the National Capital, which was commissioned by you a year ago, has now been completed in typescript form. However, at this stage copies are only available in English. We have had good cooperation from the translators of the Privy Council Office, but revisions in the past month have meant some time lag in completing the translation into French. I understand that you would prefer to defer receiving the report until both language versions are available in final form, suitable for general distribution.

While my task of preparing the report that you commissioned is now officially completed, I shall be staying on to see the two language versions through to the publication stage. I would expect that the printed volumes would be available towards the end of July.

Should you wish to receive the report in typescript in English, I should be delighted to send it to you at any time.

Yours sincerely,

Douglas H. Fullerton.

Foreword

On May 17th, 1973, Prime Minister Trudeau announced that Mr. Douglas H. Fullerton would be resigning his position as Chairman of the National Capital Commission to undertake a special study on the Capital for the Government.

The terms of reference were given in the press release as follows:

> to undertake a study of the most effective arrangements for the future administration of matters directly affecting the National Capital and its development, including the role of the National Capital Commission and its relation to other bodies concerned with the governing of the Capital Region and the coordination of those federal activities which bear upon the development of Region as a national capital

Mr. Fullerton served as Chairman of the NCC for nearly four years. Prior to that he had a career in both government and in business. In the early 1960's he was treasurer of the Canada Council and later set up his own firm of investment consultants; during this period his textbook *The Bond Market in Canada* was published. He also served as a financial and economic consultant to the Government of Quebec between 1962 and 1969. From 1966 to 1969 he wrote a syndicated weekly column for the Toronto Star and other Canadian newspapers, which he resumed in the summer of 1973. For a brief period from 1967, Mr. Fullerton was Chairman of the Cape Breton Development Corporation.

Because of his background, his special knowledge of the Capital, and his practical writing experience, the Government believed Mr. Fullerton to be uniquely qualified to undertake an analysis of the problems of governing the National Capital. The Study is a product of interviews and research carried out by Mr. Fullerton and his staff. The conclusions and recommendations are the responsibility of Mr. Fullerton alone, and are submitted to the federal and other interested governments for consideration.

Privy Council office

Preface

Residents of the Capital to-day are no doubt familiar with the background of my involvement in this Study. For readers of other times and places, I recount the circumstances in Chapter One. Although I was appointed as a one-man task force, I clearly could not do the job alone. However, I was determined to keep the staff small, since my own experience with study groups has been that the smaller they are the more productive they tend to be, and the sooner the task is done.

Because of my need for experienced help, I borrowed most of the permanent team from the National Capital Commission. Heading the list from the NCC was Mr. James Weld, my second in command. Our continuing exchange of opinions helped shape the Study, and his support in many other ways was invaluable to me. Our two-man research team combined the careful and painstaking work of Douglas Thompson (borrowed from the NCC) and André Guibord (on contract) who brought fresh insights and the journalist's flair, speed and questioning attitude. Mrs. Lorraine Dallas, my secretary, not only typed drafts at the speed of light, but ran the office, answered correspondence, and fielded questions in both languages. Mlle Louise Huot (Mr. Weld's secretary) and Mr. Gerald Reddy (general duties) helped in many ways to make the operation run smoothly. But perhaps of more importance than the contribution of any single member of the group was their good humour and ability to work harmoniously together.

The permanent staff was supplemented by the part-time assistance of a number of consultants. The contribution by Professor Donald Rowat of Carleton, a recognized authority in the study of the governing of capitals, was of particular value. He drafted one of the chapters and provided detailed and perceptive editorial comments on the remainder of the report. There were three other Carleton professors involved, David Falcone and R. J. Van Loon, who carried out the opinion survey, and Ken McRae who did a special report on education in the two languages. Mr. Murray Jones, a Toronto consultant with considerable experience in the restructuring of local government, participated as head of the group involved in most of the interviews, and prepared a special report. Mr. Raymond Poulin, a senior municipal employee, assisted in research work and also wrote a report. To all of these consultants I am very greatly indebted.

Apart from the permanent staff and the consultants, I have decided not to mention any other names because it would be invidious to do so. Political leaders—federal, provincial and municipal—received me and members of my staff most graciously, and to their eternal credit the vast majority did not speak to a brief or to special interest but as Canadians with an affection for their

Capital. I hope that the many hundreds of other people who have assisted us in so many ways will not be offended by a similar blanket note of appreciation. Their help ranged from that provided by several ambassadors in answer to specific questions, to public officials replying to requests, to the more than a hundred individuals who prepared submissions, and to the old friends who read and commented on draft chapters of the Study.

I would like to make specific reference to several organizations: the National Capital Commission, which supplied staff and facilities when it was itself hard pressed, and which made a contribution at all levels that can only be described as above and beyond the call of duty; the Privy Council Office, for clearing away administrative problems and enabling the team to concentrate on research and writing; the Department of Finance, where special staff expertise in technical matters was invaluable; Statistics Canada whose ability to find obscure facts and figures is miraculous; External Affairs for digging out information from their offices abroad; the Translation Bureau whose translators were both quick and patient; and finally the Department of Supply and Services, Printing Operations whose expert contribution is in the hands of the reader.

A few brief notes about the style of writing. It is somewhat more personal than that found in most government studies, for several reasons. One is that it is my own style; I prefer saying "I don't think it will work" to "There appears to be sufficient evidence available for one to conclude that it will not function properly". A second reason is that the report is written to be read by as wide a group of Canadians as possible, not just by officials. A personal style improves readability—and, as they say, "better read than dead". The third and perhaps most valid reason for the style is that in appointing me the government presumably wanted to obtain my personal opinions as well as my appraisal of the general situation and problems. The giving of opinions means either using the personal pronoun 'I' or 'my', or employing awkward circumlocutions of the kind noted above. However, I have tried throughout the Study to limit the first person to those instances when I am expressing my personal point of view; the use of 'we' is usually to convey the idea of a group (members of the team) judgment, or one which is based solely on objective criteria.

The English and French versions of the Study are printed separately, not together as in some government reports, because a combined document would add significantly to the expense without corresponding benefits. My final observation is the somewhat smug comment that I was happy to be able to finish the report within the one year target date, and within the original $150,000 budget (excluding costs of printing and translation). The opinions and conclusions in the main Study are of course my responsibility; those contained in the special research papers and reports in Appendices B and C are the responsibility of the individual authors.

D. H. Fullerton

Contents

VOLUME I

Page

PART THREE: Conclusions and Recommendations

VOLUME II

APPENDICES

APPENDIX A—Documentation

APPENDIX B—Research Papers and Studies

List of Tables

Glossary of Abbreviations Used Frequently in the Study

(With French Equivalents Shown)

ACFO	French Canadian Association of Ontario (Association canadienne-française de l'Ontario)
B & B	Royal Commission on Bilingualism and Biculturalism (Commission royale d'enquête sur le bilinguisme et le biculturalisme—B & B)
BC	Province of British Columbia (Province de la Colombie-Britannique—C-B)
BNA Act	British North America Act (l'Acte de l'Amérique du nord britannique—AANB); the act creating Canada, the constitution
CMA	Census Metropolitan Area (Région métropolitaine de recensement—RMR); as used by Statistics Canada
CMHC	Central Mortgage and Housing Corporation (Société centrale d'hypothèques et de logement—SCHL)
DBS	Dominion Bureau of Statistics (Bureau fédéral de la statistique—BFS); now called Statistics Canada
DPW	Department of Public Works (Ministère des travaux publics—MTP); sometimes called 'Public Works'
DREE	Department of Regional Economic Expansion (Expansion économique régionale—EER)
FLU	French Language Units (Unités de langue française—ULF)
FDC	Federal District Commission (Commission du district fédéral—CDF)
LHP	Limited Hiving Principle (Principe de la concentration raisonnable—PCR)
MNA	Member of the Quebec National Assembly (Député)
MP	Member of the Federal Parliament (Député)
MPP	Member of the Ontario Provincial Parliament (Deputé)
NC Act	National Capital Act (Loi sur la Capitale nationale)
NCC	National Capital Commission (Commission de la Capitale nationale—CCN)
NCR	National Capital Region (Région de la Capitale nationale—RCN)
ODC	Outaouais Development Corporation (Société d'aménagement de l'Outaouais—SAO)
OHATS	Ottawa-Hull Area Transportation Study (Étude du transport de la région d'Ottawa-Hull—ETROH)

OIC	Ottawa Improvement Commission (Commission d'embellissement d'Ottawa—CEO)
OMB	Ontario Municipal Board (Commission des affaires municipales de l'Ontario—CAMO)
ORC	Outaouais Regional Community (Communauté régionale de l'Outaouais—CRO)
ORCTC	Outaouais Regional Community Transit Commission (Commission de transport de la Communauté régionale de l'Outaouais—CTCRO)
RCMP	Royal Canadian Mounted Police (Gendarmerie royale du Canada—GRC)
RMOC	Regional Municipality of Ottawa-Carleton (Municipalité régionale de l'Ottawa-Carleton—MROC)
RSQ	Revised Statutes of Quebec (Statuts révisés du Québec—SRQ)

Part One

Descriptive and Historical

Chapter One

What this Study is About — A Personal Note

The building of a Capital of which the nation can be proud has been a task of many Canadians since Confederation. In physical terms their efforts have met with success, for the Capital to-day is both attractive to visitors and a good place in which to work and to live. Yet success in one area has been matched by failure in another; the past decade has seen the development in the Capital of one of the most complicated structures of local government in the world. It is with this structure, and with the problems it creates, that this Study is principally concerned.

The Capital falls short of expectations in another way. It is far from being the national symbol that many visionaries had hoped it would become—truly representative of the country, a reflection of its regional diversities and its cultural and linguistic values. We are a country desperately in need of unifying symbols, and a Capital in which all Canadians can feel pride could develop into such a symbol of nationhood.

However, the obstacles to national acceptance of the Capital are many: the physical remoteness from it of much of Canada; the limited number of Canadians who have seen their Capital; the westerner's traditional distrust of the east; the Maritimer's traditional chip on the shoulder about Upper Canada; Quebecers' resentment of English domination of the Capital; everyone's resentment about the Ottawa politicians who tax them and allegedly waste their money, and about the huge central bureaucracy which has developed. All this has posed quite a challenge for that federal agency, the National Capital Commission, enjoined by the National Capital Act "to prepare plans for and assist in the development, conservation and improvement of the National Capital Region in order that the nature and character of the seat of the Government of Canada may be in accordance with its national significance."[1]

It would be invidious to attempt to list the names of the many people since Confederation who cared enough about the Capital to support the spending of federal money to improve it, to draw plans for its future, and to implement those plans. However, the contribution of one man stands out, that of William Lyon

Mackenzie King. King was not the most popular of Canadian Prime Ministers, but his love affair with the Capital and with Gatineau Park, nurtured in his early years in Ottawa, led to decisions which shaped the growth of the Capital as we know it to-day. What King did, and what other prime ministers, ministers, parliamentarians, planners, and concerned public servants and citizens have done, before King and after him, is summarized in these pages.

The main concern of this Study, however, is not with the history of the Capital—interesting as it is—but with the problems inherent in its system of government. Of those problems, I believe that the most difficult and intractable are those which derive from the division of authority over the Capital among four levels of government, and among a multitude of federal departments. But let me explain the reasons for my own involvement.

I have lived in Ottawa during most of the years since 1940, and I acquired the average resident's views and prejudices about the city. However, on September 1, 1969, I became Chairman of the NCC, and was thrust into a more active role in the Capital's affairs. Although the work was satisfying in many ways, the rewards were more than matched by an increasing sense of frustration. As a result, in January 1973, I sought and obtained a meeting with the Prime Minister to tell him of my intention to resign the position I had then held for about $3\frac{1}{2}$ years. In partial explanation of my proposed action, I gave Mr. Trudeau a long memorandum containing my views about the problems of governing the Capital area, with particular emphasis on the role of the NCC.

I suggested in the memorandum, and in discussions with Mr. Trudeau, that the present situation could lead to increasing difficulties in the governing of the Region. The problems centred around growing jurisdictional conflicts and rivalries among various levels and bodies of government in the Region, and indeed among various departments and agencies of the federal government itself. I noted that these problems were not the sole responsibility of the federal government and the federal Parliament, since the constitution gives the responsibilities for municipal government to the provinces. However, if concerted action by all interested governments is to result, an important first step for the federal authorities would be to have a task force study the matter from the federal point of view; hopefully this would lead as quickly as possible to a more intensive public review of the question by a committee of the Commons or a joint Senate-Commons committee. Decisions taken by Parliament, as a result of conclusions by this committee, could then form the basis of negotiations with the provinces.

That's a rather condensed summary of my presentation to Mr. Trudeau; I ended up by offering to serve on any study the government would set up. He said he would consider the matter and within a few weeks I heard that the government was sympathetic to my proposals. The final decision was taken in May to entrust the study to me as a one-man task force. My resignation as Chairman of NCC was accepted effective May 31st, and the public announcement about the Study, which is printed in Appendix A-7, was released on May 17, 1973. I set up offices on June 1 at 45 Rideau Street, Ottawa.

Terms of Reference

The terms of reference cited in the foreword are worth repeating:

> ...to undertake a study of the most effective arrangements for the future administration of matters directly affecting the National Capital and its development, including the role of the National Capital Commission and its relation to other bodies concerned with the governing of the Capital Region and the coordination of those federal activities which bear upon the development of the Region as a national capital.

These are very broad terms, and anyone given a mandate to study the subject could not complain about them, except that they created the impression that tremendous powers were being vested in me to deliver authoritative answers to all the problems of the region, a task beyond any individual's capacity, the federal government's constitutional authority, or indeed my own inclination.

As the Study progressed, I found myself compelled to clarify and narrow the mandate, reiterating publicly and privately that the Study was essentially a fact-finding and opinion-finding mission, that it was mainly designed to provide useful information for the public and for the study by Parliament which would follow. In spite of the disclaimer, however, I found it difficult to dispel the idea in some quarters that I had full authority to reshape the Capital in any way I chose. This was flattering, but it invited resentment, and endangered the kind of free-wheeling discussion I was seeking.

There was a second problem with the terms of reference. They seemed so encompassing that many people and groups interested in submitting briefs didn't know where to begin in putting their views on paper. Thus our first advertisement seeking submissions produced a very limited response; it was not until October 5th, 1973, when we published locally a more informal invitation containing detailed questions (Appendix A-7) and simultaneously extended the deadline for briefs by two months, that the public began to respond. About 110 written submissions have been received, although most have been simply in the form of a letter.

Something else must be emphasized. This report concerns the *governing*, not the *planning*, of the area. Where planning matters are referred to, they are usually merely to illustrate or clarify jurisdictional or other related problems which have arisen. And if a subtitle is needed for this report it might well be "A study of power conflicts in the governing of the Capital". It never ceases to amaze me how reluctant politicians, bureaucrats, and even less exalted people are to discuss the acquisition or retention of power as motivation for their actions. Politicians will refer to the need for their party or government to be "returned to power" in order to implement its policies, but as for power for themselves—never! Yet it is the power game played in the Capital by politicians and officials at all levels which has contributed a great deal to the problems of governing the Region.

Public Hearings

The early misunderstanding about the scope of my mandate also led to some controversy about whether or not public hearings should be held. Several questions on this were raised in the House, and on July 23 the Prime Minister replied to one question as follows:

> The decision on public hearings rests with Mr. Fullerton, although the Study has not been constituted under the Inquiries Act, and he therefore does not have the power to summon witnesses. No final decision on hearings has yet been taken, although Mr. Fullerton has said in his advertisement seeking submissions that 'It is not my present intention to hold public hearings, since these would more appropriately flow from the review of the National Capital by a Special Committee of Parliament, the establishment of which the government is considering recommending at the next Session.' He has added in correspondence on this question that the time, staff, and cost involved in public hearings would make it difficult to finish the study within the time and budget allotted to it, but that the matter would be reviewed in the autumn.

Although I did not wish to close the door completely at that early date, it did seem to me that not only would public hearings further cloak the Study with an unwarranted importance, but they would be expensive and time consuming, and not particularly productive. I had found in earlier federal and provincial task forces that the written submissions and the staff studies were normally a much more useful source of information. In the case of this Study, it seemed to me particularly desirable to defer public hearings until the Parliamentary Committee meetings are held. Taking account also of the danger of hearings becoming a platform for political extremists rather than a forum for reasonable discussion, and the one-year deadline for the Study, I saw no reason later to change this decision.

Some Special Problems

A number of problems came up in the course of the Study, some foreseen and some not. One important concern was to establish my independence from the government, and particularly from the NCC with which I was so personally identified. I tried to meet this first problem by resigning from the public service, choosing instead to be hired on the basis of a one-year contract. Since then I have not sought nor been offered any employment with the federal government.

To separate myself clearly from the NCC proved a bit more difficult. I'm afraid I compounded the difficulty by borrowing staff from NCC and using some of its administrative services. However, the freedom from housekeeping problems which the arrangement provided, and the need for obtaining experienced people on short notice, overcame the obvious disadvantage of some apparent continuing NCC association. I might add that the Commission help was valuable to me, and saved a good deal of time. I found it surprisingly easy to disentangle myself from emotional involvement in the NCC, and I think I have been able to view its operations with reasonable objectivity.

Since the terms of reference referred to the NCC—"a study of the most effective arrangements for the future administration of matters directly affecting the National Capital and its development, including the role of the National Capital Commission and its relation to other bodies concerned with the governing of the Capital Region"—early in June, I wrote to the Commission seeking specific information and inviting comments and views on the subject of the Study. Individual NCC staff members were very forthcoming in providing the information I sought and the Commission files were open to me. However it was made clear to me in the autumn, when I met the Commission following the appointment of its new Chairman, that the NCC would not be presenting to me any official statement of opinion about how it saw its own future role, or about the problems it faced in its relations to other bodies or agencies in the Capital. Other departments to which I wrote also were very forthcoming about supplying information, but there were few comments of a policy nature bearing on my objectives. There was however one important exception; in February, I received a letter from the Deputy Minister of Public Works outlining that Department's views on the respective roles of the DPW and the NCC in the Capital. This led to another letter from the Chairman of the NCC who took issue with a number of points raised in the DPW letter. Both letters are reprinted in Chapter Nine.

Organization of the Study

The Study is in three parts and is accompanied by three appendices. The first part, Chapters One to Six, is mainly historical and descriptive. Chapter Two lists landmarks in the development of the Capital, with particular emphasis on the federal role. Chapters Three and Four describe the Region, the structure of municipal government, and the functioning of those federal agencies or departments which have had an important part to play in shaping the Capital's growth. In Chapter Five we discuss the federal claim to a share in the governing process, and Chapter Six is a survey of how other federal capitals are governed.

Part Two contains a number of chapters touching on problem areas, including those arising from the multiplicity of jurisdictions. Further chapters deal with the lack of coordination within the federal government itself, municipal charges of inadequate federal financial support, the impact of federal growth, and the effect of the interprovincial boundary on residents of the Region. There is a special chapter on bilingualism.

The third part of the Study contains a consideration of alternative methods of governing the Capital and the recommendations. Appendix "A" contains documents of relevance, Appendix "B" a number of studies by staff or consultants, and Appendix "C" a study prepared by Professor Rowat for the Ontario Advisory Committee on Confederation in 1966. This latter study is reprinted not only because it provides an interesting history of the Capital, but because it reviews various proposals to establish a federal capital territory.

The division of labour has been roughly as follows. Mr. Weld acted as second in command, did the special study on bilingualism and biculturalism and drafted the chapter on this subject. Professor McRae submitted a special paper on education in the Capital Region. Professor Rowat drafted Chapter Six on the governing of federal capitals, and has acted as a general adviser throughout. Mr. Jones headed a small staff task force which last autumn carried out a series of off-the-record interviews with local political figures or municipal groups, and put forward his own ideas on the future form of capital government. Professors Falcone and Van Loon organized the survey of opinion of Capital residents, and wrote the report based on it which is contained in Appendix "B". Mr. Poulin did some research work on a part-time basis, and submitted his own views on how the Region should be governed.

Messrs. Guibord and Thompson have worked full-time on the Study, have been involved in the interviewing process and in analyzing the briefs, have seen the report through to publication and worked together in drafting two of the chapters in it. Mrs. Lorraine Dallas, in addition to being my secretary, supervised the flow of paper in and out of the office, kept track of the briefs, and with the help of Mlle Louise Huot, typed the innumerable drafts that were required.

My own role was to try to assimilate as much as I could of the information that was put together by the staff and consultants, and which developed out of internal discussions and from my own interviews with many interested individuals and groups, and to assess it all against my own background and experience as NCC chairman. The product is this Study. In summary, although I have leaned heavily on my staff and many other people for ideas and opinions, and for help in drafting of parts of it, I alone must bear responsibility for it and for the conclusions and recommendations of the Study proper; material in Appendices "B" and "C" is the responsibility of each author.

An Admission

I confess to having held from the outset of the Study several reasonably firm convictions (or assumptions, or prejudices, if you like) which were not materially affected during the course of the Study. They are:

1. The governing of Canada's Capital is a jurisdictional swamp, with too many levels of authority, too many government bodies, too many elected officials and too many municipal employees.

2. The federal government has an important stake in the Capital, a national responsibility for ensuring that it meets national aspirations, and a right to some say in the governing of the Capital.

3. A federal district, run exclusively by the federal government, is simply not acceptable. Residents of Canada's Capital have had the franchise for too long to surrender it now; the trend is in the other direction, towards a form of government that is more responsive to the needs of individuals.

4. The Capital can only be truly national if the English and French languages and cultures can both flourish in it.

There is nothing new or earthshaking about my views on these four points. I made them known on many previous occasions, again at a press conference a few days after my appointment, and I referred to them at almost every public or private opportunity since. All of this may simply reinforce the opinion of some people that my mind was made up from the start. To them I can only say that the conclusions and recommendations at the end of this Study were considerably influenced in the course of the past twelve months, not only by the staff, but by the interviews we have held with a great many groups and individuals from within the region and from outside, by the many letters and briefs submitted, and by the opinion survey carried out by our consultants at Carleton University.

The off-the-record interviews with politicians at all levels of government—cabinet ministers, Senators, Members of Parliament and provincial legislatures, mayors, reeves, aldermen, councillors, and trustees—were particularly fruitful and revealing. Almost everyone spoke frankly, and without regard to party affiliations, to level of government, or to considerations of "protocol". I have tried to be as honest as I can in presenting the information and opinions that have crossed my path, including the things I learned while serving as NCC Chairman. I hope moreover that I have not violated any oaths of secrecy or official regulations, but if so I can only plead that there was no other way to make essential facts known.

Footnotes

1. R.S.C. 1970 c N-3, *National Capital Act*. 1958, c. 37, s. 1. See Appendix A-1.
2. For example, see "*The Mackenzie King Record—Volume IV—1947/1948*" (J. W. Pickersgill, D. F. Forster), University of Toronto Press, 1970, pp. 322/5, and 432/5). The book notes that before he retired, the Prime Minister was very anxious to ensure that the national capital plan would continue to be implemented, and that his diary for the first six months of 1948 contains repeated references to this subject. In May 1948, Mackenzie King noted in his diary that he told "the Cabinet that I would like to bring in a bill on the improvement of the National Capital. I said, as the Ministers knew, I had taken a special interest in the development of the Capital. We had now reached the point, however, where, if progress was to be made, the Government would have to make clear its decision to appropriate money over a term of years." It was finally decided to put the proposal forward as a Resolution to be passed by both Houses, and King spoke to it on June 28th. However, King felt he had botched the speech, saying in his diary, "A bit humiliated making such a poor fist of what ought to have been one of the best speeches of my life, with the knowledge however that the thing itself was all important and had been done, namely, the last measure introduced by me in the House of Commons was one that had relation to Canada's future and the future of its Capital."

   Later at his last Cabinet meeting before retirement, on November 12th, his final proposal to his colleagues was to fill the vacancies on the Federal District Commission. In his subsequent meeting with the press, King said: "I spoke of the interest which they knew I had always taken in the work of the Federal District Commission improvement of Ottawa as the Capital of Canada, and stated that the Order I had signed in Council today and that the Cabinet had passed today was an Order bringing the Commission up to full strength... That I thought Ottawa and surrounding district would be made the most beautiful capital in the world. Nature had made provision for such and we were still young enough to make plans that were not only necessary today but would suit the capital of the country in years to come. That Canada would be a great country and that her capital should be planned accordingly."

Chapter Two

Landmarks in the Development of the Capital

Any student of the history of Canada's Capital becomes aware early of the original battle over its location, and of several themes which continue to recur over more than a century of its life—the unsuccessful attempts to establish a federal district, and the continuing City of Ottawa demands for more federal funds. The story of the Capital has been told in scholarly but entertaining fashion by Wilfrid Eggleston in *The Queen's Choice*,[1] and summarized in Dr. Rowat's study on the federal district question which forms Appendix "C" of this Study. We therefore don't propose to cover the ground in detail, but will rather emphasize a number of landmarks in the development of the Capital. It is interesting that the significance of some of these incidents does not appear to have penetrated public consciousness.

I. Landmarks

(*a*) Late in 1857, the "City of Ottawa" was selected by Queen Victoria as the "permanent seat of the future Government of the Province of Canada".[2] The decision followed a long and acrimonious battle between proponents of it and of four other cities in Upper and Lower Canada (Canada West and Canada East)—Québec City, Montreal, Kingston, and Toronto. A private memorandum[3] to the Queen, sent by Sir Edmund Head, Governor General, appears to have had a major influence on the decision, but the bitterness of the political infighting itself may have forced the selection of the boundary city of Ottawa as the compromise.

(*b*) Following Confederation in 1867, Ottawa remained the seat of government of the new country, although some fresh attempts had been made to shift it. Section 16 of the British North America Act reads as follows:

> 16. Until the Queen otherwise directs, the Seat of Government of Canada shall be Ottawa.

Of related interest is the reference in Section 68 to provincial capitals:

> 68. Unless and until the Executive Government of any Province otherwise directs with respect to that Province, the Seats of Government of the Provinces

shall be as follows, namely,—of Ontario, the City of Toronto; of Quebec, the City of Quebec; of Nova Scotia, the City of Halifax; and of New Brunswick, the City of Frederiction.

(*c*) Eggleston notes that the constitutional position of Ottawa was "materially altered" by the decisions of 1864-67, and suggests that the change was a "retrograde step."[4] Although this is covered in Appendix "C", pp. 391/2 it bears repeating here:

As capital of the *Province* of Canada, no serious jurisdictional problems could possibly arise between the Crown and the Town in Ottawa, for the municipality of Ottawa would have continued to be under the direct control of the Provincial Government on Parliament Hill. Nor would any problem arise if government activities spread into adjoining municipalities, or even across the Ottawa River into Canada East, since between 1840 and 1867 the Ottawa River merely separated two geographical divisions of one Province.

But Confederation changed all that. Now Ontario and Quebec were autonomous states within their defined powers, and these powers included the exclusive control of municipal and local matters. Now Ottawa, by the B.N.A. Act, was a federal capital located *within a provincial municipality*, and the latter took its orders, not from Parliament Hill, but from Queen's Park, 275 miles away, and from a jurisdiction separate and autonomous and independent in broad respects from the central federal government. And the Ottawa River had once again become a boundary between two autonomous governments.[4]

(*d*) Eggleston and Rowat both refer to the significance of the views of John Hamilton Gray, a New Brunswick lawyer and a Father of Confederation, who liked the site, but foresaw the problems arising out of the change in Ottawa's status.[4] Because of the perceptiveness of Gray's view of the problems likely to arise in the future, I urge readers to turn to Appendix "C" (pp. 425/6) to get the full flavour of his comments. In essence Gray said that the Capital should no more belong to Ontario than to any other province, and that while the federal government would generate added municipal costs and responsibilities, it would have no say in whether or how these were met. He thought the federal district model of Washington was the answer.

(*e*) The problem of federal responsibility for Ottawa's municipal costs kept coming up. Sir Wilfrid Laurier became interested in this issue, and in 1899 a small ($6,000) federal grant was given and the *Ottawa Improvement Commission*—the forerunner of the present NCC—was created[5], with its main object the beautifying of Ottawa. In the same year F. G. Todd, a Montreal landscape architect was hired, and he subsequently submitted the first plan for the Capital.[6]

(*f*) In 1913, the Borden government responded to criticism by local architects of the work done by the OIC by appointing a "Federal Plan Commission" under Sir Herbert Holt of Montreal, (president of the Royal Bank) with membership including the mayors of Ottawa and Hull. This Commission was given wide powers, and in 1915 its report was tabled in the Commons. I share the view of many that this was the best planning report on the Capital ever done, not excluding that of Jacques Greber. I understand that the person chiefly responsible for the planning content was Mr. E. H. Bennett, consultant to the Committee. In addition to their detailed planning proposals, however, the commissioners made the following unanimous recommendations:

> (I) We are of the firm opinion that the future improvements in the area about the Capital at Ottawa and Hull should not be attempted without first establishing a Federal District and securing for the Federal authority some control of local government.
>
> (II) We are of the firm opinion that the pivot, on which hinges the success or failure in carrying out any comprehensive plan, lies in the proper solution of the problem of steam railway transportation.
>
> (III) In order that proper administrative and office accommodation may be provided for the work of the Government, the extension and development of the Government Buildings should be carried out on a comprehensive plan.
>
> (IV) There should be proper control of residential and manufacturing districts by enforcing building restrictions
>
> (V) The highly commendable work of the Ottawa Improvement Commission should be extended and enlarged by the development of a broad and forceful policy as to further park lands, and there should be established a National Park or Forest Reserve in the Laurentian hills, under the control of the Dominion Government.[7]

But the war was on and little was done to follow up the detailed planning proposals, let alone the main recommendations.

(*g*) In 1922 Noulan Cauchon, planning assistant of the City of Ottawa published a plan for the Capital. He is quoted by Eggleston as proposing

> a modified "Federal District" which would give a federal government commission authority over the physical features and public utilities of the capital region, but would preserve provincial and municipal autonomy in other respects, and leave the residents of the area with undisturbed rights of franchise.[8]

Again, no action was taken.

(*h*) In 1927 the Ottawa Improvement Commission became the Federal District Commission, [9] with an increased budget, and of the nine commissioners appointed by Order-in-Council at least one was to be a resident of Hull. The City of Ottawa had the power to appoint a tenth member. In 1946 the number of Commissioners was raised to nineteen; seventeen appointed by the government, one each by the Cities of Ottawa and Hull. Of the seventeen, there would be at least one representative of each of the nine provinces. Power was given to the Cabinet to designate an area "in the district surrounding the City of Ottawa to be known as the National Capital District".[10]

(*i*) In 1944 a Joint Committee of Senate and Commons was established, and proposed that the Government appoint "a special committee of experts" to study the establishment of a federal district (see Appendix "C", p. 396/7). No action was taken.

(*j*) In 1937 Prime Minister Mackenzie King had brought Jacques Gréber from Paris to advise on the planning of the Capital. Some work was done by him in 1937-39, but the war intervened. But the day after the end of the war with Japan on August 16, 1945, an area of 900 square miles was defined as the National Capital District[11] and Mr. Gréber was immediately invited over to take charge of planning for it. He became consultant to the National Capital Planning Committee, set up by By-Law of the Federal District Commission "to draw up a master plan of the National Capital District". Membership in the Committee included the federal Minister of Public Works and two members appointed by the City of Ottawa and one by the City of Hull—but with the majority of members appointed by the Federal District Commission. In 1950 the Gréber Plan was submitted to the FDC and to the Government. Although it was tabled in the House of Commons it was never officially "approved" by the federal government. In the event most of the main recommendations—creation of a Greenbelt around Ottawa, removal of railway tracks from the centre of the city, extension of Gatineau Park, and the building of a new parkway network—have since been implemented.

On the matter of a federal district Gréber deviated from most earlier commissions and advisers. As recounted by Eggleston[12] and summarized in Appendix "C" (page 398) Gréber felt that his proposals could be put into effect by cooperation between the authorities involved, "possibly through a combined planning board", and implied that no changes in jurisdiction were necessary. Mr. King apparently accepted this advice, although in earlier years he had been an advocate of a federal district.[13]

(*k*) In 1951 the federal Municipal Grants Act was approved,[14] empowering the payment of grants-in-lieu of taxes to all Canadian cities in respect of untaxed federal property. This Act was designated essentially to meet Ottawa's needs, but was understandably broadened for political reasons to cover all Canadian cities.

(*l*) In 1956 a Joint Senate Commons Committee was appointed to review the work of the Federal District Commission. Its report dealt mainly with planning matters, but it recommended changing the name of the FDC to the National Capital Commission and proposed expanding its powers and financing. On the matter of jurisdiction it said "we think that the realization of the National Capital Plan must imply the cooperation of Federal, Provincial and Municipal authorities" and proposed special consultation with the Ontario planning authorities. There was no mention of a federal district in the recommendations.[15]

(*m*) In 1958 the National Capital Act was passed[16] (it was proclaimed in 1959) changing the Federal District Commission to the National Capital Commission, and extending the size of the National Capital Region to a rough square of 1800 square miles around Ottawa and Hull. The budget of the NCC was greatly increased, and action was taken to expropriate land for the Greenbelt, attempts to achieve the same goal through zoning at the municipal level having failed.

(*n*) The Munro case[17] with Exchequer Court judgment in 1965 (Gibson J), and Supreme Court judgment (Cartwright J) on appeal in 1966, was a landmark. These judgments confirmed that the federal government had the power to plan for the National Capital Region, and to expropriate land for its purposes, including land for the Greenbelt, under the general "peace, order and good government" clause of the British North America Act. This is discussed further in Chapter Five, pp. 56 to 57. Both judgments are required reading for anyone wishing to pursue further the constitutional position of the federal government in the Capital. The Cartwright judgment is reprinted in Appendix "A". (The length of Mr. Justice Gibson's, I am afraid, precludes its publication).

(*o*) Prime Minister Pearson said in a November 1967 television interview[18] that he thought "a federal district should be created for Ottawa", and said later in Parliament that the government was discussing implementation with the two provinces concerned. On January 31, 1968 he and the prime ministers of Ontario and Québec jointly announced appointment of a Committee of officials to make proposals for the Ottawa area, but that the proposals were not to involve "changing basic constitutional jurisdiction or existing provincial boundaries". This was the beginning of the abortive "Tripartite" discussions which are reviewed in Chapter Eight (page 90/91).

(*p*) In 1966 the Québec Government set up a Commission chaired by M. Henri Dorion to study the boundaries of Québec, with special emphasis on Labrador. Its main object was to make recommendations to insure Québec's territorial integrity—"L'intégrité du Territoire Québécois". In 1967 it was given a special mandate to examine the problems "posed by the existence of the National Capital Commission". In its subsequent report brought down in May 1968[19] the Commission argued predictably that the federal government, and particularly the NCC, threatened Québec's territorial integrity, and proposed *inter alia* that Québec be given ownership of NCC land in the area.

(*q*) Effective January 1, 1969 a new regional government, Regional Municipality of Ottawa-Carleton (RMOC), was created for Ottawa, a "second tier" government made up of representatives from the municipalities.[20] Its boundaries were not very different than those of the Ontario side of the National Capital Region.

(*r*) At the Constitutional Conference in February 1969, the decisions reached by prime ministers of the federal government and of the ten provinces in respect of the Capital were stated in the conference communiqué as follows:

> 9. *Reform of institutions linked with federalism—The National Capital* (Agenda item 4(*d*))
>
> The Constitutional Conference, subject to any comments that may be submitted, agrees that:
>
> (*a*) The cities of Ottawa and Hull and their surrounding areas shall be the Canadian Capital area;
>
> (*b*) No changes be made to provincial boundaries or to the constitutional responsibilities of the government concerned.

(*c*) The boundaries of the Canadian Capital area are to be established by agreement of the governments concerned;

(*d*) In line with the aforementioned objectives, steps must be taken so that the two official languages and the cultural values common to all Canadians are recognized by all governments concerned in these two cities and in the Capital Region in general, so that all Canadians may have a feeling of pride and participation in, and attachment to, their Capital.

(*e*) That the study committee on the Canadian Capital continue its work, giving particular importance to the following:

(i) the definition of adjacent areas which would eventually constitute, along with the cities of Ottawa and Hull, and their surrounding areas, the Canadian Capital Region.

(ii) The study of the administration and the financing of a tripartite organization.

(*s*) In May 1969 the government announced the expropriation by the NCC under its Act of 15 acres in the centre of Hull, to provide land for the building of a number of federal office buildings in that city.

(*t*) In December 1969 the Québec legislature passed a bill establishing on January 1, 1970 a regional municipality, the Outaouais Regional Community (ORC),[21] roughly equivalent to the Ontario RMOC. Its boundaries were not markedly different from those of the Québec side of the NCR. It also set up at the same time the Outaouais Development Corporation (ODC), but covering a larger territory than the ORC, and with responsibilities for industrial development and tourism.

(*u*) The federal Capital was not mentioned in the detailed terms of reference of the Royal Commission on Bilingualism and Biculturalism established in July 1963. However, it is significant that the Commissioners devoted Book V of their six volume report to this subject (published in February 1970) recommending that the federal government assume a direct role in promoting equal partnership between Francophones and Anglophones in the Capital. The Report proposed a "Tripartite Agency" to carry out its other recommendations: this presumably was derived from the Tripartite discussions referred to above. Appendix III to that volume is reprinted in Appendix "A".

(*v*) The 1972 Report of the Special Joint Committee of the Senate and the Commons on the Constitution of Canada (See Appendix A-6) made two specific recommendations about the Capital:

> 47. There should be a movement by stages toward the possible creation of an autonomous Canadian Capital.
>
> 48. The Canadian Capital should be generally those areas of Ontario and Quebec now defined in the Schedule to the National Capital Act (1959).

Other more general recommendations and comments included the view that the federal government should have more say in the running of the Capital, and that a board "comprised of Ministers from the Federal, Ontario and Quebec governments, together with representatives of the Regional Communities concerned should be established to coordinate the activities of governments in the Canadian Capital". The Committee saw this as the first stage, with the second being a single new government for the Region, and then on to "fully autonomous status" if the population considered it advantageous.

II. Commentary

The list above tells the gist of the story in summary form; some subjects are covered later in this Study in more detail. But as the footnotes and text suggest, a better rounded and much more complete version will be found both in Eggleston's *The Queen's Choice*, and in Rowat's study attached to this report as Appendix "C". Students who are interested should consult the original documents. However, even this brief outline indicates the concerns that kept surfacing through the century. John Hamilton Gray's prophetic vision of the problems to come is remarkable—the proper federal concern about its own Capital and its lack of control over its development, the subordination of the Capital to the laws of one province, and the costs which would inevitably fall upon the local municipality. It is not surprising that his "federal district" proposal still keeps coming up; had it been accepted in 1867 the story we recount would have taken a much different direction.

The story of the Capital, in fact, can be condensed into rather simple terms, without doing violence to the truth. The federal government in the early years was a quiet tenant of the City of Ottawa, since its requirements were largely satisfied by the buildings on Parliament Hill. But towards the turn of the century its needs for space were growing rapidly and it was dissatisfied with the way the City's growth was managed, or not managed. So it decided to do something itself about beautification and planning (Todd). It realized soon that it lacked the authority to do a respectable job, and called on Holt, who in effect told it first to become master in its own house (federal district). But the war was on and the Parliament's Centre Block burned down, and the issue of who governed the Capital lost priority. Meanwhile the City kept protesting, with justification, that it was starved for funds because of tax-exempt federal property. In reaction to these protests, the Government kept giving Ottawa handouts on an increasing scale but in a rather grudging and parsimonious way—showing clearly federal preference to try to do the job itself rather than leave it to a municipal body in which it appeared to have little confidence.

And so the story has gone. Each time the federal government was advised to take the front door approach of seeking formal constitutional power to run the Capital, it declined, waited, and then chose instead the back door of using its money to achieve its goals.

Did Mr. King, for example, give much thought to the constitutional niceties when Gréber was appointed to plan the Capital area—a responsibility normally provincial and municipal? I think rather that he, as did most Canadians at the time, assumed with some validity that there was a vacuum there that had to be filled; if no federal action had been taken little locally would have been done to build a decent Capital. Yet why did King accept the advice of Gréber,[22] a planner, not an expert in government, that the plan could be implemented without jurisdictional changes, that is, by cooperation between the three levels of government in the region, quite contrary to his own earlier stated preference for a federal district?

In the event, the cooperative approach and zoning bylaws were tried and failed. The Greenbelt was established by expropriation and land purchase with some $50 million of federal money; the railways were paid to move most of their tracks out of the downtown area with another $50 million; the parkway land and Gatineau Park territory was also acquired by purchase or expropriation; and the centre town part of the Queensway was built on land the federal government received from the railways, or acquired specially, and then donated to the project.

Certainly implementing the Gréber plan would have required great chunks of money, regardless of how the governing of the Capital was structured. But would it have required as much? And is there not something distasteful about this massive use of federal power and money to achieve its ends, however worthy? The Munro case, of course, vested the federal actions with legality, but had there been a history of serious attempts by the federal government to obtain a more direct voice in the governing of the Capital, there would be fewer grounds for anyone challenging its position. It is remarkable that until 1967, in spite of all the recommendations and urging by commissioners and experts, there does not appear to have been one real attempt by the federal government to obtain such a voice. It is also ironic that when the federal government did make a move in 1967 it showed an astonishing lack of understanding, not only of the complicated nature of the interplay of the political forces in the area, but of the strength of its own position.

I am reluctant to leave these brief comments on the history of federal involvement in the Capital without emphasizing several important consequences of it. Whether justified or not, the federal attempts to achieve its planning ends by buying land have led to at least three very interesting results:

(*a*) There is growing world acceptance of the idea that government acquisition of land in advance of need, for housing and other municipal purposes, is a very desirable planning instrument. Because so much land in the Canadian Capital is now in federal hands—about 29% in the urban areas of the Region—the implementation of federal or municipal planning decisions about parks, recreation space, roads etc. is made much easier. In summary, the federal government, by its apparently weak constitutional position, was forced into a good forward planning approach.

(*b*) Federal land is very strategically placed around the Capital, and literally no power line, sewer, bridge, or highway of any consequence can be built without crossing federal land. The withholding of approval for encroachments proposed by municipal or provincial bodies is a powerful weapon, and although it has been used sparingly, it gives the federal government a considerable say in new developments (whether this is a good thing or not is a different aspect of the question).

(*c*) Among the levels of government the federal government is senior or paramount, and neither provincial nor municipal governments has jurisdiction over its land. Thus, possessing over a quarter of the land in the built up area of the Capital, the federal government has a constitutional right to plan and to make use of its own territory.

III. The National Capital Region as Capital

There is at least one other interesting conclusion that should be drawn from the brief history above. It is that the federal government has progressively moved to modify the narrow interpretation of the Capital as being the City of Ottawa only, by its initial action to create the concept of a National Capital District, by doubling it in size in 1959, by the proposals to the 1969 Prime Ministers' Conference respecting the Capital area, and by the subsequent building of federal offices in Hull and by the allocation of a much larger share of NCC expenditures to the Québec side of the Region.

There are some curious aspects of this business of attempting to define or bound "the capital". The BNA Act did not refer to "capital", but, as we have noted above, simply to the "seat of government". But what does this latter phrase mean? Certainly Parliament, where the laws are passed, but what about the places where cabinet meetings are held? What about the Supreme Court, or the Governor General's residence, Rideau Hall? At the time of Confederation, Rideau Hall was in the village of New Edinburgh, not in Ottawa. Several experts have pointed out a number of other anomalies, including the fact that Cabinet has met in many places in Canada.

And what is Ottawa? The tiny City at the time of Confederation? (A former Mayor is said to have supported this interpretation). The present City? Or is it some version of a "metropolitan" Ottawa that straddles the River, as in some figures put out by Statistics Canada? All nice questions, suitable for endless argument.

Most of our advisers agree, however, on two things. The first is that the phrase "capital" is vague and without constitutional significance—even the National Capital Act doesn't define "capital" but sticks in Section 10 to the words "seat of government". The second point is that changing the definition of "seat of government" in Section 16 of the BNA Act can be done by federal executive action alone, without reference to the provinces; Cabinet could pass an Order-in-Council, and that would be that. The consensus is that, however legal this might be, it would make more political sense for the government first to seek Commons and Senate approval by means of a joint resolution recommending executive action, or alternatively (and perhaps preferably) present a

Bill to amend Section 16 by Act of Parliament under authority of Section 91(1) of the BNA Act. We shall be returning to this in the final chapter.

The question of what constitutes the Capital had an interesting exposure in Parliament in the last days of April, 1974. The NCC had brought out a pamphlet, *Canada's New Capital*, which started off as follows:

> Ottawa is the Capital of Canada. Right? Wrong. It used to be that staid, musty old Ottawa was known as the nation's Capital. Technically, it still is. But let's drop the technicalities—in this case they are as out-of-date as the idea that Ottawa is bushtown. . . Sure, Queen Victoria decreed in 1858 that Ottawa all alone and by itself should be the Capital, and that's in the constitution. . . Now, what's so different about the Capital? To begin with, it's not just Ottawa any more. It's the National Capital Region. Think of Ottawa and neighboring Hull as a central core and seat of governement...

Opposition spokesmen, including the Right Hon. John Diefenbaker, attacked the pamphlet, and accused the government of trying to subvert the constitution by administrative process. Mr. Diefenbaker: "I ask the Minister, since when did Ottawa-Hull become the capital of Canada?.. When was the amendment to the British North America Act brought in?..."[23]

On April 30, Mr. Peter Reilly (Ottawa West) rose in question period to make the following motion:

> Mr. Speaker, under Standing Order 26 I ask permission to make a motion to adjourn the House for the purpose of discussing a specific and important matter requiring urgent consideration, namely, the persistence of the government of Canada in continuing to publish and to cause one of its agencies to disseminate and keep for sale a pamphlet, some of whose statements contain grave errors in fact and are in direct contradiction of articles of the British North America Act and the National Capital Act, and which statements are being promulgated to citizens of Canada as government policy despite the fact that a minister of the Crown has described the contents of the pamphlet as unfortunate and not representative of the policy of the government.[24]

The Speaker did not agree that the matter was of sufficient urgency to call for an emergency debate.

These opposition views found support from an unlikely source, the strongly separatist "Société nationale des Québécois de l'Outaouais". This group urged that the pamphlet be withdrawn, as a "political rag", "another disguised attempt to turn the Region into some kind of a federal district".[25]

I propose in the next chapter to review recent structural changes in municipal government, and describe the situation as it is today. The description will be supplemented by a map of the region and essential facts about population distribution, ethnic origins and language. In Chapter Four we consider the current role of the federal government with particular emphasis on the NCC, and the activities of other departments and agencies which affect the shape of the Capital's growth.

Footnotes

1. Eggleston, Wilfrid, *The Queen's Choice* (Queen's Printer, Ottawa, 1961) Cat. No. W93-261F
2. Ibid, p. 108.
3. Ibid, p. 102.
4. Ibid, p. 144 et seq. See also John Hamilton Gray, *Confederation of Canada*, Toronto, 1872. pp. 108-110.
5. Statutes of Canada, 1899, 62-63 Victoria, Chap. 10, *An Act respecting the City of Ottawa* (Reprinted in Appendix A).
6. Todd, Frederick G., *Preliminary Report to the Ottawa Improvement Commission*, 1903. (By coincidence, I met Mr. Todd in the 1930's when he sat in the adjoining pew in Stanley Presbyterian Church, Westmount, P.Q.)
7. *Report on a General Plan for the Cities of Ottawa and Hull* (Ottawa, 1915).
8. *The Queen's Choice*, p. 172.
9. Statutes of Canada 1927, 17 George V, Chap. 55, *An Act respecting the Federal District Commission.*
10. Ibid., Amendment to Federal District Commission Act, 1927 1946 (10 George VI, chap. 51).
11. *The Queen's Choice*, p. 184.
12. Ibid., p. 198.
13. Ibid., pp. 174/5.
14. Ibid., pp. 177-181.
15. Joint Committee of the Senate and House of Commons on the Federal District Commission. Minutes of Proceedings No. 20, July 26, 30, 1956.
16. Statutes of Canada—1958 Chapter 37: *National Capital Act.*
17. *Harold Munro v. National Capital Commission.* Judgment of Exchequer Court (Gibson J) April 28, 1965, and judgment of Supreme Court of Canada (Cartwright J) June 28, 1966.
18. Rowat, Prof. D.C.
19. *Rapport de la Commission d'étude sur l'intégrité du territoire du Québec: Les problèmes de la région de la capitale canadienne* (Dorion Report) (Quebec May 22, 1968) See p. 31-32 for further comments and Appendix A-5.
20. *An Act establishing the Regional Municipality of Ottawa-Carleton* R.S.O. 1970, Chapter 407.
21. *Outaouais Regional Community Act*, RSQ 1969 Chapter 85.
22. It is interesting to note Gréber's use of Paris as an example of such planning cooperation (Q.C. p. 198)—The failure of such an approach has led the French government in the past few years to restructure the government of the Paris area, turning it in effect into a large federal district with centralized control, and with the Prefect and a majority of councillors appointed by the national government.
23. House of Commons Debates, April 24, p. 1970, April 25, p. 1750, April 29, pp. 1826, 1829 1832 (1974).
24. House of Commons Debates, April 30, pp. 1871/1, (1974).
25. *Le Droit*, May 1, 1974.

Chapter Three

The National Capital Region—Physical Description, Population and Structure of Municipal Government

This chapter provides a brief description of the Region, of the growth and ethnic origin of the population, and of the structure of government. It is divided into three parts; (1) a general description of the area, physical features and population, (2) local government on the Ontario side, and (3) local government on the Québec side.

I. The National Capital Region: Description and Population Data

The National Capital Region, as shown on the attached map, is an eighteen hundred square mile area; 1050 square miles of eastern Ontario and 750 square miles of western Québec, in a rough square around the cities of Ottawa and Hull. It is not known why the precise boundary lines were chosen in 1958, but they appear to have been drawn to include Gatineau Park, the Greenbelt, a number of natural wonders and historic sites, and in general the dormitory towns of the metropolitan area. In 1950, Jacques Gréber believed the 900 square mile region established in 1945 to be adequate;

> The National Capital Region, as defined in the Order in Council 5635, of August 16, 1945, is amply sufficient for the planning work of the region.[1]

but a few years later, the Federal District Commission disagreed. In 1956, before the Joint Parliamentary Committee, the then F D C Chairman, General Howard Kennedy, made the following recommendation:

> that the boundary of the national capital district be enlarged from 900 to 1800 square miles... to increase the area with a view to making Federal District Commission planning assistance and advice available to municipalities in the capital's *market area*, and to encourage protection of the natural beauties of the valley of the Mississippi river in Ontario and the Lièvre river in Quebec.[2]

Since the area in which the F D C could function—plan, spend money, protect the environment, control federal buildings—was limited to the Region it naturally wanted some flexibility, and sought the power to adjust the boundaries if it so desired. However, unlike the expansion recommendation, this was not accepted by the Joint Committee.

It is a naturally beautiful area. In 1950, in his *Plan for the National Capital*, Jacques Gréber described it in the following lyrical terms.

> The National Capital Region, situated on both sides of the Ottawa River, is a harmonious blend of forests, farmlands and water, of which the Capital City is the centre.
>
> The flat lands on the Ontario side and the nonchalant courses of its rivers make, with its pastoral scenery, striking contrast with the Quebec side, its undulated hills riddled with lakes, traversed by turbulant streams and covered by thick growths of trees.
>
> South of the Ottawa River, most of the land is occupied by farms and marshlands, interspersed by countless wooded areas, over which the pine and the elm tower majestically. The north fringe of the Ottawa River has the same characteristics, while the Gatineau Hills have a reverse proportion of forests and farmlands. All of this land of low lying hills, multiple lakes, streams and small valleys, in which farms rest between its wooded slopes, is still unspoiled.[3]

The beauty, enhanced by the "striking contrasts" Gréber speaks of, is in fact the result of a process of faulting and sinking during the ancient geological upheavals that created the Canadian Shield, of which the Gatineau Hills are a part. This action together with the pre-historic occupation of the area by glaciers, followed by the presence of the Champlain Sea, left remarkably unique rock and soil formations.

Population

In 1971 the total population of the National Capital Region was 628,477, of which 24% lived in Québec and 76% in Ontario.[4] Of those living in Ontario, 91% are concentrated in largely urban municipalities (Ottawa, Vanier, Rockcliffe Park, Gloucester and Nepean). A similar urban concentration exists on the Québec side with 88% living in Hull, Gatineau, Pte-Gatineau, Touraine, Lucerne/Deschênes and Aylmer. Statistics Canada uses a slightly larger area for its category "Ottawa–Hull Census Metropolitan Area", a total for this is also shown on the following table. Thus there are three different areas which from time to time are considered in this Study, namely urban, Census Metropolitan Area, and the largest, the National Capital Region.

The issue of language is considered in Chapter Twelve; Table 3–2 shows the distribution of the Region's population by mother tongue. It is of interest to note, however, that the numbers of those of French mother tongue are not markedly different on both sides of the River. On the Québec side they form 85% of the population, against 21% on the Ontario side.

MAP OF NATIONAL CAPITAL REGION

Showing Boundaries of Municipalities, the Two Regional Governments, and the Census Metropolitan Area as used by Statistics Canada

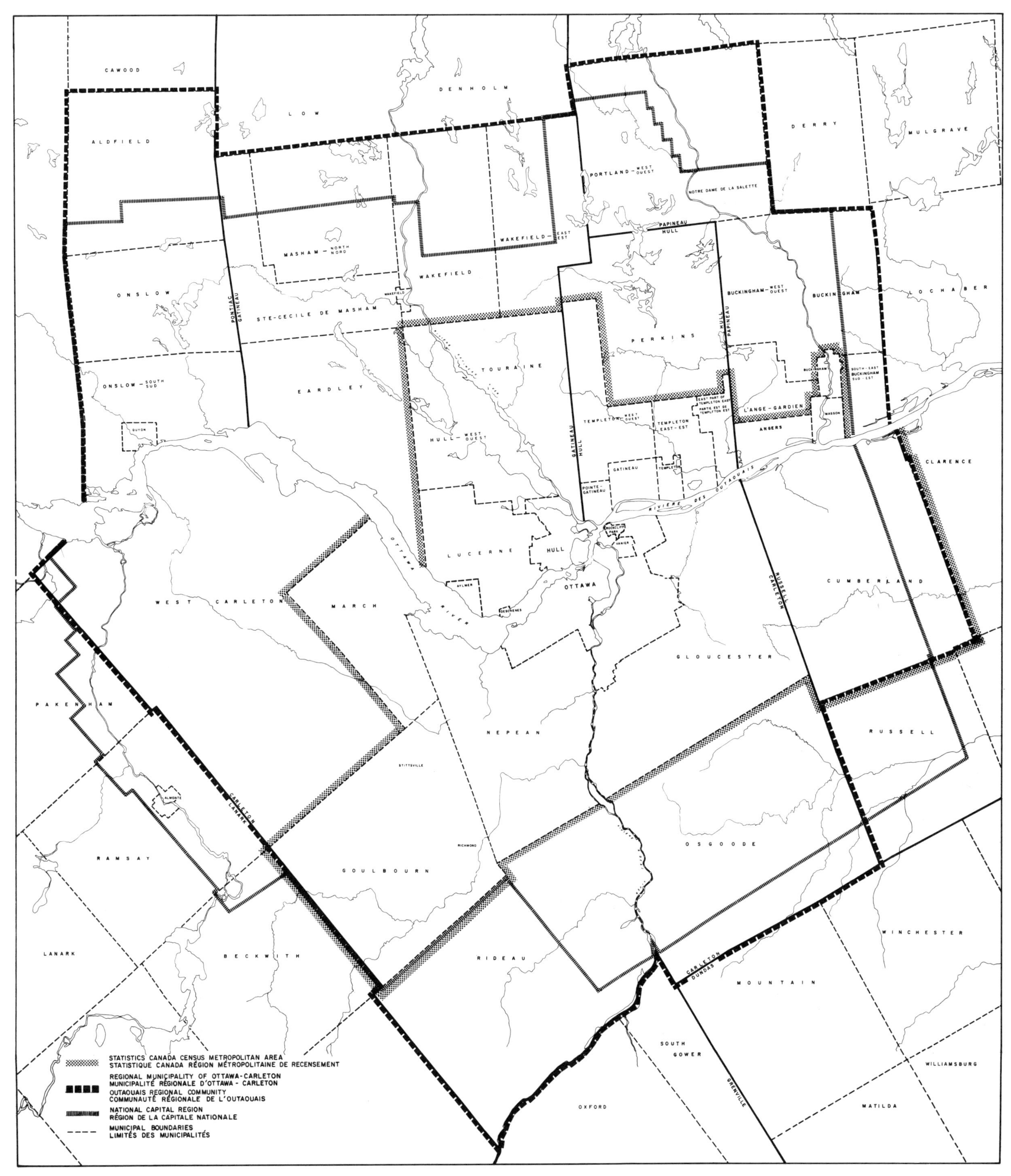

TABLE 3–1[5]

NATIONAL CAPITAL REGION
POPULATION GROWTH 1921–1971
BY MUNICIPALITY, URBAN AND METROPOLITAN AREA

	1921	1941	1961	1971
Ontario				
Ottawa	107,843	154,951	268,206*	302,341
Nepean	10,867	13,859	19,753*	64,606
Gloucester	8,397	9,871	18,301*	37,145
Vanier	5,324	7,966	24,555	22,477
Rockcliffe Park	—	1,480	2,084	2,138
Total Urban Area	132,431	188,127	332,899	428,707
Other Metropolitan	7,671	7,026	11,315	24,573
Total Census Metropolitan Area	140,102	195,153	344,214	453,280
Other NCR	12,766	11,214	14,196	18,650
Total NCR (Ont.)	152,868	206,367	358,410	471,930
Québec				
Hull	24,117	32,947	56,929	63,580
Gatineau	—	2,822	13,022	22,321
Pte-Gatineau	1,919	2,230	8,854	15,640
Touraine	900	822	2,079	9,643
Lucerne	1,917	2,321	5,762	8,611
Aylmer	2,970	3,115	6,286	7,198
Deschênes	321	284	2,090	1,806
Total Urban Area	32,144	44,541	95,022	128,799
Other Metropolitan	8,235	9,838	17,802	20,431
Total Census Metropolitan Area	40,379	54,379	112,824	149,230
Other NCR	6,116	5,714	5,580	7,317
Total NCR (Qué.)	46,495	60,093	118,404	156,547
National Capital Region				
Total Urban Area	164,575	232,668	427,921	557,506
Total CMA	180,481	249,532	457,038	602,510
Total NCR	199,363	266,460	476,814	628,477

* The City of Ottawa's growth was accelerated in 1950 by the annexation of large areas of Gloucester and Nepean Townships.

TABLE 3–2[6]

NATIONAL CAPITAL REGION
POPULATION BY MOTHER TONGUE 1971

	English	%	French	%	Other	%
Ontario						
Ottawa	210,460	70	62,235	21	29,645	10
Nepean	56,230	87	3,390	5	4,985	8
Gloucester	23,595	64	11,470	31	2,080	6
Vanier	6,590	29	14,940	67	950	4
Rockcliffe Park	1,830	86	215	10	90	4
Other	35,395	82	5,725	13	2,105	5
Total	334,110	71	97,975	21	39,845	8
Québec						
Hull	5,190	8	56,825	89	1,565	3
Gatineau	2,635	12	19,430	87	255	1
Pte-Gatineau	1,075	7	14,325	92	240	1
Touraine	1,390	14	8,090	84	160	1
Lucerne	4,405	51	3,910	45	295	4
Aylmer	2,895	40	4,145	58	160	2
Deschênes	535	30	1,255	69	15	1
Other	7,480	27	19,872	82	399	1
Total	25,605	16	127,852	82	3,090	2
Total National Capital Region	359,715	57	225,827	36	42,935	7

Note: Other figures on population breakdown by ethnic origin, mother tongue and language most often used are given in Tables 12–1 and 12-2 pages 153 and 154.

II. Local Government on the Ontario Side of the Region

Under Section 92 of the British North America Act, the Province controls "municipal institutions". The power of municipalities to raise money (business and property taxes), to plan, to develop, to provide welfare and to legislate (by-laws) is subject to provincial confirmation. Until 1972 the department concerned was Municipal Affairs, but it is now incorporated into the Department of Treasury, Economics and Intergovernmental Affairs. The power and decisions of this department, which delegates certain powers respecting municipal planning and finance to the Ontario Municipal Board, affects most aspects of municipal operations.

The historic dominance of the City of Ottawa among the Capital municipalities is shown in Table 3–1 above. Until a few years ago problems created by Ottawa's growth were resolved mainly by annexation of adjoining territories—with, however, a few exceptions such as Vanier and Rockcliffe Park. The expansion of Ottawa at the expense of its neighbours had begun as early as 1887 when the 184 acre village of New Edinburgh was annexed, including the ground on which Rideau Hall is situated. Eight major annexation followed culminating in the acquisition of 22,000 acres of the Townships of Nepean and Gloucester on January 1, 1950.

Ottawa continued to grow in the 1950's and the spillover into the adjoining municipalities, particularly the remaining areas of Nepean and Gloucester, accelerated. However, these townships were not prepared to accept further territorial acquisition by Ottawa at their expense. Clearly some new formula had to be found.

In November 1963, the Department of Municipal Affairs notified the area municipalities that

> it had been considering for some time the advisability of organizing a major study of the inter-municipal relations and regional problems. . .[7]

A meeting was held a month later at which the representatives of almost all the local municipalities expressed support for the Study proposal. In May 1964, the Minister of Municipal Affairs, The Honourable J. W. Spooner, advised the municipalities that he had appointed Mr. Murray V. Jones to conduct the Study. Mr. Jones' assignment was to enquire into the existing municipal structures and organizations, their functions and responsibilities, the anticipated future development of the area requiring reorganization or revision of the existing system of local government; and the effect of federal government operations on the responsibilities and resources of the local governments. The report on the Study was called the *Ottawa, Eastview and Carleton County Local Government Review*, and was completed and presented to the Minister the following year, June 1965.

The principle recommendation of the Study was the dissolution of existing area municipalities in order to create more evenly populated "districts" whose executive (two members from each) would form a regional council. The traditional municipal powers—legislative, executive and administrative, were to be given to the regional government, with the districts performing any functions the regional government might wish to delegate. It was Mr. Jones' belief that this was the only way that serious under-representation of the City of Ottawa within a federated municipal structure could be avoided. A month later the report was distributed to the area municipalities and to the press along with the Minister's request for comments and suggestions.

On February 1, 1967, Mr. Spooner convened a meeting at Ottawa of the local municipal representatives. He spoke of the "problems of urbanization" in the area, that necessitated some form of local government reorganization and of the failure of annexation to relieve these problems. He acknowledged Murray

Jones' pioneering procedures describing them as "a guide for similar studies now in progress elsewhere in this province", and reported reactions to the Jones Report.

> Speaking generally it must be said that while a large majority of the submissions made following the report appear to support the view that some major changes in the existing local government structure are necessary there has been a conspicuous lack of agreement with respect to the nature and extent of the changes required. As far as can be judged from the submissions received from both local and departmental sources the general reaction to the drastic recommendations made by the Commissioner (Jones) has certainly not been favourable.

Thereupon the Minister introduced the sixteen representatives of municipal governments in Carleton County (plus Cumberland) to his proposal for regional government in the area. The proposal was put forward for "discussion and consultation" with a ministerial recommendation that study and discussion committees be established. A committee was established made up of the Mayor and two Controllers of Ottawa, the Mayor of Vanier, the Reeves of Nepean, Gloucester and Cumberland together with the Warden of Carleton and a member of the Minister's staff.

The Committee appeared to have endorsed the Minister's regional government proposals almost in their entirety, for one year later on February 2, 1968, the new Minister of Municipal Affairs, the Hon. D'Arcy McKeough, addressed the representatives of the Ottawa area and announced,

> that the main features of the plan presented to you a year ago have been approved by the Provincial Government. The necessary legislation will be introduced at the session of the Legislature which starts on the 14th of this month. (February)

Regional Municipality of Ottawa-Carleton

The Act establishing the Regional Municipality of Ottawa-Carleton came into effect January 1, 1969. The area included under the jurisdiction of the new regional government was,

> the municipality or corporation of the Township of Cumberland, the City of Vanier, the Township of Fitzroy, the Township of Gloucester, the Township of Goulbourn, the Township of Huntley, the Township of March, the Township of Marlborough, the Township of Nepean, the Township of North Gower, the Township of Osgoode, the City of Ottawa, the Village of Richmond, the Village of Rockcliffe Park, the Village of Stittsville, and the Township of Torbolton.

Unlike the Ontario side of the National Capital Region (1050 square miles), the perimeter of the Regional Municipality (enclosing 1100 square miles) follows the township boundaries. As a result of this difference, the NCR includes parts of the Townships of Pakenham, Ramsay, Beckwith and Russell which are not a part of the Regional Municipality, and excludes the Township of

Marlborough and parts of the Townships of Cumberland and North Gower, which are. (see map, after page 22)

A two tier system of local government for the area was established, with a 31 member regional council for area-wide functions and responsibilities, including assessment for both local and regional purposes, arterial roads, major water, sewage and drainage works, regional planning, and capital financing for both local and regional purposes. The regional council was also "responsible for mandatory welfare services and all the present responsibilities of the county and the cities in these related fields."[8] Other responsibilities remained with the constituent municipalities.

In accordance with the Act, a "Chairman shall be appointed by the Lieutenant Governor in Council .... to hold office during pleasure for the years 1968 to 1972 inclusive ..." However, it denied the Chairman a council vote "except in the event of an equality of votes." The first Chairman of the Regional Council so appointed was Mr. Denis Coolican, a former Reeve of the Village of Rockcliffe Park. Subsequently, the office was to be filled by election:

> At the first meeting of the Regional Council in the year 1973, and in every third year thereafter .... the Regional Council shall organize as a council and elect as chairman one of the members of the Regional Council, or any other person, to hold office for that year and the two following years ...

No one contested Mr. Coolican's bid for election in 1973 and he continues as Chairman.

The legislation did not change local municipal boundaries, but did group smaller municipalities together for the purpose of representation on the regional council. This was accomplished as follows:

City of Ottawa	16 members, the Mayor, four Controllers and senior Aldermen for each of the 11 wards.
City of Vanier	2 members, the Mayor and one Councillor appointed by the Council.
Village of Rockcliffe Park	1 member, the Reeve.
Township of Nepean	3 members, the Reeve and the Deputy Reeve and one other member selected by the Council.
Township of Gloucester	2 members, the Reeve and Deputy Reeve.
Townships of Cumberland and Osgoode	2 members, the Reeves of each.
Townships: Fitzroy and Torbolton; Huntley and March; North Gower and Marlborough; Goulbourn and the Villages of Richmond and Stittsville.	4 members, one selected from each group.

However, even with the grouping of smaller, essentially rural municipalities, the City of Ottawa and the essentially urban Township of Nepean are seriously under-represented on the Regional Council, as the following figures suggest:

	Population (1971)	Representation	Ratio: Population to Representation
City of Ottawa	302,341	16	1: 18,896
Township of Nepean	64,605	3	1: 21,535
Other	104,985	11	1: 9,544

There was little reaction to the regional system until the Spring of 1970, when the municipalities began to hear from their residents about the increase in taxes for expenditures that the imposition of regional government had been intended to avoid. In the well-publicized discussions that followed, supporters of RMOC such as Regional Council Chairman, Denis Coolican argued that it would eventually bring orderly growth, particularly in land use. Other suggested advantages were economies in shared sewage, water systems and welfare schemes, elimination of small municipalities which are costly to operate, the strengthening of the municipal power base, and the elimination of the multiplicity of boards and commissions that tend to dilute authority and spread power too thinly among the local councils.[9]

The opponents, such as the then Mayor of Ottawa, Kenneth Fogarty, and Nepean Reeve Andrew Haydon, claimed that the escalating costs necessary for extensions to and higher standards of service did not benefit their municipalities directly, and indeed were largely at their expense.

During the next two years, many of the elected municipal officials (Benoit, Haydon, Fogarty, Greenberg, Jones) continued to demand of the Province the restructuring, the defederation, the amalgamation of all or part of the municipalities within the Region, or even the Region's demise. With the exception of amalgamation, provincial government spokesmen remained adamant in spite of these well-publicized appeals, stating that no major changes would be considered until "the experiment" had been given a reasonable chance (ten years) to prove itself. Thereafter, the vocal opposition subsided somewhat, though it never really stopped. The province's position was clear though—"the responsibility for basic changes in the present organization belongs to our provincial government" (Hon. D'Arcy McKeough) and apart from a few housekeeping amendments, the government restricted its changes to two relatively minor items.

The first, taking effect on January 1, 1969 was the assumption by the Province of assessment (which the municipalities had known about prior to establishment of the regional government). Then in August 1972, Regional Government assumed control of the Ottawa Transportation Commission from the City, renaming it the Ottawa–Carleton Transportation Commission and expanding its service to previously isolated suburban areas.

This was accompanied by two structural changes. One, not affecting the RMOC, was the reduction of Ottawa's aldermanic representation per ward from two to one. This revision came into effect prior to the December 1972 election, and as a result the City's elected officials all became members of the Regional Council. The amalgamation of eight small rural townships to form three new municipalities was the second change. Mr. Spooner's proposal in 1967 had hinted that the unification of some of the rural areas was necessary, so that they could be adequately represented on Regional Council. But, because of local opposition, or at best lack of consensus, the regrouping did not occur. In 1972, the Province decided that there was justifiable reason to force amalgamation, for in order to maintain a reasonable level of service and administration, some of the municipalities were obliged to compete with each other for assessment. This, in addition to the unsatisfactory rural sharing and rotating of representation on Regional Council apparently determined the action of the Province.

The Province prepared a proposal for study and discussion by the Regional and Municipal governments. In it they advocated the unification of the twelve municipalities to form four new municipalities. The Province stressed that this was a starting point only, and that if the local governments could come up with an alternative solution prior to June 30, 1973, the Province would look with favour on that proposal. The local municipalities were unable to agree on any proposal for amalgamation, or even able to discuss it unemotionally, thus forcing the Province to impose a solution, which in itself was an amendment of its original 'study and discussion' proposal. The press, which appeared to reflect the views of the people, attacked the actions of Regional Council and applauded the decisive action taken by the Province.

Thus, effective January 1, 1974, the Townships of Huntley, Fitzroy and Torbolton became the Municipality of the Township of West Carleton. The Township of Goulbourn, plus the villages of Richmond and Stittsville formed the new Municipality of the Township of Goulbourn, and the Townships of North Gower and Marlborough formed the new Municipality of the Township of Rideau, which included the police village of Manotick as well.

III. Local Government on the Quebec Side of the Region

Background: The Outaouais Region

Since Philemon Wright arrived in Hull on March 20, 1800, the development of the Hull region has occurred in five successive stages: the initial settlement period before 1855; the first urbanization period, from 1855 to 1900; the period from 1900 to 1945; the post-war period, extending from 1945 to 1968; and the period of accelerated growth, from 1968 to the present.

The period before 1855 saw the arrival of colonists from New England and was characterized by settlement, clearing of the land, fur trading and logging. Wilfrid Eggleston explains why Wright chose this site for the location of the Outaouais settlement:

> A logical site for a pioneer settlement in colonial days was a spot where the power of falling water could be harnessed for grinding grain and sawing wood. There was no lack of such power either at the Chaudière or where the Rideau River leaped forty feet over the cliff to join the Ottawa River on its way to the sea.[10]

Later, saw mills were constructed near the Columbia (Chaudière) Falls, and the Hull settlement became larger than the one in Aylmer, where the first colony had been established.

> The Chaudière Falls, which Wright saw in their natural state, could be brought under control and harnessed in such a way as to produce the driving force needed for the operation of numerous mills. It is said that for these reasons, Wright dreamed that between Aylmer and the Gatineau there would one day rise a commercial centre as large as Montreal.[11]

During this period, two significant events occurred that had a decisive effect on the region: the construction of the Rideau Canal from Ottawa to Kingston in 1826 and Queen Victoria's choice of Ottawa as the seat of government of the new Province of Canada in 1857.

The demographic configuration and the regional economy of the Hull area changed considerably between 1855 and 1900. According to Lucien Brault, it was not until the period between 1861 and 1871 that the French-speaking population became the majority in the Hull area. Until then, the little community had retained an Anglo-Saxon character dating back to its colonization by immigrants from the United States.

TABLE 3–3

GROWTH OF THE FRENCH-SPEAKING POPULATION IN THE DISTRICT AND CITY OF HULL[12]

Year	French-speaking	English-speaking	Total
	District of Hull		
1851	243	2,568	2,811
1861	420	3,291	3,711
1871	4,461	3,857	8,318
	City of Hull		
1881	5,933	957	6,890
1901	12,330	1,663	13,993

Another significant change was that now, instead of cutting down the trees and assembling the logs in rafts of booms on the Ottawa River, floating them downstream to Quebec City and from there shipping them to England, the settlers processed the lumber in local saw mills and shipped it to American markets by way of the Rideau Canal. Population growth in the Hull region during this period was largely due to this industry. In addition, several small neighbouring municipalities were incorporated during these years: Aylmer in 1855, West Hull and the City of Hull itself in 1875, Pointe-Gatineau in 1876, South Hull (Lucerne) in 1880, West Templeton and East Templeton in 1886 and East Hull (Touraine) in 1890.[13]

The period between 1900 and 1945, although it began with the Great Fire of 1900 which destroyed half of Hull and one-fifth of Ottawa, was characterized by only very moderate activity in terms of municipal organization. Several rural municipalities were subdivided, such as Templeton, and several new villages were formed, such as Deschênes and Gatineau.

From the end of the Second World War until 1968, the population of the region increased significantly, largely because of the staggering increase in federal government personnel in Ottawa. This necessitated the rapid expansion of housing developments in most of the municipalities surrounding Hull. It is interesting to note that the large-scale industry that predominated in the Hull area at the turn of the century has been supplanted since the war by the "big business" of the federal Public Service in Ottawa, and that the Hull region has even been considered in some circles as merely a suburb of Ottawa. In order to absorb the increase in population, some of the municipalities in the Hull region had to annex additional land. From 1954 to 1967, Hull carried out eight annexations at the expense of Lucerne and West Hull. Gatineau, Pointe-Gatineau and Touraine also annexed additional land because they could not satisfy the demand for new housing developments. And once more, quite recently, Hull annexed 370 acres belonging to Lucerne as the result of a Superior Court decision in a case that dated back to 1969.

Finally, the period of feverish activity currently being experienced by the Outaouais region began in 1968 with the decision of the federal government to construct office buildings in Hull and to provide the massive financial support required to establish the regional infrastructure of the Outaouais area. Since this decision, housing construction in the Hull region has increased dramatically, and at the same time, commercial complexes are being established in the Outaouais, for the first time on a large scale. Previously, people in Hull did most of their shopping in Ottawa, where the large department stores were located; they were also influenced by the considerable difference in sales tax rates on either side of the interprovincial boundary. We will deal with this thorny problem in greater detail in Chapter Thirteen of this report.

Commission d'étude sur l'intégrité du territoire du Québec (*Dorion*)

Thus, during the decade from 1961 to 1971, the Outaouais area experienced a period of rapid change. One of the factors which had a significant effect on the course of history of the Hull Region during this period was the study undertaken by the *Commission d'étude sur l'intégrité du territoire du Québec*, which dealt with the Outaouais region and influenced the Québec Government in its decision to create structures.for regional development in the area.

Formed in 1966 by the Québec government, the CEITQ, which subsequently came to be known by the name of its chairman, the geographer Henri Dorion, was assigned various tasks, one of which was to study the maintenance of Québec's territorial integrity in the Hull region and to recommend the establishment of structures which would insure optimal conditions for the development of the Outaouais region.

After 18 months of research, the Dorion Commission submitted its report to Québec's Premier Daniel Johnson on May 22, 1968.[14] The postulates and recommendations of the Dorion Commission appear in Appendix "A" of this report.

Briefly, the Commission supported Québec's territorial integrity and rejected any form of government of a purely federal nature. The Commission reaffirmed Québec's provincial jurisdiction in the Outaouais region and called for a more equitable distribution of federal investment on each side of the Ottawa River. The Commission also proposed that a permanent Tripartite Commission be created and given authority to draw up and periodically update a development plan covering the National Capital Region in its entirety. Finally, the Dorion Commission recommended the creation at the earliest possible date of a Western Québec development commission, empowered to formulate policies and projects that the Québec government could propose to a Tripartite Conference, to prepare all other plans involving the development and construction of facilities for the Western Québec region, to work out the details of projects arising from the plan accepted by the Tripartite Conference and to see that the projects were carried out by the Québec government departments concerned.

The Dorion report was favourably received in the Outaouais region and the Québec government was not long in acting on many of its recommendations.

Municipal Organization in the Outaouais

Of the 12 municipalities in the urban part of the Outaouais, five are cities and are therefore governed by the Québec Cities and Towns Act, and the other five come under the jurisdiction of the Municipal Code: two villages, one township and four municipalities that have no official designation. Of the five cities in the first category, Hull and Aylmer are situated west of the Gatineau River and Gatineau, Pointe-Gatineau and Touraine lie to the east.

Since 1970, with the formation of the Outaouais Regional Community, these 12 urban municipalities, as well as 20 other rural municipalities, have been brought together on a regional basis within the boundaries of the ORC, which has certain municipal powers on a regional scale, in accordance with its establishing statute. The new Outaouais Regional Community also has its own public transit system, serving its urban sector. Finally, the Outaouais Development Corporation, a government agency for regional development has jurisdiction in the four counties of the Outaouais region: Hull, Pontiac, Gatineau and Papineau.

In December 1969, the Québec government adopted Bill 77 creating the Outaouais Regional Community[15]; the Act was designed to consolidate local governments in the Outaouais in order to counterbalance the new Regional Municipality of Ottawa-Carleton, established in June 1968 on the Ontario side of the National Capital Region, as well as to create for the Outaouais a structure comparable to those established in Quebec City and Montreal. The ORC takes in an area of 908 square miles. The territorial boundaries of the ORC do not correspond precisely with those of the Quebec side of the National Capital Region; the latter encompasses only parts of the townships of Aldfield, Ste-Cécile-de-Masham, Masham North, Wakefield, Wakefield East, Portland and Portland West, Buckingham and Buckingham South East, while these townships are included in their entirety within the ORC. The Quebec side of the National Capital Region represents an area of 750 square miles.

In addition to creating the ORC, this Act implemented one of the principal recommendations of the Dorion Commission by establishing the Outaouais Development Corporation and the Outaouais Regional Community Transit Commission, which was henceforth assigned responsibility for public transit in the Outaouais region.

Under the ORC Act the Outaouais Regional Community has jurisdiction over 32 municipalities located on either side of the city of Hull. The Outaouais Development Corporation's authority extends over the four counties of Hull, Pontiac, Gatineau, and Papineau and represents an area of 14,000 square miles and 102 municipalities.

The Outaouais Regional Community

The Community is divided into five sectors. The City of Hull and the town of Gatineau each constitute a sector in themselves, and the other three sectors consist of a number of municipalities around an important centre or axis in each area; Aylmer; Pointe-Gatineau and Touraine; and finally, Buckingham and Masson.

The Outaouais Regional Community is administered by a Council and an executive committee of eight members designated as follows: the chairman, who is appointed by the Lieutenant-Governor in Council, three members appointed by the City of Hull, one member appointed by the town of Gatineau, and one member appointed by each of the other three sectors. The Council of the Community is composed of the mayor or another council member from each of the 32 member municipalities. The members of the executive committee of the ORC must be chosen from among the members of the local councils of each municipality. The decisions of the ORC Council are taken by a majority vote of the members present. Each one has one basic vote plus one additional vote for every thousand inhabitants in his municipality beyond the first thousand, which means, for example, that the mayor of Hull exercises 65 of the 142 votes in the ORC Council.

According to the provisions of the Act, the ORC has competence in the following matters: the valuation of property in its territory, the preparation of a development plan, the establishment of a data-processing department, the uniformity of traffic regulations and the synchronization of traffic control systems, the billing of tax accounts, the preparation of minimum standards for construction and for the supply of drinking water, sewers and residential garbage disposal. The Act also authorizes the ORC to prepare a plan for redefining municipal boundaries within its area and to extend its competence to the following matters: regional recreation, construction of low-rental housing, co-ordination and integration of police and fire departments, and public health.

The Outaouais Development Corporation

The ODC is a crown corporation composed of five members appointed by the Lieutenant-Governor in Council, with powers delegated to it by the Quebec government. The object of the Corporation is to promote the economic progress of the Outaouais region and to carry out projects for industrial, commercial, recreational and tourist facilities. It finances its own activities by means of its revenues and its loans, which are guaranteed by the Quebec government. Since its creation in 1970, the Corporation has received an annual subsidy of $5 million from the Quebec government.

The Outaouais Regional Community Transit Commission

The Commission is composed of a chairman and general manager, appointed by the Lieutenant-Governor in Council, and two commissioners appointed by the ORC Council for a period of ten years.

The Transit Commission's budgets and loans are subject to the approval of the Council of the Community, but only representatives from municipalities in the urban area served by the Commission have the right to vote on these matters. These same municipalities assume the Commission's deficit. For the purposes of the Transit Commission, decisions of the Council are taken by a majority of "A" and "B" votes; each municipality has one "A" vote and a number of "B" votes in proportion to its financial contribution to the Commission.

Soon after coming into being in 1971, the ORC Transit Commission applied through the ORC for a $2.5 million loan to enable it to acquire two private companies, Transport urbain de Hull and Transport métropolitain de Hull, which had been providing public transit in the Outaouais region in recent years. However, the $1 million grant promised by the provincial government did not come through until the end of April and, at the time we went to press, the ORC Council had not adopted the Transit Commission budget for 1974.

Amalgamation

Towards the end of the 1960's, the Québec Department of Municipal Affairs began to encourage the amalgamation of a number of municipalities in the province in order to make better use of their resources, to ensure a more equitable sharing of the revenues and services among component units, and to obtain better planning of public utilities. In the Outaouais area, the Member of the National Assembly for Hull, and Minister of the Public Service and Minister of State for Inter-governmental Affairs and Finance, the Hon. Oswald Parent, followed up this initiative. In a letter addressed to the Chairman of the Executive Committee of the Outaouais Regional Community, he proposed that the 32 municipalities of the ORC be amalgamated into five new municipalities, a change which should not, however, cause the Québec government to "contemplate the dissolution or disappearance of the Outaouais Regional Community." He proposed that the first amalgamation encompass West Hull, Lucerne, Aylmer, Deschênes and Hull; the second would include Touraine, Templeton West, Pointe-Gatineau, Gatineau, Templeton, Templeton East, Templeton East (east part); the other three amalgamations would group together all the other municipalities, which are mainly rural.

On December 23, 1971, exactly two years after adopting the Act creating the Outaouais Regional Community, the Québec government adopted Bill 276, an Act to promote the regroupment of municipalities. In January 1972, the Québec Minister of Municipal Affairs ordered a study concerning financial data from the region's municipalities for the purpose of selecting the best amalgamation alternative for the municipalities located within the ORC. This study, made public on June 6, 1972, recommended to the department that the 32 municipalities in the ORC be amalgamated into five new municipalities. The City of Hull and the other 11 urban municipalities surrounding it, from Aylmer to Templeton, were chosen to form an amalgamated urban unit. This area encompasses 13 per cent of the territory in the ORC and 84 per cent of its population; as an urbanized area its needs are different from those of the surrounding rural sectors.

Lately, however, there have been increasing suggestions that the Outaouais Regional Community territory would be divided into three urban and three rural municipalities and this may have been announced by the time this report is published. The three urban sectors would be formed by Aylmer, Lucerne, Deschênes, Hull and the southern portion of West Hull; by the seven urban municipalities immediately to the east of the Gatineau River; and by the towns of Buckingham and Masson further east.

In an address delivered in Hull on January 28, 1974, the Minister of State for Intergovernmental Affairs and MNA for Hull, Mr. Oswald Parent, admitted,

> ...it is obvious that reform is urgently needed on both the local and regional level. It is also obvious that the problem of municipal amalgamation must be solved this year. Having too many municipalities has long been an obstacle to regional development as a whole.[16]

In a letter to all the mayors of the 32 municipalities of the Outaouais Regional Community, on April 10, 1974, Mr. Parent urged all municipal councils to adopt a motion in favour of amalgamation as soon as possible, and to submit their final decision to the Department of Municipal Affairs before August 31st 1974:

> There is no longer any point in continuing discussions which cannot add anything more and it is time to go right on to the negotiation phase... I am counting on your cooperation in achieving before the end of the summer the objective for which we have been working so hard for several years.[17]

At the same time, Mr. Parent specified to the municipalities that they should retain the general principle that amalgamation should be along the lines of the five municipal units defined by the minister of Municipal Affairs in July 1972. He added:

> For serious and completely justified reasons, however, the Quebec Government could accept that a municipality's territory be divided into several parts or that a regroupment unit be modified in one way or another.[17]

Footnotes

1. *Plan for the National Capital*, Ottawa, 1950, p. 287.
2. *Joint Committee of the Senate and the House of Commons on the Federal District Commission, Minutes of Proceedings* No. 19, June 27, 1956, p. 909.
3. *Plan for the National Capital*, pp. 119-120.
4. Statistics Canada *1971 Census of Canada*, Catalogue 92-702, Vol. 1. Statistics Canada does not provide population figures relating directly to the National Capital Region. It does, however, provide census information for metropolitan Ottawa–Hull and for the local municipalities in Ontario and Québec. From the two, it was possible to arrive at reasonably reliable figures—those quoted, which may suffer marginally because the NCR boundaries bisect some of the rural municipalities.
5. Ibid.
6. Statistics Canada, *1971 Census of Canada*, Catalogue 92-773 (Sp. 3).
7. *Ottawa, Eastview and Carleton County Local Government Review, Report on Research Findings*, (Ottawa 1965), p. II. Letter from Hon. J. W. Spooner to Ottawa Mayor Charlotte Whitton, dated May 26, 1964 referring to previous correspondence his department had had with the Mayor.
8. Address by Hon. D'Arcy McKeough to a meeting of local municipal representatives, Ottawa, February 2, 1968, p. 6.
9. *Ottawa Journal*, "Reaction Varied to Regional Government" by Joe Dupuis, April 2, 1970.
10. Eggleston, Wilfrid, *The Queen's Choice*, p. 67.
11. Brault, Lucien, *Hull 1800-1950*, University of Ottawa, 1950, p. 24-25.
12. Ibid., p. 229.
13. *Étude de regroupement, City of Hull*, March 1973, p. 12.
14. *Rapport de la Commission d'étude sur l'intégrité du territoire du Québec, Les problèmes de la région de la capitale canadienne*, Quebec City, May 22, 1968.
15. Outaouais Regional Community Act, RSQ 1969, Chapter 85.
16. Parent, the Hon. Oswald, *La présence du Québec dans l'Outaouais*, an address to the Hull Chamber of Commerce, January 28, 1974, p. 15.
17. Parent, the Hon. Oswald, *Letter to Mayors of Municipalities* in the Outaouais Regional Community, April 10, 1974.

Chapter Four

Evolution of Federal Role in the Capital: The NCC and Other Federal Bodies

Concurrently with the evolution of local government, which we described in the last chapter, the federal role in the Capital has been shifting and changing. We now turn to record and assess federal operations which are particularly relevant to this Study, although as we note elsewhere, the federal impact on the Capital is so enormous and so pervasive that it cannot possibly be fully reviewed. The emphasis in this chapter will therefore be mainly on the physical impact of federal activities—planning, building, land acquisition, and on the areas of real or potential overlap among federal agencies, and between the federal government and the other governments involved in the governing of the Capital. The discussions of some of the problems generated by conflicting jurisdictions will be considered in more detail in Chapters Eight to Ten.

I. The National Capital Commission

Two organizations in particular dominate the federal role in the Capital, the National Capital Commission and the Department of Public Works (DPW). Since our terms of reference give prominent place to the role of the NCC, the story which follows pays special attention to that agency. The historical development of the NCC has already been touched on briefly. Perhaps the simplest way to grasp the NCC's role in the growth of the Capital is to consider it as being composed of five different phases, all with a different pace and emphasis:

(*a*) *1899–1926* as the Ottawa Improvement Commission (OIC). The beginning of planning under its first adviser, Montreal landscape architect Frederick Todd. His major contribution was beautification, the building of parks, and the beginning of the parkway system. OIC had a limited budget, but Todd's emphasis on trees and greenery, and on the need to preserve the forests at the lower end of what is now Gatineau Park, set a commission pattern which has persisted to this day. However, no action was taken on the 1915 Holt Commission planning or governing proposals.

(*b*) *1927–1945* as the first phase of the Federal District Commission, (FDC). A larger budget, increased number of commissioners, but when the depression arrived in the 'thirties, forward progress slowed. By 1939 the system of parks had been extended to cover some 900 acres, the driveway system had grown to 22 miles, the Champlain Bridge built, Confederation Square had been created, and the Commission had taken over landscape construction and maintenance of the grounds for all federal buildings in the Capital. The most noteworthy event of this period was in 1937 when Prime Minister King brought in Jacques Gréber as adviser on planning. Little was done during the war.

(*c*) *1945–1958*—The FDC—the Gréber period. The National Capital District of 900 square miles was set up, and Gréber was brought back again immediately after the war. The Commission had established a National Capital Planning Committee, with Gréber as consultant; the function of the committee was to draw up a master plan of the National Capital District. The committee's report was completed in 1950, and made public in 1951. In 1951, the federal Municipal Grants Act was passed, entitling Ottawa and other cities across Canada to grants-in-lieu of taxes on federal properties. In the early 'fifties progress was made on implementing the Gréber plan, including the Mackenzie King Bridge, the extension of the parkway system, the beginnings of railway relocation and the Queensway, and various shared cost programmes undertaken with the City of Ottawa (roads, bridges, sewers). Efforts were made to establish the Greenbelt by zoning, which failed, but substantial land purchases were made in Gatineau Park. In 1956 came the Joint Parliamentary Committee on the FDC, and their hearings and recommendations led to the creation of the NCC in its present form.

(*d*) *1958–1969*—The NCC—post-Gréber period. The National Capital Act[1] was passed in 1958 and proclaimed the following year. It enlarged the National Capital District to 1800 square miles, and changed its name to National Capital Region. It strengthened the NCC's powers of expropriation and, with government approval, the Greenbelt was largely acquired in this manner. Railway relocation was completed and the new station built. The parkway system was extended and much land acquired for future parkways around and through Ottawa and the Hull area. The main new parkways built included the Gatineau Park network; the Ottawa River Parkway, and Colonel By Drive along the Rideau Canal. Gatineau Park was developed to provide recreation, in particular at Lac Philippe. Lac Mousseau (Harrington) was set aside as the summer home for the Prime Minister. The LeBreton Flats area was expropriated, in part a consequence of the railway relocation programme and the displacement of industry which resulted. Joint projects with the provinces included the MacDonald-Cartier Bridge crossing the Ottawa River.

In summary, in this period the main features of the Gréber plan were put in place, but there were few new initiatives taken. The Commission planners were heavily involved in highway projects and studies, including that of the Ottawa-Hull Area Transportation Study.

(*e*) *1969 to date*—The most recent NCC period has been dominated by these developments:

(i) In the spring of 1969 the federal government decided to build office buildings in Hull, and to expropriate land through the NCC for this purpose. This led to a substantial shift in NCC spending to help on a shared-cost basis in the building up of municipal services in the Hull area, including the water—filtration plant, a sewage system, and an extensive road network. It led also to changing the concept of a single (Ottawa) core to a bi-polar core, one pole in the concentration of government buildings in Hull, the other in downtown Ottawa. The Portage Bridge was built, a key link in the new core concept.

(ii) Roads were de-emphasized, and work on parkways was largely halted, except for the Airport Parkway, badly needed for access to Uplands Airport. Cooperation began with citizen groups to slow arterial road and expressway construction, and to limit their adverse environmental effect. Much greater emphasis was placed on people things, on liveliness in the centre of the Capital—pedestrian and bicycle paths, skating and boating on the Rideau Canal, toboggan runs, vegetable gardens on NCC grounds. Gatineau Park plans were steered away from development and recreation and towards conservation, and snowmobiles were banned from the Park.

(iii) The share of NCC funds devoted to shared cost projects, in cooperation with municipalities and provinces on both sides of the river, steadily increased. This had the effect of reducing the NCC's own construction activities.

(iv) Two specific transactions might be noted. Discussion with the E. B. Eddy Company had begun in 1969 with a view to moving the factories away from the riverfront site. In February 1972 the Company closed its sulphite plant, a major polluter of the air and of the Ottawa River, and its newsprint machine; this freed some 44 acres of riverfront property (40% of the Eddy site) which it sold to the NCC at a price of $29.5 million. Conditions of the sale were that no employee would be laid off as a consequence of the transaction, and that the NCC has first call on the remaining property. In 1973 there was an exchange of administration of land with the Province of Québec, whereby control over some 12,500 of acres of bush in the north-west part of the Park (15% of the Park's area) was transferred to the NCC in exchange for 255 acres of urban land in the south-east corner of the Park, and elsewhere in Hull; 193 acres for educational purposes and 62 acres for roadways. In value terms the exchange favoured Québec by about $1 million.

NCC Expenditures and Operations

The historic expenditure figures, I am afraid, are not very significant, because of the changing value of the dollar, and the rise in land values. About all that can usefully be said is that up to March 31, 1973, expenditures "for development and improvement" by the NCC and its predecessors amounted to about $300 millions, with about half of this in the form of property acquisition. To this should be added some $38 millions interest on loans to acquire property.

The current value of NCC property is very difficult to estimate, because so much of it is dedicated to parks and parkways, but in 1972 one internal NCC calculation put it in excess of $800 million.

The net operating expenses of the NCC in 1972–73 were about $10.0 million, and in 1973–74 $11.4 million, with an additional $3.2 million in each year in interest on loans. Capital expenditures, largely financed through a non-lapsing National Capital Fund, vary widely because of the swings in the timing of payments (e.g. the Eddy transaction), but they have been running in recent years at about $25 million to $35 million annually. Grants-in-lieu of taxes paid to local municipalities amount to about $1.5 million.

Organization and Relationship with the Government

The National Capital Act provides that the Commission consist of twenty members, with at least one member from each province, at least two from Ottawa and one from Hull, and at least one each from another local municipality in Ontario and in Quebec. The Chairman and Vice-chairman are designated by the Governor in Council, but only the Chairman serves full time; he has the rank of deputy minister. The Executive Committee acts for the Commission between meetings. There are three other committees (not all members of each are Commissioners): the National Capital Planning Committee, the Land Committee and the Design Committee.

As a Crown agency the NCC reports through a minister to Parliament, with the Minister designated by Order-in-Council; following World War II the minister designated was the Prime Minister of the day. In 1957 responsibility passed to the Minister of Public Works where it remained until 1968, when it was transferred to the Hon. Jean Marchand, Minister of the Department of Regional Economic Expansion. In October 1970 a further shift was made to the Hon. Robert Andras, Minister of State responsible for Housing, and in January 1972 to the Honourable Ron Basford when he replaced Mr. Andras. These shifts affected the nature of NCC relationships with other departments, particularly Public Works, and also affected the scope of its operations.

Federal Crown (government) corporations or agencies are created to manage those public services where business enterprise and public accountability must be combined. Of the three main varieties—"department corporations", "agency corporations", and "proprietary corporations"—the NCC falls into the second group, described in the Canada Year Book 1972 as "responsible for the management of trading or service operations on a quasi-commercial basis or for the management of procurement, construction or disposal activities on behalf of Her Majesty in right of Canada."

In summary, a Crown corporation or agency is given a measure of independence from the government because of the nature of its work. However, the idea that the NCC has really much freedom to act on its own is in many respects a myth. It is set up in corporate form—"3. (1) There shall be a corporation, to be called the National Capital Commission.... 4. (1) The Commission is, for all purposes of this Act, an agent of Her Majesty, and its powers under this Act may be exercised only as an agent of Her Majesty."[1]—but it operates much more as a small department of government. The degree of NCC independence, of course, varies from time to time, and may reflect the interest of the responsible Minister in the Commission, his desire to run it himself, and the relationship between him and the incumbent Chairman.

All the significant powers to spend money conferred by the Act are hedged by regulations or by such clauses as

> Sec. 14. Except with the approval of the Governor in Council, the Commission shall not (*a*) dispose of any real property for a condideration in excess of a value of ten thousand dollars; (*b*) acquire any real property for a consideration in excess of a value of twenty-five thousand dollars; or (*c*) enter into an agreement or lease enduring for a period in excess of five years.

As a Crown agency the Commission has to provide estimates, operating and capital budgets, and five year forecasts, but it is also subject to all the requirements of financial reporting imposed on the departments. In summary, most decisions taken by the Commission, have little validity until approval is received from Treasury Board or the Cabinet itself. Every negotiation in which the Commissions is involved, every property transaction, every agreement, is always subject to approval by the Governor in Council.[2]

There are a few areas in which there is a bit of freedom from departmental regulations, including the hiring of staff. But the pay structure is almost entirely controlled by the government, the chief limitation being that rates of pay of the Chairman and General Manager, the two senior full-time jobs, are set by Order-in-Council. The pay of almost all staff up to senior managerial level is determined by negotiation between Treasury Board and the public service unions for the various classifications. Rates between the NCC and government departments are kept in line by common classification standards, and linked through a number of NCC "benchmark" positions to equivalent positions in departments. The straitjacket thus fits rather tightly, and leads to some anomalous situations. Although the NCC's operational role is more like that of a municipality than a government department, in the past few years senior NCC staff appear to be paid less than those in equivalent positions in the City of Ottawa or the Regional Municipality of Ottawa–Carleton.

It would be improper to conclude from all this that the NCC is a powerless agency, because it had been allocated generous budgets, and most of its proposals tend to be well-received and endorsed by Cabinet or Cabinet committee. And when approval is not forthcoming, it does not mean automatically that the government is behaving capriciously; it may sometimes be applying different priorities or exercising political judgment. What I am saying, however, is that when a Crown agency is viewed from outside as reasonably autonomous, and the reality is very different, it poses a variety of problems for those who administer it.

This will be discussed later from several different aspects, but let me mention two particular problems of which I became well aware during my stay at the

NCC. One is that the Chairman is forced to wear two hats. As head of a Crown agency he is expected to provide leadership, to speak for his agency, to negotiate with municipalities and the private sector, to keep his Commissioners happy, and to act as if the agency were really independent. As a deputy minister he is expected to defer to his Minister in all things, to obey all the rules of the public service, and in general to be as anonymous as he can. The second problem is the frustration of the Commissioners. They find out at their first meeting that they are really only an advisory body to an agency which itself is only an adviser to the government, instead of being directors of a fairly autonomous corporation.

Objects and Powers

But what is the NCC formally directed to accomplish, and what are its legal powers—even if it is subject to the inhibiting factors noted above? The Act is printed in Appendix A, and clauses 10 to 12, under "Objects, Purposes and Powers" provide a very broad base for the Commission's operations. Section 10(1) sets the object clearly as preparing plans for and assisting in the development, conservation and improvement of the National Capital Region "in order that the nature and character of the seat of the Government of Canada may be in accordance with its national significance."

Section 10(2) allows it to buy, sell, lease, and develop property, construct parks, highways, parkways, bridges, buildings, maintain and improve its own property, engage in joint projects with municipalities, or make grants, conduct research, preserve historical places or buildings—and in 10(2)(i) do anything else incidental to the attainment of its objects.

In Section 11, the Commission is instructed to coordinate the development of federal public lands in the Capital, to screen proposals for new buildings on such lands, or alterations thereto, and to require that the site, location and plans be approved by it before work can begin (all subject to overriding veto by Cabinet). Section 12 authorizes the Commission to build railway lines and facilities, and to enter into agreement with the railway companies; this was specifically designed to cope with the problems arising out of the relocation of the railway lines proposed by Gréber.

Internal Organization and Functions

The Commission is organized to carry out its day-to-day operations on the following basis:

(i) *Headquarters*—Under the chairman and general manager are five assistant general managers, one for each of three planning divisions, one for development, and one for finance and property. The chairman is assisted by a small staff of senior advisers—legal services, social development, intergovernmental affairs, and the NCC Secretary.

(ii) *Planning*—NCC planning is divided into three divisions, Ontario, Quebec, and research and services. The first two divisions are concerned mainly with specific planning issues for their respective areas, and are involved in constant liaison with the municipal planning authorities. Associated with the work of all three groups is the National Capital Planning Committee, about half of whose members are commissioners and half drawn from outside government circles.

In recent years the planning emphasis has been largely (a) planning for the new federal developments on the Québec side, for the Eddy site and for LeBreton Flats, and cooperating in planning the associated services; (b) the linking together of the two regions through the so-called "core" plan, involving the whole centre town region on both sides of the river; (c) the preparation of a "guide plan" or set of long-range policies designed to create the framework for the capital of the future; (d) the consideration of alternative policies for certain specific Commission areas of responsibility, for example, Gatineau Park, the Greenbelt, housing for the centre of the Capital, and the development of the proposed new South East City.

(iii) *Development*—Those basic duties associated with managing most of the large federal land holdings in the region—landscaping in all its forms, snow removal from parkways, canal rink and parking lots, the preservation and maintenance of Gatineau Park and recreational areas, care of mechanical equipment, etc. This involves about 500 of the Commission's regular staff of 700, and up to 200 additional summer employees. Construction has been a steadily diminishing part of the Commission's activities, as work on new parkways has declined, most of the Gréber projects completed, and as the Commission emphasis has shifted to assisting in works carried out by the provinces and municipalities.

(iv) *Land*—The Commission's large land holdings—124,000 acres—grew out of land acquisition programmes, which were expanded greatly at the time of the Greenbelt expropriation. About 1000 leases are in existence. Legal operations are closely linked: over half of some 3000 property transactions since the Greenbelt acquisition involved expropriation; of these, 119 reached litigation. About 20 cases are still unresolved, 58 were settled out of court, and of the 41 that went to court, 6 went on appeal to the Supreme Court. I might note that the NCC dependence on expropriation has fallen off sharply in recent years; in July 1970 its expropriation powers, as well as those of all federal departments, were transferred to the DPW. During my tenure as NCC Chairman not one expropriation was carried out, either by or for the NCC.

All Commission land transactions are screened by its Land Committee, which is chaired by a commissioner, and whose members are chosen for their special skills or experience. All valuations must be based on several appraisals, and be approved by the Commission or its Executive Committee upon the recommendation of its Land Committee, before going up to the government for final approval.

(v) *Design*—Responsible for screening and approval of design for buildings and other structures on government land in the Region, and for the design of the Commission's own construction and landscaping programmes. All proposals are reviewed by the Design Committee, composed largely of architects drawn from across Canada.

II. The Department of Public Works

The DPW has been responsible for construction and maintenance of federal buildings in the Capital from the time the first Parliament Buildings were constructed following the naming of Ottawa as the seat of government of the Province of Canada. Its current operations in the Capital are perhaps best described in the following information taken from the 1972-73 annual report:

(i) Approximately half of the net $291 million capital and operating programme for accommodation is spent in the "Capital Region" (defined roughly as the National Capital Region with extensions southward to the St. Lawrence and northwestwards along the Ottawa to Temiskaming Co., Québec).

(ii) With further reference to the Capital Region, "The task of looking after the accommodation needs of a public service population of some 78,000 requires the full-time services of nearly 1,600 employees of the Property Administration Branch, under the supervision of six divisional chiefs." ...The real estate portfolio, the largest in Canada, embraces some 30 million gross square feet of space in more than 750 Crown-owned and leased buildings. The Crown-owned assets are valued at more than $750 million and include 7,000 acres—almost 11 square miles—of prime land."

(iii) "Other Property Administration branch tasks include the operation of a number of multi-million-dollar heating and air-conditioning plants. One of these, the Cliff Street plant behind Parliament Hill, is said to be the largest single heating plant in the Western Hemisphere.... Control of some 18,000 parking spaces is a responsibility of the branch, as is the supervision of contract catering in more than 160 Crown equipped food service outlets dispensing up to 55,000 meals daily."

The size and scale of the DPW operations in the Capital speaks for itself. Our review here is simply to examine briefly three areas of particular interest to this study: government leasing policy, the DPW's involvement in property, and other areas of actual or potential overlapping jurisdiction between the DPW and the NCC.

Build or Lease?

Until 1963 government policy was largely to build its own office accommodation. Needs were limited until the rapid growth in federal employment in World War II, and then a crash programme of "temporary" wooden office structures was undertaken; some of these buildings remain to this day. In the early years after the war a number of new large buildings were built in the core, mostly on Wellington Street. In the 1950's, following the recommendations of Gréber, federal construction was largely concentrated on sites several miles from downtown, such as Tunney's Pasture, Confederation Heights, Carling Avenue, and in the Greenbelt. Emphasis was on functional and economical structures rather than on the monumental form of many of the core buildings. However, the external appearance of all government buildings is subject to the control of the NCC through its Design Committee.

In the 1960's public service growth accelerated, and demands mounted for space better than that available in the temporary wartime structures. In 1963 there was growing government reluctance to grant the DPW the construction funds it needed to meet burgeoning demands, and a new policy of leasing office space from speculative builders was adopted. The race was on, and since the government made no formal advance commitment for such space, and since rental competition was on a price basis, the downtown area soon became dotted with cheaply-built structures, leased as soon as completed because of the compelling demands of government growth. This led to a battle over building heights, a subject which is discussed in detail in Chapter Nine.

In 1969 the government attempted to shift back to a policy of building most of its own space requirements, and a large new programme was launched including seven proposed new buildings for the Quebec side of the river. This programme is being carried out, but the very rapid growth of the public service in 1972 and 1973 meant that the need for rented space continues unabated.

I can add a rather wry personal postscript to this story. By the fall of 1969 a government drive to slow the growth of the public service was in full swing, and it became concerned about the undiminished pace of speculative office construction by the private sector. At one Treasury Board meeting, I was instructed to go out and spread the news to the developers of the expected combined impact of the cessation of growth in the public service, and the upsurge of new government building plans, on future federal needs for rental space from the private sector. This was all done with the best of intentions, and with the object of limiting losses for the speculators. I followed my instructions, crying woe in public statements; a study was prepared at the NCC reflecting the effect of slower federal employment on population, and on the reduced need for homes and office space. The builders were slowed briefly, but they had a much greater trust in the inherent tendency of governments to grow rapidly than in my judgment or in federal preaching about economy. In the event, bulldozers kept scooping out new excavations for still more speculative office buildings to house still more public servants, and still the space in these new buildings—plus that in new federal buildings—is inadequate to the rapidly growing federal bureaucracy!

DPW As Federal Property Agent

In recent years the government has been reviewing its policies for the use of federal land to achieve a more effective and coordinated land management operations. Pursuant to this, the DPW effectively became the chosen instrument, and progressively a number of measures were taken to strengthen its role. The land inventory was set up in the DPW and federal expropriation powers transferred to it (as principal or as agent for departments), as was the large property division of the Ministry of Transport. As the *DPW Annual Report, 1970-71* said,

> These various activities were related to the ultimate destiny of Public Works becoming the federal government's designated agent in the areas of land acquisition and disposal, development of Crown-owned lands, and design and construction. Public Works would, in fact, become Canada's largest construction and property management "firm".

The problem that this poses for the National Capital Commission is that for 70 years *it* has been the federal government designated land agent in the Capital, it holds nearly twenty times as much land as the DPW in the National Capital Region, it has acquired an exceptional expertise in property management and expropriation, and its legal department has developed a solid base of case law, backed by Munro[3] and many other judgments based on the National Capital Act. Finally, in many ways the NCC is more a land developer than a planner, and there is no doubt that land holdings, and its knowledge of land and control of federal land, is vital to its continuing function. However, one searches long and hard through DPW reports and studies relating to its new challenge in the field of federal land management to find any reference at all to the NCC, or to the special needs of the Capital. As we recount in Chapter Nine[4], this has led to conflict between the two bodies.

Other Areas of Potential Conflict

Land management, and the absence of design control of leased office buildings, are two particular sources of difficulty between the DPW and the NCC. Another is the arbitrary division of responsibility for maintenance of federal property in the Capital. In brief, the DPW is responsible for such maintenance inside the building skin, the NCC outside it. For example, the flowers inside the Governor General's greenhouse are managed by the DPW, those outside it by the NCC; every spring the NCC takes formal custody of the greenhouse goldfish when they are shifted to the outside pool, and returns them to DPW's custody in the fall! The DPW covers the cost of the initial landscaping of a new government building, the NCC the cost of the continuing maintenance.

The DPW provides parking lots for public servants—some of it on land provided by the NCC. One problem the DPW has faced is its attempt to conform to City by-laws, which have required one parking lot for each 500 square feet of office space—except in the down-town core where there has been no standard imposed. In this respect it is the City by-law more than the demands of public servants which has shaped the decisions. The NCC, however, has been concerned about the impact of free federal parking on public transit in the region, and on transportation planning, and has been doing its best to persuade the government to restrict the number of parking spaces made available.

III. Other Departments and Agencies

Central Mortgage and Housing

The CMHC since World War II has been a powerful force in the housing field in Canada. Under the National Housing Act it insures mortgage loans, makes direct loans for home-ownership and rental housing, carries out land assembly, subsidizes public housing, and makes loans and grants for urban renewal, sewage treatment projects, urban research. It is perhaps fair to say that, by the emphasis and direction of its lending and insuring operation, the CMHC has been a major factor in the building of post-war Canadian cities.

We do not propose to argue here whether the results of CMHC operations on balance have been good or bad. The point we wish to make is first, that the type of single family home on its own lot, which CMHC policies have encouraged, has greatly influenced the shape of the Capital's growth as it has that of other cities across Canada. The second point is that the giving or withholding of CMHC insured mortgage loans can be a powerful force in supporting—or weakening—federal planning policies in the Capital. One example occurred in the early 1950's, when the NCC was trying to establish the Greenbelt by zoning. The municipalities did not go along, and in 1955 the CMHC was instructed by the government[5] to restrict its loans for Greenbelt housing. This had a very considerable impact on slowing undesirable growth, but eventually the federal government, to preserve the Greenbelt concept, was forced to buy or expropriate most of the land within it. CMHC restrictions were then lifted. To the best of my knowledge, CMHC powers have not again been employed in this fashion.

Other involvement by the CMHC includes land assembled in the Capital over a long period for eventual housing projects; some of this land has been made available to other agencies or to other levels of government for such institutional projects as hospitals and for roads. At the present time the CMHC is a partner with the NCC and with the Ontario Housing Corporation in the assembly of land for the proposed South East City, in the area of Carlsbad Springs.

Department of Agriculture

The main Central Experimental Farm in Ottawa occupies 1100 acres of land in a completely urban setting and is surrounded on three sides by housing. Its north-east corner in fact is just over two miles from the Parliament Buildings; in many respects it was the Capital's first Greenbelt. As such it has provoked the usual complaints from the City of Ottawa—it provided no tax revenues, but added substantially to the costs of providing services to the rapidly growing area beyond it—water, sewers, roads and public transit. In recent years, Agriculture has acquired from the NCC an even larger block of land in the Greenbelt to expand the Farm's operation.

One interesting thing about the Farm is how firmly the jurisdiction over it still rests with the Department of Agriculture. This urban land would be very valuable (perhaps $200,000 per acre) if used for housing or related purposes. But if anyone questions the economics of growing experimental crops on land of this value, the answer is usually that the maintenance of the Farm, as an undeveloped island of open farm land and park, is a "good thing" for the Capital. Undoubtedly the preservation of this land for public use has made enormous sense in the past, and from the public's point of view the land is almost sacred. Nevertheless, the judgment of whether the present use of land is good for the Capital or not is essentially an urban planning decision, and hardly one over which Agriculture should have complete control.

My purpose in raising this point is to emphasize the role that departmental ownership of land plays in urban planning in the Capital. This does not mean that departments should be deprived of a measure of control over land needed for their operations, but that some internal federal mechanism should exist for a continuing review of existing federal land use.

Other Federal Involvement

The Department of National Defence is another large land owner in the Region, including the Rockcliffe and Uplands air bases, and a wide variety of military installations such as armouries and proving grounds. Total holdings amount to 5,550 acres. Decisions affecting its land are subject to the same type of stricture we apply to the Experimental Farm—it tends to be regarded as the preserve of the military, and is not always subject to urban planning scrutiny. A similar comment might be made about the 6,100 acres held in the Region by the Ministry of Transport, mainly at Ottawa International Airport. The Department of Indian Affairs and Northern Development controls the Rideau Canal and owns land along it, including the land on which about one-fifth of the City's Lansdowne Park is situated.

In the field of cultural amenities, the city has been richly endowed by the federal government. Heading the list is the $50 million National Arts Centre, the National Gallery, and a wide variety of museums that are national in nature. These not only serve as a showcase and storehouse of Canada's cultural heritage, but represent a great attraction for residents and tourists alike.

All departments have some impact on the Capital, but we will refer to two only at this time, Finance and Treasury Board. Finance is responsible for the administration of the Municipal Grants Act, and in this capacity negotiates annually with local municipalities to determine the amount of grants to be paid in lieu of taxes. The formula is complex, and involves exclusion of certain buildings and lands from the calculations, but the amount paid in the Region in 1973 by federal departments and agencies was $18.6 million. This is expanded on in Chapter Ten. Treasury Board is involved from time to time in decisions on personnel matters that have a bearing on the functioning of the city, including parking policy for public servants and the staggering of working hours for government employees in order to spread the load on public transit and ease traffic congestion.

Footnotes

1. R.S.C. 1970 c. N.3. *National Capital Act*, Appendix A.
2. Ibid.
3. *Harold Munro v. National Capital Commission.* Judgment of Exchequer Court, April 28, 1965, Gibson J, and judgment of Supreme Court of Canada, June 28, 1966, Cartwright J.
4. Chapter *Nine*, page 108.
5. *Proceedings of Joint Committee of the Senate and the House of Commons on the FDC*, 1956, p. 66.

Chapter Five

The Federal Claim to a Seat at the Table

I. The Capital as a National Symbol

Why should the federal government be involved at all in governing the Capital when Section 92 of the BNA Act gives responsibility for "municipal institutions" to the provinces? Over the century of the Capital's history, this is the view that has been put forward again and again by many local municipal, provincial and even federal politicians, most of whom make the argument that there should be less, not more, federal say in the running of the Capital—but of course more federal money allocated to the municipalities. "Just give us the tools. . ."—they suggest.

In this chapter we put forward a number of reasons why federal involvement in the Capital is not only defensible on legal or constitutional grounds, but eminently desirable as well. But whatever the validity of the case, the rationale which underpins federal participation rests on the role the Capital plays in the functioning of the nation, on its national symbolic importance. This obligates the federal government to ensure that, as the National Capital Act enjoins in Section 10, "the nature and character of the seat of the Government of Canada may be in accordance with its national significance".

Oddly enough, the national symbolic role of the Capital, and the consequent federal obligation, have seldom been publicly articulated except in the most general terms, and then almost as an assumption that did not require explanation. Most Canadians have tended to take for granted that it was a good idea to have a "beautiful" Capital, and could see no reason why the federal government should not help bring this about. This proved to be enough justification for the government to take the various steps it did to improve the Capital, and to obtain funds for these activities from Parliament.

The question is whether mild benevolence towards the Capital is enough in Canada today, a country lacking in established symbols of nationhood, a country with strong regional differences and subject to many centrifugal forces. But even if one accepts that a stronger national feeling about the Capital would be a good way to bind the nation more closely together, how does one go about achieving this objective? How does one sell the idea to Canadians? How does one put this concept of the symbolic capital into words? One correspondent put it this way:

> ..."How do you define a Capital" I think of it as a nucleus, an attraction, an embodiment, and a source. It must draw together, and it must reflect (and by its Parliament think on) and radiate the distillation of the nation's thoughts.
> ...I conclude that the site, the place, must be the Capital, and must be the magnet for the Canadian thought, and it must be brought about by the supreme attractiveness and beauty of its collection of Canadian artifacts, traditions, in the Archives, Museums, buildings, parks, and in its service to the citizens. It must be respected and appreciated by Canadians.
> ...What could be more glorious than to sit on Parliament Hill about September the 25th any year, and look across at maples right to the hills?

A few years ago the NCC made an attempt to describe its objectives in summary form for the purpose of introducing its 1972–73 Annual Estimates:

OBJECTIVE

To help develop the National Capital Region so that it will be:

(*a*) a fitting symbol of Canada's cultural and linguistic values;

(*b*) an efficient and esthetically satisfying place in which to carry on the nation's business;

(*c*) a model of urban planning and development that will benefit other parts of the country and be a source of pride for Canadians.

There have been a number of other attempts to find inspiring words to describe the national significance of the Capital. Gréber had the following comments:

> A Capital is the reflection, the symbol, of the whole nation. The Capital of Canada, as in all federated states, such as in the case of Washington, or Berne, has special importance; it is the city which, to every Canadian and to all foreigners, must be representative of all of the ten confederated provinces, without, however, prejudicing the attributes and prerogatives of their respective capitals.
>
> ...now a link between the two provinces of Ontario and Quebec, which are symbolic of Canadian greatness: ....Extending beyond this initial symbolic development, Ottawa has since become truly representative of the whole of Canada. ....The planning of the Capital is therefore a national undertaking, of which each Canadian can be proud and through which national desires and aspirations can be expressed through material accomplishments. The first accomplishment, initiated by the Federal Government, will go down in history: it is the decision that the planning of the National Capital be dedicated to the memory of Canadians who gave their lives to the nation in the second world war.

> This heroic symbol will be materialized in the heart of the territory of the Capital, not by an allegoric sculptural composition, sometimes subject to controversies, but by an objective reality: the living panorama of the Capital.[1]

In his judgment on the Munro case Mr. Justice Gibson quoted Gréber and then had the following things to say himself:

> The National Capital Region belongs to the nation in the sense that it can be said that the aspirations, hopes, attainments and way of life of the citizens of Canada are exemplified to themselves and to all the visitors to Canada in the nature and character of the east of the Government of Canada. Concern for and interest in the seat of the Government of Canada are the affair of all the citizens of Canada and of all ten provinces. A worthy seat of Government can be achieved by the adoption and implementation of a general plan under the provisions of section 10 of the *National Capital Act*.
>
> Every country must have a capital worthy of it, and the evidence indicates that throughout history this has always been recognized. As indicated earlier, the national significance of ancient Greece was exemplified in its capital Athens, of Italy, in its capital Rome, of France, in its capital Paris, of Great Britain, in its capital London, and of the United States, in its capital Washington.
>
> In the result, therefore, I am of opinion that the words "national significance" are meaningful and are apt in describing the goal sought to be attained for the nature and character of the seat of the Government of Canada.[2]

One interesting attempt to articulate the place of the capital in the Nation was made in 1969 in an official paper concerning the development of the capital region. Referring to the "future needs and aspiration" of the Capital, four objectives are cited:

> *As a Symbol, to:*
>
> ... be the true reflection of Canada, the major element contributing to national pride; strong, continuing, visible.
>
> ... epitomize every Canadian's wish for achievement and recognition by the excellent appearance of every facet and by provision of elements of vitality designed to evoke identification and response.
>
> ... reflect the multi-national fact of Canadian life, particularly the dual aspect of our basic heritage.
>
> *As a Capital Region and Metropolitan Centre, to;*
>
> ... function well as an urban concentration.
>
> ... be economically healthy.
>
> ... exhibit the highest standards in the readily visible portions of the City scape.
>
> ... provide a suitable, convenient, comfortable, satisfying milieu for the citizens who include M.P., Senators, foreign diplomats, the permanent executive and the senior judiciary, and for visiting dignitaries.
>
> ... provide for future growth and renewal.

As an Inspiration, to:

... display intellectual activity of a high order by accommodating a significant proportion of the valuable elements of Canada's scientific and educational estate.

.... be a repository for the nation's art, archives and artifacts and to provide a brilliant showcase for display of these and the nation's lively arts, and whatever cultural manifestations from other countries may appear in Canada.

As an Exemplar, to:

... reflect Canada's activities in communications, physical and intellectual, and any special characteristics peculiar to Canada that are recognized as being of the highest international standard.

... perform a catalytic function by providing a full-scale urban laboratory for design, testing, construction and display of model solutions to the physical and social crisis in Canada's cities and for other social and technological innovations.

... be a centre of communication for information and ideas, and creativity however expressed.

... be adaptable so as to reflect the changing nature of Canada in whatever form and direction this may take.

This is a comprehensive list, and I find little to quarrel with in it. The reservations I have about it derive mainly from my suspicion that it loads too much on to the backs of those charged with trying to build the Capital; it may be too ambitious in establishing so many goals. When one has too many targets there is a tendency to scatter one's shot. Still, its probably as close as anyone is likely to come to a comprehensive description of what a capital might aspire to become.

Mind you, there are different opinions about the merits of building up the Capital as a symbol. One correspondent wrote as follows:

> It seems to me that the notion of a national capital as exists in more established nations than Canada, e.g., the United States, should be questioned before we attempt to embark on a similar route. Ottawa (as far as the rest of the country is concerned) has never been the heart beat of the nation. Few Canadians outside Ottawa look to the capital for their information and attitudes. It is no accident that the best newspapers in Canada are not Ottawa editions. I think this tells us something we should closely examine. If we can agree that most Canadians do not await Ottawa's pronouncements with bated breath, should an effort be made to make Ottawa to be seen by its citizens in a way most U.S. citizens view Washington? I think not. I think the fact that most Canadians view Ottawa with less interest and awe than we should push for something else. I would suggest that rather than try and make the pilgrims look toward Mecca, we inject aspects of Mecca into various urban centres in Canada. (This correspondent is quoted further in Chapter 11 page 142-3).

I found some of this attitude in my travels across the country; there was little of the feeling Americans have for Washington. In one speech I made in

Sydney, Nova Scotia, about the capital being a needed federal symbol, one member of the audience commented "the federal presence to us is symbolized by the Coast Guard Academy across the harbour. Don't let them take it away!" (Some attempts to move it had been rumoured).

However, if the national interest imposes obligations on the federal government to see that a capital worthy of the country results, what powers has the government to meet this obligation? We turn now to this question.

II. Acquired or "Squatters" Rights

A good argument can be made, whatever its legal status, that what the federal government has done during the last century in the Capital and continues to do, entitles it to a say in the governing process. Few will disagree with the contention that most of the "good" things found to-day in the Capital (apart from the generous endowment of nature) were put there by the federal government, were built on land provided by the federal government, or were otherwise heavily subsidized with federal funds. If the Capital can be regarded as reasonably well planned, as I think it can, then most of the imaginative plans were prepared by the federal government or by the planners it hired. Until very recently there was very little local planning done except by the NCC and its predecessors; the federal government filled a huge gap in an area normally of municipal responsibility.

Furthermore, until very recently the NCC was the only body concerned with the overall planning of the Region as a whole, and in particular with the meshing of the plans for both sides of the Ottawa River. Until the advent of regional government, each municipality tended to plan almost as if it were independent of federal planning and totally isolated from other municipalities in the Capital. One attempt at combined planning was made in 1965 in the efforts to coordinate transportation plans through the Ottawa-Hull Area Transportation Study, but these plans were so automobile-oriented and costly that they proved unworkable.

I realize that a display of medals by a battle-scarred veteran may arouse sympathy or pity, but will not necessarily guarantee respect, and the federal display of its past activities as a justification for a role in governing may be subject to the same weakness. Whatever the legal grounds for putting "acquired rights" forward, it provides a good moral case for federal participation in local government in the Capital, and particularly if backed by some of the legal arguments and the undoubted sources of independent federal power which are commented on below.

III. The Concept of a Federal Municipality

The federal power to act has been strengthened, as we have noted in Chapter Two, by the acquisition of land by purchase or by expropriation under the National

Capital Act. The amount of land now held by the federal government in the Region is substantial, amounting to over 12% of the 1800 square miles, and an estimated 29% of the total land in the urban part of the area. Neither the municipal or provincial government has jurisdiction over this land, and the federal government is not required to conform to local by-laws or to provincial licensing requirements. The laws of the provinces, and of their creatures, the municipalities, cannot take away or abridge any federal right without the federal government's consent. Under the paramountcy doctrine, federal legislation prevails over provincial legislation in cases of conflict.

However, federal policy is generally to conform to municipal ordinances to the maximum possible extent. One reason lies in the advantages in avoiding the setting up of parallel facilities. For example, elevators in federal buildings are inspected and licensed by the appropriate provincial government branch, which has special expertise. Another reason for federal cooperation is its desire to be, and to be seen to be, a "good citizen".

Mr. Alex Morin, General Manager of NCC, put forward the novel idea of looking at federal property in the Capital as a separate municipality run by NCC for the federal government. It is a very oddly shaped municipality, mind you, with tentacles running through almost every part of the NCR; if pieces of federal property were coloured on a map it might resemble a Riopelle painting. However, there are a few municipal enclaves in the region like Vanier and Rockcliffe Park which are completely surrounded by the City of Ottawa, so the idea is not quite so far fetched as it seems at first glance. And from the federal point of view, a more wide-spread understanding both within and without the government of what this land means to the NCC, and how important an instrument it is in achieving federal goals in the Capital, would give everyone a much clearer view of the scope of real federal power in the Capital. It would have particular value in displaying how federal land powers can be weakened by the dispersion of control over such land among the various departments and agencies, a matter referred to in a later chapter.

A wide appreciation of the "federal municipality" concept should also make it easier to understand the role of the NCC, which in its structure is in many ways similar to a municipality. The NCC Chairman is appointed, not elected, and he is responsible to a Parliament elected by the people of Canada, rather than to local citizens, but in many respects he has to function as a mayor of a municipality, or a regional chairman, and to deal on that basis with officials of other municipalities in the Region. One hesitates to draw a comparison with the District of Columbia, but there is a parallel between the status of the appointed Mayor of Washington and that of the NCC Chairman (although changes are now occurring in D.C. government which are expected to lead to a civic election of a mayor and council in 1975, and to a substantial devolution of much federal power to the elected government).[3]

IV. *Federal Constitutional and Legal Rights*

No one can dispute the provinces' control over municipalities; the BNA Act is clear. Equally clear, however is that the Capital has a special role which distinguishes it from other cities in the country. This special role of the Capital, as we have noted above, is what led Parliament to approve the spending of federal money on the Capital, and to pass the National Capital Act in 1958. This Act created the National Capital Commission, gave it in Section 10: "*Objects, Purposes and Powers*", and in Section 23 declared that all works of the Commission were "for the general advantage of Canada". (See Appendix A).

But how far did these powers extend? We have referred several times to the Munro Case. In 1959 the NCC expropriated the property of one Harold Munro, whose land was needed for the Greenbelt around Ottawa, an integral part of the Gréber proposals. On 21 February 1965, Mr. Munro's lawyers took the matter to the Exchequer Court, seeking clarification of the following question:

> Whether, on the special case stated by the parties, the expropriation of the lands of the defendant by the National Capital Commission therein referred to is a nullity because the legislative authority of the Parliament of Canada under the British North America Act, 1867 to 1960, does not extend to authorizing the expropriation.

On April 28, 1965 Mr. Justice Gibson in his judgment[2] answered the question in the negative. He concluded that "the legislative authority of the Parliament in Canada, under the *British North America Act* 1857 to 1960, does extend to authorizing the expropriation of the lands of the defendant..."

This ruling was upheld in June, 1966 on appeal to the Supreme Court of Canada, with judgment written by Mr. Justice Cartwright.[4] The appellants had argued in effect that the expropriation was for planning purposes, and hence a provincial matter. The judgment stated that Section 92 of the BNA did not give the subject of the Capital exclusively to the Provinces, nor indeed is it referred to anywhere in either Section 91 or 92 of the Act. The judge therefore concluded that the sole power rested with the Dominion under the preliminary words of Section 91 relative to "laws for the peace, order and good government of Canada". In referring to the National Capital Act, Justice Cartwright noted:

> I find it difficult to suggest a subject matter of legislation which more clearly goes beyond local or provincial interests and is the concern of Canada as a whole than the development, conservation and improvement of the National Capital Region in accordance with a coherent plan in order that the nature and character of the seat of the Government of Canada may be in accordance with its national significance. Adopting the words of the learned trial judge, it is my view that the Act 'deals with a single matter of national concern'.
>
> There is no doubt that the exercise of the powers conferred upon the Commission by the *National Capital Act* will affect the civil rights of residents in those

> parts of the two provinces which make up the National Capital Region. In the case at bar the rights of the appellant are affected. But once it has been determined that the matter in relation to which the Act is passed is one which falls within the power of Parliament it is no objection to its validity that its operation will affect civil rights in the provinces.[4]

The Munro judgment has to be regarded as a landmark decision, confirming the place of the National Capital Act almost as the Magna Carta of federal rights in the Capital. Section 10 of the Act confers very wide powers indeed on the NCC to operate in fields hitherto regarded as the sole responsibility of municipalities, and so long as the action taken derives from powers given under the Act, then the federal legal right to undertake a wide variety of functions in the Capital appears unquestionned.

We thus see that, historically, the importance of the Capital city to the life and spirit of the nation has long been recognized; that the federal government has, in fact, been involved in the shaping of the Canadian Capital; that its interests have created something like a federal municipality; and that the Courts have recognized the constitutional right of the federal government to act in the planning of the Capital for "peace, order, and good government". We now should ask ourselves "what is sensible, practical, pragmatic?". A most important factor guiding our approach to this question is considered next.

V. Living with an Elephant

Prime Minister Trudeau's phrase about the problem of existing beside the United States—"sleeping with an elephant",—may be a trifle overworked these days, but it is an apt way of describing the problems facing Capital municipalities in their relations with the federal authorities. The federal government, as noted earlier, has a tremendous and obvious *physical* impact on the Capital, through its public buildings and the expenditures by the NCC and other federal bodies. Decisions to build or lease office and cultural buildings, and as to their location, the expenditures on green belts and parks, the removal of railway tracks and the creation of new roads, parkways and bridges, the sharing of costs in certain essential municipal projects—all these have had an enormous effect on the shape of the Capital as it develops.

The visible physical consequences of federal decisions is of course only part of its total economic impact on the Region. First is the employment it provides, and the rate of growth in the creation of new jobs. How many government employees are there? Strangely, this is a difficult figure to find, apparently because of the multiplicity of departments and agencies, the different types of employment provided (full time public servants, casual employees, military, RCMP, summer students, people on contract), and the constant movement in and out. We discuss this and other aspects of federal growth in some detail in

Chapter Eleven (pages 144-5), and suggest that early in 1974 total federal employment was close to 100,000.

But this is only part of the story. The construction industry is geared to building (*a*) office structures either for the federal government or for speculators who hope to lease all or most of their buildings to the federal government, (*b*) housing, largely for public servants or those who cater to them, or (*c*) highways which are at least partially federally financed. One could go through all the other ramifications of the secondary effects of federal spending, but it is enough to say that the federal elephant takes a lot of servicing, and the direct and indirect employment this produces completely dominates the local scene.

Two other consequences might be noted. Federal pay levels appear high by business standards across the country, and there has been a demonstrable reluctance of industry to move in to the Capital to compete for employees, unless the government is itself an important market for their product or service.

A second point—the rate of growth in government employment in the Region—may be even more important. Since 1971 this growth appears to have been of the order of 10% per year, and has had tremendous implications for municipal planning and for the economy of the Region. Competition for houses has pushed up property values in the Region faster than almost anywhere else in the country, despite the highest per capita rate of housing unit construction. The municipalities' resources are stretched to meet the costs of services related to new housing—as well as of office buildings. The important thing is that the rate of growth really is determined almost exclusively by the federal government, and it is to that government that the rising chorus of protests against such growth must be directed.

All this leads us to our final point, that the impact of the federal government is so great and so pervasive in the Region that local municipal governments must have some way of being informed about federal decisions and plans. In our discussions we found a considerable measure of municipal discontent with their lack of knowledge of what the federal elephant would do next. I felt some sympathy because there were times at the NCC when we were unable to push the beast into making up its mind either to zig or to zag.

The municipal need for information is certainly proven, but the unanswered question is how to go about getting it to the municipalities. I suggested above that the federal government has constitutional, legal acquired and moral rights to a seat at the table. One way of achieving the necessary improved liaison would be for the municipalities and provinces to offer such a seat. In this connection we will look briefly at how other federal countries deal with the relationship of the national government and the Capital, and in this next chapter we lean heavily on the pioneering work of Dr. Rowat, a recognized authority in the field.

Footnotes

1. *Plan for the National Capital*, General Report (1950) pp. 157/8.
2. *Harold Munro vs National Capital Commission*, Judgment of the Exchequer Court, April 28, 1965, Gibson J. pp. 80/81. See also Chapter Two, page 14.
3. U.S. Public Law 93-198, 93rd Congress, S. 1435 (87 Stat. 774) *District of Columbia Self-Government and Governmental Reorganization Act*, Dec. 24, 1973.
4. *Harold Munro vs National Capital Commission*, Judgment of the Supreme Court, June 28, 1968. Cartwright J. (see also 2 above).

Chapter Six

How Other Federal Capitals are Governed

The governing of any capital city presents a special problem, that of achieving a just balance between the interests of the local residents and the interests of the nation or state. The governing of *federal* capitals presents an additional basic problem: the question of the relationship of the federal capital to the state or province in which it is geographically situated. For guidance as to how other federal countries try to cope with these problems we examine in this chapter a number of examples drawn from the study "*The Government of Federal Capitals*[1]" edited by Professor Rowat. This volume contains a chapter on each capital written by a different expert. Professor Rowat wrote the chapter on the Canadian capital and the concluding comparative essay.

His study, which covered all seventeen of the then existing federal capitals and countries having federal constitutions, reveals that there is no standard model or general solution for the government of federal capitals upon which all federal countries have agreed. The Fathers of the American Constitution took the view that, as a basic principle of federalism, the federal capital should come within a special federal territory, so that it would not be governed or dominated by any single state in the federation. This reasoning was adopted by the Latin American federations and others, such as Australia and India. But it was by no means adopted by all federations. Several, like Canada, accepted the view that the federal capital should continue to be under the jurisdiction of the province (or state) in which it was situated, and should be treated in much the same way as any other city within that province. Examples of such capitals are Bern and Bonn. Indeed, Professor Rowat found that the existing federal capitals are about evenly divided between those that are governed by the central government within a federal territory and those that are not, while the capitals of two federations—Austria and Nigeria—are actually member states of the federation, with their own state governments.

Professor Rowat makes a distinction between centralized federations (i.e. where the states have little autonomous power) and decentralized federations (where states enjoy a large degree of independence). The experience of the relatively decentralized federations would clearly have more relevance to this study, particularly those with systems of governments analagous to our own. To keep this chapter within reasonable compass, I have selected from among these federations seven capitals as having particular relevance for Canada: Bern (Switzerland), Bonn (West Germany), Canberra (Australia), Caracas (Venezuela), Delhi (India), Vienna (Austria), and Washington (U.S.A.). Two of these capitals are governed under the laws of a state in the federation (Bern and Bonn), four are inside a federal territory (Canberra, Caracas, Delhi and Washington), while the seventh, Vienna, is itself one of the states of the Austrian federation. To those who wish to pursue this more deeply I commend Professor Rowat's book.

For purposes of comparison I have grouped the seven capitals into the three basic types mentioned above. I will first review the state-governed capitals, whose type of government is similar to that of Ottawa, then Vienna as a city-state, and finally the capitals within federal territories. In doing so, I will comment on Professor Rowat's conclusions about each type, and will then discuss the relevance of experience elsewhere to the problems of governing Canada's capital.

I. State Governed Capitals

Bern

Bern is a city of only 180,000, but with a metropolitan area of 300,000 persons. The city of Bern is the capital of the state (the canton, also called Bern) within which it is situated. Otherwise, the similarities between Bern and Ottawa as federal capital cities, are rather striking. Since Bern is centuries old and has had a long tradition of independence, it is completely self-governing and the central government has no formalized control over it. Even the state of Bern does not control it directly, so the independence of its city government is quite comparable to that of a Canadian city.

That Bern cannot be controlled directly by the central government has brought it face to face with the same problem of divided jurisdiction that we find in Canada's Capital. The city complains that it does not get enough financial help from the central government, in much the same way that Ottawa and other Region municipalities do, and the Swiss central government complains that it does not have enough control over its own Capital. For example, not only can it not control planning for the area, it cannot even control the location and external design of its own buildings! If it wishes to put up a building, it has to secure the approval of the Bern city planning department. The planning and architecture of the downtown area are taken very seriously in Bern, because it is an ancient city with many historic buildings to preserve. In this sense Bern's planning problem is different from that of Canada's Capital. It is not how to tear down and rebuild the centre of the city, but how to preserve its historic flavour. The Bernese are therefore understandably concerned about the kind of building the federal government may wish to put up in the area around the parliament buildings, near the city centre.

An even more difficult planning problem is what should be done about the suburbs. Bern is growing like most cities and is overflowing into the suburbs. A serious problem of planning and metropolitan government is developing there, as it has in Ottawa-Hull. However, there are not as many automobiles as in Ottawa, and the city has not been growing quite so fast. Perhaps for these reasons, the jurisdictional problems have not been quite so obvious as in Ottawa, but it is illustrative of typical problems of government faced by federal capitals not situated within a federal territory.

Perhaps the most important parallel between Bern and Ottawa-Hull is that both have the problem of a minority language and culture. Switzerland's two main languages are German and French, and the French language and culture are in much the same minority position as they are in Canada. Bern is a predominantly German-speaking city in a German-speaking province, and its French-speaking minority, particularly federal civil servants, naturally want to use their own language in daily life, and to have easy access to their own culture.

As Professor Rowat points out, the language issue in Bern is not as acute as in Canada's capital for several reasons:

> In the first place, the German-speaking majority in Switzerland have been more generous in meeting the language requirements and wishes of the minorities. For instance, nearly all of the educated majority have learned to speak French, and usually make a point of doing so socially when French-speaking persons are present. They even go more than half way in this respect by not expecting a French-speaking social group to speak German when German-speaking persons are present. Also, the French-speaking population are well represented in the federal civil service. French is used more there than in the Canadian federal civil serivce, partly because French rather than German is the traditional diplomatic language. The French-speaking minority are therefore over-represented in the Ministry of Foreign Affairs.[2]

Clearly, in trying to solve our language problems, we have a good deal to learn from the Swiss.

Bonn

Bonn's status is somewhat different, because when it was chosen in 1948 it was intended to be only a temporary capital. After the war, the West Germans held tenaciously to the view that Germany would soon be reunited, and that Berlin would again become the capital of the new, united Germany. Partly in order to symbolize the capital's temporary nature, a small, rather inconvenient university town was chosen. The choice also represented a compromise similar to the selection of Ottawa; other large cities in Western Germany were contending for the honour, and Bonn was geographically located between some of them. Perhaps not entirely coincidentally, it happened to be the home territory of Chancellor Adenauer, who had a considerable say in the decision. It is situated in the State of North Rhine Westphalia, the largest and most economically powerful state of the West German federation.

Bonn has been growing very rapidly, and the greater Bonn area now has a population of about 500,000. Yet this is small for the capital of a country of over sixty million people, and its relatively small size still appears to reflect the federal government's original policy not to develop Bonn monumentally as the permanent capital and as a national symbol. There is some indication currently that West Germany's views on this are changing. When I visited Bonn last October I was shown a number of more monumental buildings on the drawing board.

Professor Rowat has noted that, of all the federal capitals, Bonn seems to be the closest parallel to Ottawa:

> In the first place, the city has had a long history of independent self-government. Second, it is one of the few state-governed federal capitals that is not also the capital of the state in which it is situated. Like Ottawa, it is governed from a state capital, Dusseldorf, which is a considerable distance away. Like Ontario, the state of North Rhine Westphalia, which governs Bonn, is the most populous one in the federation and its government has several larger cities to worry about. Like the residents of Ottawa and Hull, the citizens of Bonn feel that they are being neglected by the state government. Third, the federal government has no direct control over or financial responsibility for Bonn or its surrounding area. The residents complain that the federal government does not pay a large enough share for new facilities, such as bridges, highways and cultural centres, which are required because Bonn is the capital city; others complain that it is not a capital worthy of West Germany; and so on, in much the same phrasing that one hears about Ottawa.[3]

Another parallel is that Bonn is divided by a river as are Ottawa and Hull. The small part of it that is on the east side of the Rhine corresponds to Hull, so that there are similar problems of bridge-building and public transportation. Before the massive extension of Bonn's boundaries in 1969, this part of Bonn was a separate city like Hull, called Beuel, but unlike Hull it was in the same state as Bonn, and does not have a different language, culture and body of law.

Before 1969 the Bonn area suffered from a serious need for metropolitan government. Because of the small size of Bonn, the embassies and many government departments had to locate outside its boundaries. Most of the embassies settled in Bad Godesberg, a city adjoining Bonn's southern border, which had a population of about 80,000, while some of the ministries moved to a town on Bonn's western border. New federal buildings were placed mainly in the fringe area between Bonn and Bad Godesberg. Bonn's population rapidly spread far beyond its boundaries with little planned control, and the difficulties for the federal government and its employees of conducting business in several different municipalities were becoming insurmountable. Because of this, the government of North Rhine Westphalia had been considering, in consultation with the local governments, a plan for a second tier of regional government for Bonn's urban area that would have been much like the present regional governments for the metropolitan areas of Ottawa and Hull. But it decided instead to consolidate the whole area under a single government, and therefore in 1969 expanded Bonn's boundaries to include Bad Godesberg, Beuel and many of the smaller suburban municipalities.

Conclusions on State-Governed Capitals

In a centralized federation, there is little chance of serious disagreement between the federal and state governments, because the federal government is likely to wield enough control over the development and nature of its capital to meet national objectives. But as our survey shows, this may not be true in decentralized federations like Switzerland, West Germany and Canada. Professor Rowat observed that:

> Though state-governed national capitals in decentralized federations usually enjoy a high degree of self-government, they suffer from serious problems of divided jurisdiction, financial insufficiency, cultural domination by the governing state, inadequate metropolitan government, and the inability of the central government to control the capital city or its development in the interests of the nation.[4]

Most of these problems arise from the lack of a central governing body for the national capital area, and the absence of an agreed approach between the central and state governments. Where there is a metropolitan government for the whole area, as there is now for Bonn, and where there is agreement between the central and state governments on the development of the capital and on the sharing of the costs involved, as seems to be the case in Western Germany, these problems can perhaps be overcome.

Professor Rowat's conclusions were based on his observation of Bonn before the massive consolidation of 1969. The federal and state officials I talked to in Bonn were satisfied with the new structure, and pointed out that there is now a specific agreement between the central government and the state of North Rhine Westphalia about the arrangements concerning Bonn, including the sharing of financial support. The central government is represented on the state's regional planning bodies, and these in turn establish land-use plans to which the local governments, including Bonn, must adhere. Early in 1974, the two levels of government, along with the City of Bonn, were in the process of negotiating an "agreement for the future planning of Bonn as the federal capital" and the establishment of a "development corporation of the federal capital of Bonn".

II. A Capital as a City-State

Vienna is one of the few examples in the world of cities which are at the same time states in a federation. And, except for Lagos (Nigeria), it is the only example of a city-state which is at the same time the federation's capital.

With a population of nearly two million, Vienna contains over one-fifth of Austria's population and is the largest state as well as the largest city. The next largest city, Graz, has a population of only about 250,000, and the next largest of the nine states, Lower Austria, has a population of about 1.5 million. Thus Vienna is a powerful force in its own right in the federation; its position has been buttressed by its historic role as the capital of the giant Austro-Hungarian Empire. One unusual fact about Vienna is that its population is lower now than it was in 1910—a rarity among world cities. Another unusual fact is that, besides being the capital of the federation, it is also the capital of Lower Austria, which does not have a capital of its own. The latter's parliament buildings and administrative departments are located in Vienna.

Because Vienna is a city-state, its government acts as both a city government and a state government. Interestingly, these two roles are kept separate in law and practice, so that one day the elected body will meet as the state legislature, and the next day as the city council, with quite different procedures. Similarly, the prime minister of the state is also the mayor of the city, and wears different hats on different days, so to speak. The state and city administrative departments, however, are not separated, and the term "city" tends to predominate in common usage and in the names of the city-state governmental organizations.

From the beginning of the Austrian federation in 1919, Vienna has been predominantly Socialist, while the federal government has been dominated by the conservative Christian Democrats. Austria's history is mainly a history of struggle between urban Vienna and the federal government, which mainly represented the rural interests of the rest of the federation. Thus, the example of Austria indicates that turning a federal capital into a state does not solve the problem of how to unify the conflicting interests of the residents and of the federal government in the capital city.

In Austria's case, giving the federal capital the status of a state may have been justified because Vienna was so large and important a city, with many commercial, industrial and other interests to be represented, and with a long tradition of independence. But where the capital is relatively small, and the federal government's predominant interest is that of developing the urban area as a national capital, as in the case of Ottawa-Hull, a federal capital with the autonomy of a state would pose a number of problems. As Professor Rowat pointed out[5], if the National Capital Region were to become Canada's "eleventh province," as some people have proposed, this would place the federal government in much the same position in relation to the new province as it is now in relation to Ontario and Quebec regarding the Region. It would still have no control over the Region, and much the same difficulties of divided jurisdiction would remain. However, these problems might be partially overcome by limiting the constitutional power of the new province, that is by making it a "special" province.

III. Capitals in Federal Territories

Canberra

Australia's population is about half that of Canada's and the federation has six states and two federal territories. Its constitution provides a division of powers between the central and state governments that is surprisingly similar to Canada's. The federation is relatively decentralized, with the residual powers remaining with the states, rather than, as in Canada, with the federal government. Canberra, like Ottawa, was chosen to be the capital as a compromise between the two largest cities in the country, Sydney and Melbourne, and is located inland about half way between them in the Australian Capital Territory, a 900 square mile area carved out of the State of New South Wales. Unlike Canada's Capital, Canberra and its environs are governed exclusively by the central government.

Construction in Canberra began in 1913; at first it was slow to attract population, and by the end of the second world war, it was still a city of only 17,000. Although fully planned and architecturally attractive, Canberra's amenities were not comparable with those of Melbourne, then the home of most federal departments. With the resumption in 1959 of the programme of transferring federal departments to Canberra, the city developed quickly and became large enough to include most if not all city facilities, and to be regarded as an attractive place to live. This development was heavily subsidized by the government, and individuals were attracted by low cost government housing. All land is owned by the government and leased for private development in accordance with established criteria. Since 1959 Canberra's population has grown astronomically. It is now close to 200,000 and is expected to reach 250,000 by 1980. However, the programme of transferring government departments to Canberra has lately been slowed, and consideration is being given to diverting further transfers to new growth centres in Australia.

The Federal department responsible for governing Canberra, until recently, was the Ministry of Interior, but the very important powers of planning and building were largely the responsibility of an independent agency, the National Capital Development Commission. Canberra has no elected city government, but for some 40 years there has been an advisory council with locally elected members. Eight of the twelve members are elected, the remainder being federal officials appointed by the Minister. Last March I spoke to some of its members, who expressed considerable frustration at their inability to affect events. The residents also elect a member to the federal House of Representatives. At first he had a vote only on matters relating to Canberra, but in 1965 he became a full member of the House. It is now being proposed that the Capital Territory should elect two members to the House and one or two to the Senate.

As Canberra's population grew, proposals were made for a partly or fully elected governing council for the Territory. In 1965 a study group of

Australia's Royal Institute of Public Administration proposed a completely elected council, with full legislative and executive powers subject only to ministerial veto.[6] In 1967 the Ministry of Interior produced a report on self-government for Canberra,[7] and in 1968 the Capital Territory branch of the governing Liberal Party sponsored a three-day seminar conference on the subject. A serious but probably diminishing concern is the fear of Canberra's residents that self-government will mean higher taxes, the loss of benefits which they now receive from the federal government, and less efficient management of the city's affairs.

A new government in Australia was elected in 1972, the first change in 23 years. The Whitlam government has placed a particular emphasis on urban policy, and appointed the former chairman of the National Capital Development Commission (NCDC) to head a new Cities Commission, which is to study and report quickly on Australia's urgent urban problems. A former Assistant Commissioner of the NCDC has been appointed permanent head (deputy minister) of the new Department of Urban and Regional Development. The old Department of the Interior has been broken up. The functions of administering Canberra's urban services and of collecting municipal taxes there have been taken over by a new Department of the Capital Territory, but the NCDC has been left with its original responsibilities of planning and construction in the Territory.

A measure of self-government for Canberra is now being considered, with elections at first proposed for some time in 1974. For this reason the term of office of the partly elected advisory council was extended in 1973 for one year. An inquiry by a Parliamentary Joint Committee on the costs of Canberra, which began in 1972, was continued in 1973 with some new members. A central objective of this inquiry is to try to establish the proportion of state-type and municipal-type facilities and services that should be paid by local residents. Its terms of reference were extended in 1973 to include "an appropriate form of self-government". In addition, a number of special agencies have been proposed for the Capital Territory—an Education authority, a Health Authority, a Housing Commission, a Land Commission, and a Fuel Commission (extending the Electricity Authority). There is much concern, both in and out of government, at this trend toward fragmentation of authority. It is possible that the new self-government, if and when it comes, will take over some or all of these special agencies and thus help to coordinate the federal government's activities within the capital Territory.

Caracas

Caracas is a modern city with a population of about a million nestled in a valley about twenty miles from the sea. The Federal District, however, which extends to the sea, is much larger and contains nearly two million people. The urban population of Caracas has spread beyond the District, forming a sizeable city. Sucre, outside the eastern boundary. Since Venezuela's population is under ten million, the concentration in the Federal District gives it a larger population than any of the states. The most populous of the twenty states, Zulia, has just over a million, and its capital, Maracaibo, has about half a million.

The Federal District, like the states, elects two senators, and also elects members to the house of representatives in accordance with population (one for each 50,000 inhabitants). Like the Federal Districts in Argentina and Brazil, it has a governor, appointed by the President. But it also has a governing council elected by its residents. The council chooses its own chairman as mayor, and unusually has a party majority different from that of the federal government. For administrative purposes the District is divided into two Departments, the Libertador Department (433 square kilometers) encompassing Caracas, and the Vargas Department (1,497 square kilometers) covering the part along the sea. The governor is the chief administrator of the District's public services. Thus the government of the District strikes an interesting balance between local and central control, and its residents have a fairly high degree of self-government.

In 1972 the federal government created a planning authority for the whole Caracas region, including Sucre. Caracas and Sucre are to share the costs of its planning, and consideration is being given to unifying their most important public services.

Delhi

The Union Territory of Delhi is more relevant to our experience because India inherited the British system of parliamentary government, and because it has a relatively decentralized federation. Of course, the proportions are vastly different from ours. India has a population of over 500 million, with a complex federation of seventeen states and ten territories, of which the Union Territory of Delhi is one. Created in 1956, the Union Territory has a population of about four million, and its urban area includes the two contiguous cities of Delhi (with a population of over three million) and the official capital, New Delhi, (with about 400,000). The Territory also encompasses a large rural area, with about 360 villages having locally elected councils. While New Delhi is governed by an appointed committee, Delhi has its own elected governing council, a huge one of 106 members. On the executive side, however, it has a commissioner who is appointed by the central government.

The Territory was formerly governed for state and federal purposes by a Chief Commissioner and his Advisory Council, who were responsible to the Minister of Home Affairs. In 1966, however, the federal government created an elected Metropolitan Council for the Territory, with five members appointed by the federal government and 56 directly elected. The federally appointed Administrator now chairs an Executive Council of four other members who, though appointed by the federal government, are chosen from among the members of the Metropolitan Council. Thus a second tier of government for state and federal functions has been installed above the local governments.

In the election of 1967, the opposition Jan Sangh Party won a majority on both the Delhi and Metropolitan Councils, and thus was able to choose the mayor and the chairman of the Metropolitan Council. It also obtained all of the seats on the Executive Council because the federal government followed the parliamentary convention of appointing the executive body from the majority on the Metropolitan Council. From this it is clear that, while the federal government exercises ultimate control over the Territory, its residents enjoy a relatively high degree of self-government.

Washington

Few of those in Canada who oppose the idea of a federal capital territory seem to know that in the 19th century the local governments within the District of Columbia were elected. In fact, Washington was self-governing until 1871. The main reason for the abolition of Washington's city council was that an energetic mayor decided to modernize Washington with ambitious construction projects, but overspent the budget and got the city into serious debt; another reason was opposition to the enfranchisement of negroes in Washington after the Civil War. The federal Congress therefore decided to abolish the elected government and have federal agencies administer the city services. Ever since Washington has had no self-government, and until recent years its residents had no vote in federal elections. This has made it the traditional "bad example" for those opposed to a federal district in Canada. The rallying cry has always been "we don't want a Washington here".

Since the war, however, there has been a strong and successful movement towards more voting rights and self-government for the residents of Washington, although there are special reasons why these were not granted sooner. Most of the white population moved into the surrounding metropolitan area in Maryland and Virginia, where they have full voting rights and elected local governments, leaving a large black majority, over two-thirds, in the city. Many whites therefore opposed the extension of voting rights to Washington's residents, and the Southern Democrats in control of the Congressional committees that govern the federal district were reluctant to create an elected city council which would have a black majority. In 1961, however, an amendment to the American Constitution gave the residents of Washington a vote in presidential elections. In 1968 they gained the right to elect a school board, and in 1970 the right to elect a non-voting member to the House of Representatives.

Until recently Washington (which is coterminous with the District of Columbia) was governed for legislative purposes by Congress and its committees, and for executive purposes by the President and his executive agencies. The main agency administering the city was a three-man board of commissioners, all appointed by the President. In 1967, however, the board was abolished in favour of a new city council of nine, plus a so-called mayor as chairman and administrative commissioner. Though the President still appointed all of these officials, President Johnson took the unusual step of appointing a majority of blacks to the council and also a black, Walter Washington, as the first "mayor." Mr. Washington was later reappointed by President Nixon. Finally, in 1973 Congress passed a bill, which was signed by the President on December 24, providing a large measure of self-government for Washington[8].

If the new city charter is approved in a referendum to be held in 1974, the city's 750,000 residents will then be able to elect their own mayor, a governing council of thirteen members, and advisory neighbourhood councils. But Congress has retained certain powers over this new city government, including approval of its expenditures and the power to disallow its acts within 30 days. Also, it may not change such things as the building height limitations and the local court system, or such national institutions as the National Zoo or the National Capital Planning Commission. However, many other District bodies which are now federal agencies will be consolidated under the city government. The mayor may veto acts of the council, and though his veto may be overridden by a two-thirds vote of the council, the President has been given the power to sustain the mayor's veto.

Because Washington's urban population long ago overflowed the District's boundaries, the federal government has inevitably become concerned with the development and government of the whole national capital area. In fact, the problems of government in Washington's national capital area are in many respects similar to those in Canada's National Capital Region. Only a small portion of the present built-up area is within the District, which has an area of only 69 square miles (compared with 1,800 square miles in Canada's National Capital Region). The urban population has spread into some sixty municipalities in the two surrounding states, Maryland and Virginia, and the whole metropolitan area now has a population of more than 2.5 million—three times that of Washington. Therefore, despite the existence of a federal district, the problems of planning, governing and controlling the development of the whole area are very much like those of the Ottawa-Hull area. The federal National Capital Planning Commission has no more jurisdiction outside the District than the Canadian NCC has over non-government land within the National Capital Region. Another source of difficulty is that, as in Canada, various federal departments and agencies have become involved in the development of the area.

Although the area's governments have formed a co-ordinative council, the involvement of the federal government, two states and sixty municipalities in governing the area means that the difficulties of co-ordination are almost insurmountable. To extend the boundaries of the District would require Maryland and Virginia to surrender large portions of their territory now containing whole cities. It would also require an amendment to the Constitution, which must be approved by three-quarters of the states. Thus American experience with the District of Columbia demonstrates the problems that can be caused by creating a federal district that is too small.

Conclusions on Federal Territories

In summary, Professor Rowat concludes[9] that a federal capital territory is particularly appropriate in a decentralized federation because otherwise the sharp division of powers between the central and state governments prevents the central government from having effective control over its own capital. Certainly where the federal capital has a relatively small population and is primarily a "civil service town" this would seem to be true, because the federal presence and interests clearly predominate.

At the same time, as our survey reveals, federal territories often leave other basic problems of governing the capital city unresolved. A federal territory may not permanently solve the problem of governing the capital's metropolitan area because the urban population may expand beyond the boundaries of the territory, as it seems to have done in most cases—even in Australia. However, as Professor Rowat points out[10] this problem will not arise if the territory is made big enough to contain any conceivable future growth of the capital's urban population. More serious is that federal territories do not seem to have solved the problem of co-ordinating the local activities of the federal agencies within them, and often they have not provided self-government for their residents. However, the latter situation has changed in decentralized federations, as we have noted, and the residents of Caracas and Delhi already have self-government, a significant measure of it will soon be implemented for Washington, and it is being considered for Canberra.

IV. Relating this Experience to Canada

Our examination of the experience of other federal capitals supports Professor Rowat's conclusion that a federal capital territory is particularly appropriate for a decentralized federation, especially if the population of the capital area is relatively small and federal interests predominate. Our survey also shows that the commonly-held view in Canada that a federal district means no self-government is false: it is quite possible to have a relatively high degree of self-government, including municipal governments, within a federal capital territory. However, a federal capital territory is no panacea, and may leave important problems of governing the capital unsolved.

We must also recognize that Canada's capital has unique problems because it has a unique combination of characteristics. These are: (1) the capital area is divided by a river; (2) the population on each side of the river has a different predominant language, culture, and civil law and education system; (3) each side is governed by a different province; and (4) neither Ottawa nor Hull is the capital of its province. It will be noted that the latter two characteristics are "man-made", so to speak. They are parts of the political structure, and could be changed by a political decision, such as the decision to create a federal capital territory. But the other two features are geographical and historical, with the river reinforcing the cultural division. No other federal capital area has both of these characteristics. Similarly, no other federation has Canada's peculiar features, and no other federation is so decentralized. Hence, Canada's capital has special problems of government for which the experience of other federal capitals provides no firm guide. We are therefore free to develop a governmental arrangement which can best meet the special needs of our own capital.

Footnotes

1. Rowat, D.C., *The Government of Federal Capitals* (University of Toronto Press, 1973).
2. Ibid., p. 347.
3. Ibid., p. 348.
4. Ibid., p. 349.
5. Appendix "C" p. 438-9
6. See J. D. Miller, "*Self Government for Canberra?*" *Public Administration* (Australia) 26 (September 1967), p. 220.
7. *Self-Government for the Australian Capital Territory: A Preliminary Assessment* (Canberra, 1967).
8. U.S. Public Law 93-198, 93rd Congress S1435 *District of Columbia Self Government and Government Reorganization Act*, December 24, 1973.
9. *The Government of Federal Capitals*, p. 350.
10. Ibid., p. 347.

Part Two

The Problem Areas

Chapter Seven

How Well is the Capital Governed? An Appraisal of its Municipal Government

The development and structure of local government in the Capital was examined in Chapter Three. We now attempt to appraise its effectiveness, having particularly in mind the special characteristics which distinguish the Capital from other municipalities in the country, namely the strong federal presence and the two-province location. In Chapter Eight we consider the interaction of local municipalities, the two provincial governments, and the NCC and other federal bodies.

1. Too Much Government: the prima facie case

The regional governments on each side of the River comprise some 43 municipalities. Of these, 32 are on the Québec side (a reduction to 5 or 6 appears imminent), and 11 on the Ontario, the latter having been reduced from 16 on January 1, 1974. These municipalities vary greatly in size, with the population of the City of Ottawa forming over 60% of that of the Regional Mnicipality of Ottawa-Carleton in 1971, and Nepean nearly 15%: Hull's population formed 40% of that living in the Outaouais Regional Community. However, assuming present growth trends and no further annexations by the largest units, these percentages are expected to fall gradually over time.

Although the creation of RMOC led to an integration of a number of municipal services which could only be dealt with sensibly on a regional basis, such as sewers, water and arterial roads, it created a new and powerful force in the Region, directly competitive with the City of Ottawa. One immediate result was the rapid rise in RMOC staff, partly the product of transfer of some functions from the City and from other municipalities, but also apparently due to overlapping responsibilities with the City, notably in the fields of planning, transportation, engineering, and administration. As might be expected, this led to a substantial increase in both employment and expenditures by municipalities in the Capital.

On the Ontario side, estimates of the size of these increases were obtained from two sources, the figures provided annually by each municipality to the Ontario government, and those of Statistics Canada. These figures are shown in Table 7–1. The approximately $80 million difference in 1972 appears to be explained almost entirely by the fact that the municipal returns are net of provincial grants to the four RMOC school boards. In 1972 these grants amounted to $83 million; Statistics Canada includes the grants in their aggregate expenditures figure.

TABLE 7–1

REGIONAL MUNICIPALITY OF OTTAWA–CARLETON
EXPENDITURES AND EMPLOYMENT, 1968 AND 1972

	1968	1972
Municipal Employment (continuous full-time[1])		
—RMOC (staff)	—	1539
—City of Ottawa	3451	2954
—Other RMOC municipalities	495	741
—All RMOC municipalities—TOTAL	3946	5234
Expenditures by Area		
	($ millions)	
1. *"Ten Year Financial Review"*[1]		
Current:		
—RMOC itself	—	$ 44.7
—City of Ottawa	$ 80.4	107.7
—Other RMOC municipalities	20.8	38.2
—All RMOC municipalities—SUB-TOTAL	$101.2	$190.6
Capital-RMOC	18.6	49.6
—All RMOC municipalities—TOTAL	$119.8	$240.2
2. Statistics Canada[2]		
—RMOC —TOTAL	$171.3	$324.9

In the four year period, 1968 to 1972, the number of continuous full time employees of municipalities in the Region rose by one-third, current expenditures nearly doubled and capital expenditures more than doubled. Such evidence as is available suggests that this trend continued in 1973. By way of comparison, NCC's salary and wage bill increased from $4.9 million in 1968 to $7.3 million in 1972. (NCC employment figures are not too meaningful because of the large number of casual and seasonal employees). On the Québec side, current expenditures net of grants rose from $10 million to $21 million[3]. The equivalent Statistics Canada gross figures, and including capital as well as current expenditures, show an increase from $28.6 million in 1968 to $64.0 million in 1972.[2]

It is interesting to compare trends in municipal employment in the Capital with those in other large Canadian cities. Table 7–2 is based on figures of local government employment supplied by Statistics Canada, and is on a different basis from the "continuous full-time employment" figures used in Table 7–1.

TABLE 7–2

GROWTH IN EMPLOYMENT 1968 TO 1972
URBAN MUNICIPALITIES IN SELECTED METROPOLITAN AREAS[4]

	Population 1971 Census	Number of Employees		
	Metropolitan area (urban & rural)	End June 1968	End June 1972	Percentage Increase
Ottawa–Hull				
Ontario Side	453,280	4,358	5,948	36.5
Quebec Side	149,230	635	891	40.3
TOTAL	602,510	4,993	6,839	37.0
Quebec City	480,502	3,370	4,384	30.0
Edmonton	495,702	6,061	7,205	18.9
Hamilton	498,523	4,421	5,124	15.9
Calgary	403,319	5,188	5,772	11.3
Vancouver	1,082,352	11,035	12,023	9.0
Winnipeg	540,262	6,484	6,727	3.8

The above evidence suggests that regional government has caused an abnormal expansion in municipal employment and costs, even allowing for the rapid population growth and for inflation. Another test of the efficiency of local government is the opinion of those who have to work with it, either from outside it or inside it. As NCC chairman, I can only say I found that rather than the simpler NCC-municipal relationships which might have been expected, the establishment of RMOC complicated matters. In 1968, for example, there were only two bodies in the Region with much of an interest in planning and transportation, the NCC and the City of Ottawa. When the RMOC was created, the NCC faced the immediate problem of finding out who was responsible for what, and of determining whether one discussed a particular issue with the City or the Region. I recall one instance when, to improve traffic, we proposed a few changes in the road system at the west end of the Pretoria Bridge, where three kinds of roads converged—the NCC Driveway, a Regional arterial, and a City street; changes in traffic lights were needed as well. The negotiations for this minor change—all to be paid for by NCC—took well over a year!

Certainly there is evidence of a large growth in the planning staffs at the municipal level as well as the RMOC. Some growth undoubtedly was needed to fulfil the obligation the province imposed upon RMOC to prepare a master plan for the area; some of it may well have been due to the growing recognition in our society or the need for better urban planning. Yet many observers suggest that an important cause was competition between the Region and the City, and between both of them and the planners at the NCC. There was evidence of a similar trend on the Québec side, with new planning staffs being established in Hull and in the ORC; on some issues these staffs were reinforced by planners from the province. Formerly the only planning on the Québec side had been done by the NCC, which invited considerable resentment; there is no doubt that the NCC monopoly was a major target for this new planning capability on the Québec side.

Whatever the cause, I suspect that to-day there are probably more urban planners per head of population in the Capital than in any other metropolis of comparable size in the Western World. Predictably, the quality of the planning has not necessarily improved with the numbers of planners, and the multiplicity of jurisdictions has led to frustration among the planners, and confusion and differing goals among the administrators and politicians. One measure of this discontent may have been the number of resignations in 1973 and 1974 of senior planning staff at all levels of government in the Region.

II. Differences in Objectives Among Ontario Municipalities

A second consequence of the setting up of RMOC was its polarizing effect on existing rivalries and objectives, notably those between the urban area on the one hand and the outer suburbs and rural townships on the other. The Regional Council provided a natural arena for the display of these differences, which proved in some respects to be fundamental. If there is much to be said in favour of a vehicle to expose such problems, a better mechanism should bc provided for resolving them.

We encountered some of these basic issues in meetings with municipal politicians, and found our impressions confirmed by press reports of Council meetings and from Council minutes. One constant complaint of the City of Ottawa was its underrepresentation at the Regional level: it contained over 60% of the population, and paid 72% of the taxes, but was entitled to only 16 of the 31 regional councillors. Unless City representatives voted in a block, they tended to be outnumbered by the more solid non-city forces, often united to oppose "big" Ottawa. Moreover, on many issues there was usually enough internal dissension in the Ottawa contingent for one or two or more councillors to cast their votes the other way, but when the Ottawa group did unite they were accused of bullying tactics! It is no wonder that each Ottawa mayor and council has tended to favour one-tier government, with the usual proposal being the annexation to Ottawa of the area inside the Greenbelt, leaving the rural areas to fend for themselves. A corollory to this is the view of such leaders as Reeve Haydon of Nepean, who has sought the breaking up of Ottawa to achieve a more equitable distribution of population among constituent regional municipalities.

The rural townships do not appear very enthusiastic about regional government, in part on economic grounds. Many of them believe that "regionalization" has forced them into more expensive spending habits, services most of their residents don't need such as water and sewers. Others believe it raises wages, e.g. for rural policemen, without gains in efficiency. Still others contend that regional taxes have gone up without any corresponding benefits; all are concerned about the tax burden on the farmer which forces him to sell his land to speculators for eventual development. (However, some of the farmers have an ambivalent feeling about this, tending to want to keep things as they are but welcoming the rising land values which they regard as a form of pension for themselves). Then there are the new farm "settlers" who moved out to the country area from Ottawa "to get away from it all". They saw their newly acquired peace and quiet threatened by the advancing suburbs, and wanted to preserve the *status quo*—that is, with immigration from the city restricted by such controls as minimum acreage per house. And many rural spokesmen resented the loss of contact between residents and their elected representatives which they believe to be inevitable with larger and more centralized municipal government.

One direct conflict of objectives has become increasingly evident during the past year or two in various schemes to enlarge arterial road connections between the suburbs and downtown. Councillors from the rural townships and outer suburbs tend to be strongly in favour, the Ottawa councillors—reinforced by the support of many community groups in the path of the proposed arterials—strongly opposed. An example was the proposal of regional planners to acquire a large block of centre-town land needed for a new crossing of the Rideau Canal at Somerset Street; this purchase has been approved first and then reversed at a later meeting. One reporter described the discussion as "one of the most heated invective (sic) debates in regional government's five year history", and said the decision was "a victory for a giant group of community associations who applied intense pressure on council to scrap the bridge plan, describing it as 'communicide'."[5]

Another key issue in the field of planning concerned the location of government buildings and of industry. Reeve MacQuarrie of Gloucester township wants new federal work centres decentralized to Gloucester, to "solidify our assessment base".[6] The response of Nepean Township to the draft Regional official plan, made a similar point: "A definite policy on decentralization of employment could make the satellite towns to a very great extent viable and self supporting, and eliminate the necessity for the reliance on transportation to the centre core which is the basic developmental constraint of the plan".[7] This is clearly in opposition to the federal advocacy of a strong, liveable core, a policy which the city of Ottawa appears to endorse. These positions appear difficult to reconcile, and represent two fundamentally different views of how the Capital should develop.

Another area of difference concerned welfare. The suburbs and rural areas are reluctant to contribute to the fast growing welfare costs which originate largely within the City of Ottawa. One reason for this stand is the belief that centralization of the Region leads to loss of contact between local officials and welfare cases. As Reeve Haydon of Nepean noted,

> Before, we had hundreds of people in the Community who would give us feedback on families receiving welfare and we were able to give a much better assessment of their needs.
>
> Our welfare officers knew everyone in the township, and we were able to weed out the gold-brickers. Now if you want welfare you just trundle down to the regional office in downtown Ottawa where nobody knows you, and we have no idea who is being paid or if they really deserve it.[8]

The City quite properly argues that people who work in centre-town but sleep in the suburbs have no right to evade urban costs, which inevitably are heavily concentrated in older downtown sections of the metropolitan area. There is in fact a continuous migration into the city from the outlying areas of people in search of better welfare benefits and subsidized housing.

The existence of conflict may blur the fact that RMOC has been successful in a number of its functions. Certainly progress has been made in coordinating water and sewer developments which really could not have been carried out efficiently by the municipalities themselves. But the differences are there, and must be taken into account when appraising RMOC's performance. One press comment on an RMOC executive committee meeting noted this problem:

> Factionalism is nothing new for regional government—Mr. Coolican regularly asks for divine help in avoiding it, in the prayers he gives before monthly council meetings—but Monday's meeting was one of the most extreme recent examples.
>
> The fragile coalition of Ottawa and non-Ottawa representatives on regional government fell apart Monday, shattered by bickering, intransigence and mutual mistrust.

The reporter also said,

> Resentment and fear of Ottawa's power aren't the only reasons for regional government's present disunity. Personalities played a part in Monday's discord.[9]

There is nothing new either about personality clashes in politics, but it does seem to me that personal ambitions are often underestimated as a source of division in such bodies as RMOC. It usually gets good press coverage, but we have no way of measuring the intensity of it as a cause of divisiveness at the RMOC Council. However, many local politicians suggested to us that the real problem with RMOC has been its lack of strong leadership, and that this weakness at the top has encouraged factional divisions on the Council.

III. The Problems on the Québec Side

In the Outaouais Region, the conflicts have in some respects been the same, e. g. rural vs. urban, but within a rather different framework of government. In the first place, instead of a single regional authority as in Ontario, the province set up several bodies: the Outaouais Regional Community, and the Outaouais Development Corporation (although the latter had a somewhat different territory and mandate). For both, the post of chairman remains a provincial appointment. A third body of importance is the Outaouais Regional Community Transit Commission, in which the Chairman and both commissioners are provincially appointed; on the Ontario side, the members of the Ottawa-Carleton Regional Transportation Commission are drawn from the RMOC Council.

Even apart from the control exercised through these appointments, the Province of Québec has been playing a much larger role in Outaouais local government than is the case in Ontario. Provincial power has been concentrated in the person of the Honourable Oswald Parent, Member of the National Assembly for Hull, Minister of the Public Service and Minister of State for Intergovernmental Affairs and Finance. He has provincial responsibility for liaison with the federal government on matters concerning the National Capital Region. Mr. Parent is widely regarded as having had a say in every local municipal decision of consequence, and as having exercised a considerable measure of control over local councils, including the ORC.

When Mr. H.-Léon Leblanc, first Chairman of the ORC's Executive Committee, retired last January, he seemed to realize himself that the Regional Community had to assume its own responsibilities. This was evident in his review, submitted last January 26, of his four years at the helm of the ORC:

> In accordance with the provisions of section 93 of its Act, the Community should be accredited to negotiate on all matters under its authority with the Government of Canada or any of its agencies, any regional or local municipality in Ontario, and any public body including school boards, and to conclude all agreements deemed to be in the Community's interest.[9] (*translation*)

To further emphasize the ORC's right to assume its responsibilities, Mr. Leblanc stated that the ORC was a municipality under the terms of the Municipal Affairs Department Act (RSQ 1964, chapter 169), that it had all the powers of a municipality and that the laws governing municipalities applied *mutatis mutandis* to the Community.

He added:

> In my opinion, the Council must be aware of the powers granted by its Act and those mentioned above; it must accept these responsibilities and function in the same way as all other independent municipalities in the Province of Québec. . . I wanted to present a review of the Community's true situation in the midst of this maze of federal, provincial and municipal government meddling. [9] (*translation*)

A number of other people have confirmed to us the assumption of the ORC's authority by the Minister of State for Intergovernmental Affairs (Mr. Parent), in the area of negotiations between the ORC and the NCC, the Ottawa-Carleton Regional Municipality, and the federal government as a whole.

I raised this question with Mr. Parent in a meeting with him on February 22, 1974. He acknowledged that provincial intervention had been excessive in recent years, and explained the reasons for it in these terms:

> The federal government's move to expand its offices in the Québec side in 1969 caught us unprepared—a relatively backward municipal structure, a severe lack of the basic municipal needs such as water, sewers and roads, and a group of municipalities that had been fighting each other rather than working together. The only way we could get things going, and persuade the municipalities to think and act regionally, was to apply a degree of centralized control that admittedly could be regarded as authoritarian or dictatorial. However, we have now progressed to the stage of being able to relax the provincial control and begin to hand the powers back; in fact this relaxation began last fall.

Mr. Parent's recognition of the need for greater responsibilities for ORC was further revealed in a speech in Hull last January 28. He said:

> . . . Everyday experience shows that the Outaouais Regional Community should play a broader and more dynamic role, assuming immediate control of the following: planning, garbage collection and disposal, snow removal, regional recreational facilities, creation of a regional road system through by-laws, study and implementaiton of uniform traffic regulations on major arteries and inter-municipal roads, development and implementation of construction standards, construction of low-rental housing and control of the municipal bonds and debentures market.[10] (*translation*)

Finally, Mr. Leblanc accused the Québec government of not lending moral and financial support to the ORC, because it had so far failed to pass a series of 22 amendments to the ORC Act considered vital to the effective functioning of the Community. In addition, it had subsidized the operating expenditures of the Québec City and Montreal Urban Communities to a greater extent than those of the ORC. He neglected to mention, however, the massive investments the Québec government had poured directly into the Outaouais region for its highway system, filtration plant, sewage disposal system and the main regional sewer, the costs of which were shared among the NCC, the Québec government, and local municipalities.

It was generally agreed among the people we met in the Outaouais region, that the ORC has not shown the leadership expected of it. In some areas it is even considered, at least in its present form, as a restraint placed on the municipalities in the hope that they would one day put aside their parochial outlook and finally begin thinking in terms of the best interests of the region as a whole.

Constant friction between urban and rural municipalities has therefore been the order of the day since 1970. In 1971 the rural municipalities threatened to withdraw from the ORC, claiming that it was costing them too much for the services they obtained. For their part, the urban municipalities found that they had almost nothing in common with their rural counterparts. Local politicians we talked with wondered whether the ORC's territory should not be restricted to the urbanized part of the Outaouais region and that part of the rural area absolutely essential to the former's development in the next 20 years. Another structural weakness is that it is possible for certain municipalities in the Regional Community to draw more money from it than they contribute in their annual levy.

Mr. Léon Leblanc places the blame squarely on certain municipal representatives on the ORC's Council; he criticizes their lack of interest and their negative attitude. He also finds fault with the Outaouais Regional Community Act for not granting the ORC the authority required to implement the development plan drawn up by it. Others attribute part of the ORC's failure to its lack of energetic leadership.

Certainly, ORC meetings appear disorganized, and lacking focus, and unquestionably Hull and Gatineau, which control 85 of the 142 votes on the Council, have the deciding voice. Whether the weakness of ORC is due to the division of authority among several regional bodies, to the dominance of the provincial authority, to the urban-rural split, or to its own internal failings, the Community to date has never played a role approaching that of its Ontario neighbour, the RMOC.

IV. Community Groups and Associations — A new level of government?

Community and neighbourhood groups and associations are becoming a growing factor in urban politics and planning, not only in the Capital but all over the world. Residents of a particular area in a city no longer seem prepared to place as much faith in the municipal elective process as they once did; the old method of voting a group in, giving them a free hand for two or three years, and then kicking them out if they fail to perform, doesn't appear to provide enough responsiveness or accountability to satisfy the younger generation of voters. If these groups are occasionally led by political activists, the usual initial cause of their banding together is to protect themselves against a particular threat to their own environment, often a proposed arterial road or a new high-rise apartment. Sometimes when the threat disappears their reason for existence does too, but their adhesiveness and staying power has increased recently through association with other like-minded groups to fight for common principles or against a common enemy.

In the Capital, most of group activity in respect of planning has been on the Ontario side. The evolution of community groups began in the late 1960's, a time when the increasingly rapid growth of the Capital began to threaten the character of core area residential neighbourhoods. Originally the groups consisted of loosely organized rate-payer and home-owner associations who concerned themselves with such things as garbage pickup, snow removal and taxes, but never involved City Hall in serious controversy. These evolved into vocal action groups attacking municipal and planning decisions on zoning and traffic that threatened the character of their communities. Among these was Action Sandy Hill, which in 1969 was one of the first citizen groups to succeed in blocking several proposed developments, including a freeway to connect the MacDonald-Cartier Bridge to the Queensway.

On the Québec side, the community associations appear to be more politically oriented with left-wing and separatist involvement. The emphasis had been less on planning, except on the social consequences of planning decisions, and more on causes such as legal aid and housing. A spokesman for the Québec group, in comparing their operations to those in Ontario said: "Their approach is quite different from ours. They are more worried about urban growth, high rise buildings and the aesthetics of the city, whereas we are still contending with economic survival, serious housing problems, and the invasion of the Island of Hull by the federal government"...

Although the community groups are usually more effective in stopping things than in proposing alternatives, I am confident that they are here to stay, and most be considered as almost, if not quite, a new level of government. Certainly in the Capital they have acquired muscle, and their efforts have been significant in preventing the building or widening of several arterial roads and commercial developments. The problem remains how to fit them into a system where too many layers of government exist already, and to keep them really representative of the community rather than of small special interest groups.

V. Summing Up

If my term as Chairman of NCC gave me some contact with the problems of local government in the National Capital Region, and if our discussions with local political figures and others has broadened our knowledge somewhat during the course of this study, I have some diffidence about attempting to appraise the overall appropriateness of present structures to meet the Region's needs. Local politics is an intricate game, and anyone who has not been elected to municipal office should be cautious about judging the actions and motivations of those who have had to make their judgments and decisions in full public view. Nevertheless, I think there is general agreement that the local government process has not been working very effectively, a judgment in which I concur, and it is essential for purposes of this study for me to try to assess where the problems originated. If it is convenient to divide these problems into four categories:—flaws in the structure of the two regional governments, fundamental differences in objectives among component groups, the lack of interprovincial liaison, and inadequate recognition of the special needs of the federal government—I have no doubt that some problems reside in the calibre of the people who achieve political office. Unfortunately, this latter issue is much too subjective for analysis by anyone except the politicians themselves.

(*a*) *Structural Flaws*

In the setting up of RMOC, the Ontario government disregarded the Jones recommendations (see Chapter Three, page 25) for establishing new districts of more or less equal size, and chose instead, admittedly with strong backing from the affected municipalities, to adhere to the old municipal boundaries. This left the City of Ottawa in much too dominant a position; although this was recognized, the attempt to compensate for it by limiting the City's voting power has only compounded the mistake. As one prominent local politician noted "The Region was set up on the basis of political expediency and nothing else. This is why it is having problems to-day and why it will continue to have problems as long as it is in its present format". Other people have suggested that "political expediency" was not only to accommodate the wishes of local politicians, but to give more voting power to the rural areas which were known supporters of the party in power in Ontario, and fewer votes to the urban areas which were not so strong in the faith. I have no way of checking the validity of this theory.

One comment on some of these problems was the statement in the Ontario Legislature by Michael Cassidy, M.P.P. (Ottawa Centre)

> the problem of rivalries in the Ottawa area between the Mayor and the N.C.C. chairman, and between the regional chairman and the mayor and so on, is a consequence of a system created by this government in putting two-tier regional government into an area which is already very heavily governed because of the federal presence right now. This area could have had lost of other systems of government, but it had this one put on it.
>
> Now you put two more chiefs into an area where there is already a chairman of the National Capital Commission, and it is no wonder you get the kind of difficulties you have right now.[11]

The fact remains that the division of responsibility between the Region and the City of Ottawa has not taken very much power from the City, but has created another large municipal unit which competes with it. This competition is inherently wasteful, and the existence of the two large units presents a confusing picture to the outside world. Who is most entitled to speak for the municipalities of the Region, the RMOC Chairman or the Mayor of Ottawa? With which body, for example, should the federal government deal?

But an essential flaw remains, the mixing together of one very big municipality and a host of smaller ones. It is a formula that seldom works anywhere; either the big unit effectively takes over and imposes its will on the group, or the devices designed to protect the smaller units lead to injustice and frustration for the large, and sometimes eventually to the break-up of the union.

On the Québec side, the same problem exists to some extent in the dominance of Hull. But the structural basis of ORC has been so different from RMOC that there are few other parallels. In Ottawa-Carleton, municipal government is much more solidly established and proven, and indeed in many respects is more responsible than its Québec counterpart. ORC has been much more subordinate to provincial control, and although one may object to the partial emasculation of municipal government which is implicit in such provincial intervention, we have noted that there may have been special reasons why it was necessary. In any event, provincial control is firmly based on the constitution, a great deal of progress in the physical development of the Outaouais Region has been accomplished in the last five years, and events seem to be moving in the direction of a diminution in the extent of provincial involvement.

(*b*) *Differences in Objectives*

We have noted a few of the obvious differences in objectives: the rural areas' complaints about urban domination, the divided view of arterial highways, the desire of suburban townships to get government buildings, the clash over welfare costs.

These problems are inherent in any attempt to group radically different municipalities, and are common to other regional municipalities in the world. What is lacking in RMOC is an effective method of reconciling or arbitrating the differences; either they are resolved in the City's favour by block voting, or in favour of suburbs and rural townships by defecting City votes; in either case it leaves a legacy of bitterness; when it came to the crunch of a necessary municipal amalgamation in 1972, the RMOC was so helpless that it could not even put together any kind of an agreed solution, and the matter was thrown back into the Province's hands.

On the Québec side the more coercive provincial role from the outset, if less democratic in appearance, at least forced necessary cooperation upon the constituent municipalities of ORC. We have seen that this did not sit too well with them, although there seems to have been a quieter acceptance lately of the regional approach. The proposed expanded powers of the Community, and greater devolution of power from the province, may be contributing to this.

(*c*) *The Two-Province Location*

One fundamental flaw in the structure of two regional governments is the absence of formal arrangements for cooperation between them. While the legislation establishing each made provision for joint projects with the other and with the federal government, no provision was made for a method of bringing liaison about. Partly under the stimulus of NCC, some encouraging steps have been taken in the past year, notably the cooperation of the transit systems on the interprovincial bus loop and free transfer privilleges. On December 17, 1973 a meeting was held—described as "historic" by the chairman of NCC—and involving the federal Minister of State for Urban Affairs (Mr. Basford), the Ontario Minister of Transportation and Communications (Mr. Carton), the Québec Ministers of Intergovernmental Affairs, Transportation, and Municipal Affairs (Mr. Parent, Mr. Berthiaume and Mr. Goldbloom) met with the chairmen of NCC, RMOC and ORC. Its purpose was to launch "a unique step in federal-provincial regional government cooperation on transportation planning in and for the National Capital Region".[12] In addition, periodic meetings of Ontario and Québec ministers are being held to improve the liaison on matters affecting the two regional governments.

All this cooperation is to the good, but tremendous gaps remain. The RMOC draft master plan, for example, had little or no input from the Québec side; can either side really draw up such plans without the other? The Québec road network, being build and paid for by the Province and NCC, will have an important impact on traffic in downtown Ottawa, but that city was not consulted. Good liaison can hardly be effectively achieved by periodic meetings of senior officials and ministers. If such liaison is a move in the right direction, and is to be applauded, it is the day-to-day contact at the planning and working level, *within a framework of legislative authority*, that is more likely to achieve the degree of coordination needed.

(*d*) *The Existence of the Federal Government*

We have observed the economic force and the power of the federal government on both sides of the River, and its claim to a seat at the governing table. In the new arrangements for interprovincial cooperation referred to above, federal representatives are involved. Before coming to conclusions about these new moves, we will examine in the next chapter how cooperation among all the different levels of government has worked to date—or has failed to work.

Footnotes

1. "*Ten Year Financial Review*" for RMOC and component municipalities, dated 1973, as submitted to Local Government Services Division of the Ministry of Treasury, Economics and Intergovernmental Affairs.
2. Statistics Canada, *Local Government Finance, 1972* Catalogue 68-203 p. 54. Municipalities covered are almost identical to RMOC.
3. *Etude de regroupement—Groupe de Travail, Cité de Hull*, March 1973. (Mandat confié le 3 octobre 1972 en vertu de la résolution CE-72-1087).
4. DBS—*Municipal Government Employment* April-June 1968 (8505-606) Vol. 2 No. 2 Statistics Canada—*Local Government Employment*—April-June 1972 cat. 72-009.
5. *Ottawa Journal*, June 14, 1973.
6. *Ottawa Journal*, February 4, 1974.
7. *Ottawa Journal*, February 1, 1974.
8. *Globe and Mail*, November 21, 1971.
9. *Ottawa Citizen*, April 17, 1973.
10. *Rétrospective—mes quartre années à la présidence du Comité exécutif de la Communauté régionale de l'Outaouais* (*Retrospect*—my four years as Chairman of the Executive Committee of the ORC), H-Léon Leblanc, January 1974, p. 4 (translation).
11. Parent, the Honourable Oswald, *La présence du Québec dans l'Outaouais* (Quebec's presence in the Outaouais region), speech before the Hull Chamber of Commerce, January 28, 1974, p. 15. (translation).
12. Notes for address by Edgar Gallant to Ottawa Kiwanis Club, January 18, 1974.

Chapter Eight

The Interaction of NCC and Other Levels of Governments — Why Don't They All Get Together?

We saw in the last chapter some of the problems inherent in the relationships among Capital municipalities, particularly on the Ontario side of the Region, and the very considerable differences between the way local government has functioned on the two sides of the River. We turn now to examine the more complex relationship among the three levels of government, the provinces, the municipalities and the National Capital Commission.

1. The Role of the Provinces

For the first century after Confederation there were really only two effective bodies concerned with the governing of the Capital, the federal government—largely through the medium of the NCC and its predecessors—and the City of Ottawa. The attitude of the Province of Ontario might reasonably be classed as "benign neglect"—the province content to let federal money be used to embellish the Capital (at some saving to itself). The Province of Québec at first hardly recognized the existence of Hull[1]. Later, on grounds of sovereignty, it resisted federal initiatives in the Hull area, but offered little to replace them. Amounts spent by each province in the Region were appreciably below the provincial average, particularly on highways connecting the Capital to the outside world.

It was only in the last half of the 1960's that either province became very aware of the Capital, and then it appeared largely a response to new federal moves. In Québec the aroused provincial interest appeared to originate in the "encroachment" of NCC activities and land ownership on Québec territory. This had been reflected in briefs of Québec groups to the Québec Tremblay Commission in 1954; in some instances the same submissions were presented to the Joint Committee of Parliament[2] in 1956. These Québec concerns led in turn, to the Dorion inquiry[3] in 1966, and to its slogan "intégrité du territoire". The Dorion recommendations formed the basis of the provincial position in the Tripartite discussions initiated in 1967 by Prime Minister Pearson, and were the inspiration for the new Outaouais municipal structures. In Ontario, new interest developed in 1963 because of the growing municipal problems in the Ottawa area, which led to the Jones study and eventually to the establishment of RMOC[3] in 1969.

Mr. Pearson's initiative on Tripartite proposals was responded to by Premiers Robarts and Johnson, and undoubtedly stimulated further interest by the provinces in the Capital. The ensuing discussion at the Prime Ministers' Conference in January 1969, and the statement which resulted[4], probably confirmed to the premiers of both provinces that the federal government was really interested in a new approach. It was followed in the spring by the announcement about federal office buildings for Hull and the expropriation of land for them. This move was welcomed in Québec as a start on correcting a long-standing injustice and as providing an economic spur to the Hull area.

Meanwhile, beginning in January 1968, a number of meetings were held of the Tripartite "Preparatory Committee (later "Study Group") on the Capital Region of Canada", involving senior federal officials and officials from Ontario and Québec. Their instructions were to consider the establishment of a "Tripartite planning and development agency" for the Capital Region. One proposal suggested that the executive of this body would be composed of nine members, to be drawn in equal numbers from each of the three governments. Since no public reference by governments has been made to these discussions, it is difficult for me to report on them; I attended only the last meeting which was held on September 17, 1969, two weeks after my appointment as chairman of NCC.

However, the talks broke down, for reasons which I suspect include:

(i) Naïveté that some kind of tripartite organization could be established without surrender of any powers, territorial rights or constitutional jurisdiction by either the federal government or that of each of the two provinces.

(ii) The preoccupation of both Ontario and Québec with their own embryonic regional governments, and their concern that the proposed agency would affect these new governments substantially, just as they were being established.

(iii) The growing narrowness of the mandate of the proposed Tripartite Agency as the talks developed. It finally appeared to be conceived mainly as an overall planning body charged with preparing and coordinating plans for the area.

(iv) The Québec position was based on Dorion recommendations and predictably followed a nationalist line. *Inter alia*, Québec wanted title to federal land in the Capital passed to the Tripartite Agency, the abolition of the NCC, the execution of works in a province to be left to the provincial government, and the right of veto over Agency decisions affecting Québec.

(v) Ontario, while more prepared for change than Québec, was not likely to pursue major initiatives that might not find agreement of the other two governments, and which therefore might only serve to upset the local electorate and local municipal officials.

(vi) The federal government, although it had originated the discussions, found itself steadily being asked to give up more and more in return for a new agency of increasingly dubious merit. Its spokesman finally declared that the federal government would not place itself in a position where, as a result of the establishment of the new Agency, it could not do in the Capital Region what it had been doing very successfully for a number of years through the NCC. The federal authorities may also have become apprehensive about the proposed voting structure of the new agency which would give Québec and Ontario two-thirds of the votes.

When the Tripartite discussions were dropped, federal negotiations with the two provinces on Capital matters continued on a bilateral basis. This posed no hardship for Québec, because of the burgeoning federal expenditures on the Québec side. As the Québec minister then responsible for relations with the Capital put it to me late in 1969—"we (NCC and Québec) will have a lot to do together over the next few years, and it will be much simpler for us both to sit down and work things out, rather than proceeding through some new and complicated tripartite body". The first important agreement between Québec and NCC involved the desperately needed water filtration plant, to cost between $5 and $6 million; Hull had called for tenders on September 1969 but couldn't raise all the money. On behalf of the NCC, I volunteered to the provincial minister (Hon. R. Lussier) to recommend, to the federal government a contribution of one-third of the cost, if matched by the province. He agreed to go along, Hull and the Outaouais Community managed to find the remaining third, agreement was reached, and the filtration plant was built. This form of bilateral negotiation continued through the change of Québec government in 1970, and set the pattern for a series of agreements between that government and the NCC in the following four years.

During the period I can recall only one serious difference of opinion with Québec, that of the location of a new arterial road crossing Leamy Park and Brewery Creek. Although the NCC had in 1971 initially agreed to an urban arterial along this route, it became clear as time passed that this route would solve few traffic problems, and that the funds would be better spent on public transit. Moreover the road would seriously damage the Park, lead to a complicated connection with Québec north-south Highway A-5 (3 major interchanges within one mile), and spoil Brewery Creek's potential as a recreation area. Local municipalities, nevertheless, had for years sought an east-west expressway across the Island of Hull which would be equivalent to Ottawa's Queensway, regardless of environmental considerations. But construction of the connecting bridge over the Gatineau had begun in 1972, and the NCC faced the added problem of coping with a fait accompli. The matter was eventually resolved in Québec's favour.

We noted in the last chapter that the extent of provincial control over the Outaouais municipalities was not viewed too happily by them, and led to some public (but mostly private) criticism by municipal politicians of the minister concerned, the Hon. Oswald Parent, and of the NCC. I also recorded

Mr. Parent's reasoned explanation. I can only add the personal comment that during my term as Commission Chairman the many essential shared cost programmes undertaken could only have been brought to fruition because of the concentration of power in the province's hand. If I found it trying to be criticized frequently by Outaouais municipal leaders for being unwilling to negotiate directly with them—when we both knew that it was at the province's insistence that all policy discussions were channelled through Mr. Parent—at least the basis for the negotiations was on solid constitutional grounds: municipalities have been known to play one level of government off against another.

The relations of the NCC with Ontario have been less close. One important reason was that province allowed the RMOC and the municipalities a much freer hand in their dealings with the NCC than did Québec with its municipalities. It is also possible that the ending of the Tripartite discussions aroused some resentment on Ontario's part; they had participated in response to federal initiatives, and believed that the federal government must accept a considerable part of the blame for the breakdown.

Early in 1970 an event occurred which did damage Ontario's relations with the NCC and with the federal government. I refer to it in some detail, not only because of its particular significance, but because it illustrates how negotiations between governments are often soured by the desire of politicians to get maximum press coverage for themselves or for their own government. Good coverage normally flows from an element of surprise, a goal more likely to be obtained from secrecy than from consultation.

The Portage Bridge across Victoria Island was an NCC project, designed to link the new federal complex in Hull to Parliament Hill and to other federal buildings in central Ottawa. More a road than a bridge (only 10% of the route involved bridging), it had been proposed in the Holt plan in 1915, but was dropped in the Ottawa-Hull Area Transportation Study in 1965 in favour of a bridge above the Chaudière Falls at Lemieux Island. Although in the eyes of the NCC at least the auto-oriented OHATS Study had been invalidated by its huge cost, even before the federal move to Hull, Ottawa road plans still appeared based on it at the end of 1969.

A number of meetings about the proposed Portage Bridge were held between the NCC and the RMOC planners at the technical level in the early months of 1970, and intensive discussions were begun with the Québec authorities to tie the new link directly into a widened Maisonneuve Boulevard in Hull; the costs for this latter were to be borne by Québec. The $13 million project was approved in principle by Treasury Board in February 1970, but with the rider that, before it was announced, I (as NCC chairman) was to be given at least a month to consult with Ontario, in order to fill them in and to see if they could be persuaded to contribute to part of the cost. I made contact with the Ontario officials, a meeting was arranged, and then to my surprise I saw the next day in the papers that the Bridge project had been announced by the federal Minister of Public Works, and belatedly confirmed several hours later by my equally surprised Minister, the Hon. Jean Marchand.

Ontario provincial politicians rose in their collective wrath, and denounced the bridge as going nowhere, as not having been subject to discussion, let alone negotiation, as costing local municipalities millions in developing proper approach roads, and as being a typical example of federal arrogance. The impression was also widely circulated that the Chairman of the NCC had a good deal to learn about cooperation with other levels of government, an impression which lingered on to haunt me. As I write these words in February, 1974, a newspaper report quotes a former area federal member of Parliament as considering "Mr. Fullerton's four years as NCC Chairman a disaster as far as over-all planning of the region is concerned. The Portage Bridge debacle is cited as a prime example of the breakdown of consultation under Mr. Fullerton."[5] Oddly enough I had always thought that, in our system of government, it was ministers rather than officials who bore the responsibility when things went wrong.

There is no doubt that the Portage Bridge, however urgently it was needed, did leave a legacy of distrust between the federal and Ontario governments, and made effective liaison more difficult. Opposition to the bridge would have arisen in any event, (its purpose was definitely to meet federal, not municipal, priorities) but had there been time for adequate consultation in advance of the premature federal announcement, I am sure the criticism would have been muted. As it was, the release of the story turned the bridge into a fait accompli, made the proposed consultation a farce, and laid the federal government open to the charge of bad faith.

The federal government has no monopoly on a preference for secrecy and surprise rather than consultation. Premier Davis of Ontario announced on Nov. 22, 1972 that the Krauss Maffei system of intermediate capacity rapid transit was to be built in Toronto, Hamilton and Ottawa, and maps showing projected routes in each city were published. Yet there had been no Ontario consultation whatever with RMOC and the City of Ottawa, let alone the NCC—and part of the proposed route crossed federal lands! Premier Davis obtained the media coverage he sought, but the operation hardly represented a good beginning for intergovernmental discussion on ways and means to improve public transit in the Capital.

Notwithstanding the Portage Bridge, the climate between Ontario and NCC did improve over the years, and several cooperative projects, involving the province, federal agencies, and RMOC, were brought to fruition. One of these was the extension of the sewer system or sewage treatment facilities in the Ontario side of the Region (politicians from every conceivable level were present at the November, 1972, opening of the new Watts Creek plant). Another combined operation was the joint approach to the creation of a new city in the Carlsbad Springs area outside the Greenbelt. Ontario Housing, Central Mortgage and Housing and NCC, were the principal participants in the venture, which has involved initially the acquisition of thousands of acres of land, and the setting up of a planning team. And, also notwithstanding the Krauss Maffei announcement, considerable progress has been made in cooperation in transportation planning along with Québec; we referred to this in Chapter Seven (page 87).

Finally, I had a most cordial reception from the Honourable John White, Ontario Minister of Treasury, Economics, and Intergovernmental Affairs, when in February 1974 I met him and members of his staff to exchange views on the governing of the Capital. He agreed to give a sympathetic hearing to proposals which might result from the Study.

II. The Local Municipalities and NCC

That the NCC is not exactly loved by municipal politicians in the Capital will not be news to anyone who reads the newspapers in the Region or listens to news broadcasts. We heard many complaints about the NCC in the course of our interviews. As the main federal agency in the Capital, it has been the object of attack from many leaders at the municipal level: "too authoritarian", "benevolent dictator", "doesn't consult enough", "too powerful", "unpredictable and inconsistent in its policies", "too secretive", "needs municipal representation on it", "NCC planning role is no longer needed", "failed to develop LeBreton Flats", "Gatineau Park has hurt Hull's growth", and so on. If some of this criticism may be unfair, it at least suggests that a wide gap exists between the public's image of NCC as a benevolent provider of good things, and the views of local politicians. In the paragraph which follows I therefore consider the criticisms in some detail.

(a) Inadequate Consultation

Not only local policitians but the public has been concerned about lack of consultation, and there were many references to it in the briefs and interviews. One example is contained in a letter of the president of the Ottawa Real Estate Board, Mr. Leo Brule, commenting on RMOC's official plan:

> Ever since the Official Plan was announced, it has become quite evident that the lack of co-operation and co-ordination among the Planning Boards within the Region have resulted in duplication of planning efforts. This lack of co-operation and co-ordination has become painfully obvious as public discussions of the proposed Regional Plan have been held...
>
> We feel strongly that the Federal Government, the Provincial Government and Planners from the municipal bodies comprising the Regional Municipality of Ottawa-Carleton should hold informal sessions on a regular basis to discuss their respective areas of progress or disagreement...
>
> The Planning Boards must establish better lines of communications if planning in a Regional basis is to be expedited in the proper manner."

This problem is one which the NCC has been aware of for a long time, without finding a satisfactory solution. We have referred to several reasons for it elsewhere in this Study. One is the difficulty of consulting or negotiating with a municipality on any proposal which ultimately will require federal approval at the Treasury Board or Cabinet level—and most of them do. Such consultation is difficult to carry out in secrecy, since municipal governments function in a fairly public manner. Federal ministers, however, do not like to see the public debating issues which have not yet reached them for consideration and decision. They may have reason for this—often governments are stampeded into taking decisions as a result of the effect of calculated leaks on public opinion—but the other side of the coin is that once a cabinet decision is taken it is very difficult to change, leaving the agency or department little room for manoeuvre. And, as I have noted, secrecy contributes to maximum publicity.

(b) Municipal Representation on the NCC

A common complaint from the municipalities is that the twenty-member Commission, drawn as it is from all over Canada, is not accountable to Capital residents. Most municipal spokesmen believe that NCC membership should include a number of elected local representatives—say the mayors of the largest municipalities, or the chairmen of the regional councils. The argument is plausible, and indeed there is a good historic basis for the request. In "An Act respecting the City of Ottawa" (Ottawa Improvement Commission Act) of 1899[6], one of the four commissioners was to be appointed by the City of Ottawa. In the Federal District Commission Act of 1927[7] one of ten commissioners was to be appointed by the City, and in 1946 an amendment to the F.D. Act provided that of 19 members, one each would be nominated by the Cities of Ottawa and Hull[8]. At least since 1927, successive mayors of both cities filled the seats.

However, when the NCC Act was passed in 1958 no provision was made for these city appointments (although there is no legal barrier to appointments of mayors). According to NCC files, the reason is that the presence of the mayors on the Commission caused a number of problems. A summary of the NCC position is given below, and is based largely on a memorandum sent in 1965 to the Minister of Public Works by the then Chairman of the NCC, General S. F. Clark. In his accompanying letter General Clark explained the sources of his information:

> Because I was not a member of the Commission when the Mayors of Hull and Ottawa were members of the Federal District Commission, I prepared the enclosed memorandum after consultation with two former Chairmen who were with the Commission when the Mayors of Ottawa and Hull were members. Also, I have had the benefit of the views of the staff of the Commission who served at that time.

The main points covered were these:

(i) *Mayors' Conflict of Interest*—The allocation of Commission spending among the various municipalities (mayors tending to lobby for their City), and differing federal and City policy objectives, placed the Mayor in a conflict of loyalties or judgment; this was intensified if the proposal might lead to negotiations or outright conflict between NCC and the municipalities or the province. Similar difficulties arose in specific proposals for the Mayor's own municipality to which he and his fellow City councillors might be opposed. Either the Mayor had to sit on the fence—not always palatable politically—or he or she was sometimes led to play both sides of the fence. It was this latter kind of activity in fact, with a Mayor taking one position at Commission meetings and a different one publicly at Council, which finally precipitated the exclusion of City appointments from the National Capital Act.

(ii) *Confidentiality of NCC meetings*—General Clark noted:

> ... One or other of the mayors on the Federal District Commission sometimes released information about Commission business that had not been cleared with the Government. It was given to the public either at press conferences or at meetings of the Board of Control or City Council. This situation is difficult for a mayor to avoid. The Board of Control and the City Council will consider the mayor as their representative on the Commission and expect him to report fully to them on the Commissions' actions and recommendations.

The leaks eroded the confidentiality of Commission meetings and led to public discussion in those City councils which had Commission representation; we have noted how popular this is with the federal cabinet.

(iii) *Mixing of elected and appointed members*—This is difficult to achieve harmoniously. Some mayors, of Ottawa in particular, leaned heavily on their elected status and demanded a special say (rivalling the Chairman's) in the running of Commission affairs.

In summary, if the case for elected representation on NCC has a superficial logic, the experience suggests that it has some inherent weaknesses. The appointment of the two regional chairmen might be less objectionable, although it is difficult to see how they also could avoid interest conflicts. But one reason why the issue itself keeps coming up may well be the widespread ignorance of how NCC really functions.

(c) *Ignorance, Misunderstanding and Anti-Federal Bias*

After meetings with politicians at all levels of government, and with the public at large, I have come to the conclusion that many complaints about NCC have their source in the widespread lack of understanding of what NCC is and how it works. If conflicts on particular issues are sometimes inevitable, critics often attribute to NCC powers it does not possess, or motives it never entertained, or, more simply, suspect it of trying to take over municipal functions. Suspicions, about NCC, however, have been fed by the NCC's inability to consult adequately with municipal leaders. and by its use of land acquisition and ownership to achieve federal objectives in the Capital.

In appraising the NCC performance, another factor has to be taken into account on the Québec side of the region, the existence of a group which holds strong anti-federalist views; their political allegiance tends to be in the direction of the separatist Parti Québécois. I won't attempt to explain their doctrine, except that it leads them to ascribe all kinds of sinister motives to the NCC. They accuse it of being a kind of "Trojan horse", leading the federal invasion into that part of the sacred soil of Québec which happens to lie in the "federal" National Capital Region. In one respect, this can be regarded as a left-handed compliment. An important federal goal is to build its Capital into a national symbol, and clearly the separatists recognize it as such. But there are some by-products of their activities that have hurt the NCC and federal image in Hull and in the area around it.

Any healthy democratic society thrives on the clash of views honestly held and vigorously expressed. While those who believe strongly in Canada may be shocked at separatist views, those who believe in democracy can scarcely question the rights of other citizens to express their ideas, no matter how personally distasteful. But the history of the twentieth century has shown that democracy itself can be undermined by the unscrupulous distortion of truth. The technique has invariably been to pick an issue which stirs strong popular feelings and to twist it for political purposes.

This is what, I believe, has happened to some extent in the Capital, where genuine and widespread fears about the survival of the French language and culture have been exploited by French-speaking separatists or ultra-nationalists in the teaching profession and in the press and broadcasting media. It would be most unfair to label all reporters and broadcasters separatists, of course, but we have witnessed for the past few years a steady distortion of news about the federal government and about the NCC in the local French-language paper, *Le Droit*[9], and in some broadcasts, including those of the CBC Inevitably it is these anti-federal stories which get picked up and reprinted in other French publications across Québec.

This distortion occurs in many ways; the slanting of news stories, the prominent placing and large amount of space given to anti-federal statements, headings which twist an honest report, the use of pejorative phrases in editorials or stories. Let me give one example of this latter. *Le Droit* keeps referring to the NCC "expropriation" of Eddy's despite the fact that no such expropriation ever occurred (see page 39) and despite repeated public statements and letters (most of which were published) to the *Le Droit* editors to this effect. The linking of "NCC" and "expropriation" has occurred in other contexts in the newspaper, and appears to be associated with separatist attempts to show that not only is the federal government intent on driving industry out of the Region, but it is using force to achieve its ends. For example, in *Le Droit* of January 25, 1973, there was an accurate story referring to the negotiated purchase by the federal DPW of the head office of the Metropolitan Life in Ottawa (page 108); the heading, however, read "*La CCN exproprie la Métropolitaine*". A minor annoyance, to be sure, but the steady drip has had an effect; I find many people who refuse to accept the truth—that the NCC expropriated nothing during my tenure as Chairman—because they have seen the contrary so often "in the paper".

Another consequence of the continuing bias is that some municipal leaders on the Québec side, to obtain good coverage in the French media, may adopt a public anti-federalist stance at variance with the views of their constituents or indeed with some of their own private opinions. No doubt they consider it safe to attack the federal government because they believe that there are benefits to be obtained from acting like a David facing a federal Goliath. Yet the effect is certainly to make the NCC's task more difficult at a time when almost everything the NCC does on the Québec side has been in close partnership with the Québec government and with the municipalities.

A further unfortunate effect of the propaganda is to divide the French-speaking communities on the two sides of the Ottawa River. An example of this was the insistance of Franco-Ontarians in obtaining equal representation in the directorship of the new cooperative television station, CFVO, before giving it their financial support. The Study has been told that this was due specifically to guard against this new organ falling in the hands of separatists. How much more effective would be the Francophone voice in the National Capital Region, where they form more than a third of the total population, if there were complete solidarity on both sides of the River!

In some respects this complaint is directed at professional ethics rather than excessive political zeal; I think the NCC can survive the continuing barrage of misinformation about what it does and how it functions. And, fortunately, there has been some moderation in the extent of the distortion since last October's Québec election. Moreover there are some signs that the media bias is becoming counterproductive—the people of the Region, particularly those who are employed by the federal government, and who use its parks and recreational facilities, find it hard to believe that it can be all bad; there is a good deal of active resentment about the tone of *Le Droit*, for example. The school children are beginning to challenge the separatist line of some of their teachers, and may be becoming more open minded and apolitical. In the interest of everyone I hope these trends continue; a press and media slanted and dominated by ideology is widely discounted by its readers, as anyone knows who has lived in a country with a one-party political system.

(*d*) *The Personality Factor*

Another factor in the NCC-municipal relationship in recent years might be described as the visible clash of personalities. When I was Chairman of NCC, I was frequently described as "controversial" or "abrasive" or as having too high a profile for a public official. I'll admit at least to having a highly developed sense of outrage. If my organization or group is attacked or threatened, or my motives questioned, or my statements misrepresented, then I'm inclined to do battle, if necessary in full public view. I have also not been unaware that controversy is a good way to bring issues before the public. The media are interested and give it exposure, and people start thinking about it and reacting to it.

Public controversy has its defects. The papers tend to exaggerate the extent of differences, to personalize matters rather than stay on the real issues, and to pick away at the participants to try to push them into yet one more statement, all of which is wearing on everyone. It may intensify inherent divisions between levels of government, and leave scars. To what extent this controversy had adversely affected relations between the NCC and the municipalities I find difficult to judge objectively, but at least the public in the Capital has become aware of some important issues, and is much more conscious of the NCC than it was before.

But however problems in the NCC's external relationships are rationalized, there are clearly enough stresses and strains in the system to threaten the stability of the existing governing structure. Readers to this point will have sensed a considerable degree of scepticism on my part about the ability of this structure to survive, but there are different opinions. Some believe that what is needed is more formal consultative arrangements among the different levels of government—a little shoring up of the foundation here, a little cross bracing of the rafters there. In a sense it is an attempt to answer in a positive way the perennial cry for cooperation: "why don't they all get together?".

III. Coordination by Consultation

Consultation among governments in the Capital has undoubtedly increased during the past year. One reason may have been the growing awareness of these governments of their interdependence and of their inability to do things alone. Another may be the approach of my successor as NCC Chairman, and his greater confidence in the consultative process. In a speech Mr. Gallant said:

> From time to time we are shocked to be reminded that in the small territory with which we are concerned there are so many levels or orders of government —the federal, two provinces and over 50 municipalities and two new "supra or super municipalities", the RMOC and the ORC. It's quite natural to react—even yearn for something more simple, more efficient and manageble. We could eliminate so many dog fights, jealousies, elections and even politicians. But if all the lumps and bumps and warts were shed we might find ourselves a pretty plain-faced lot. And we might lose more than our charm. A federal district! Noting our achievements to-date, I would be inclined to suggest to the politicians: "Dither on for awhile yet!" Who knows, maybe our funny system works best under these so-called unreasonable pressures.[10]

He returned to this general theme in a speech on April 18th; referring to the greater extent of recent consultation:

> We are breaking down some of the barriers and problems which often lend support to the notion that the present system is unworkable. We are building a general framework which can encompass the RMOC and ORC plans and the new NCC concept which I will tell you about in a few minutes. We are confident that this framework can accommodate federal, provincial, regional and local goals in a compatible and consistent planning approach... Our system of consultation and compromise is proving productive. We have reached some tentative agreements already.[11]

Along similar lines is the idea that the Capital, if it to be a symbol of Canada, should reflect in its government the stresses and strains of federal-provincial-municipal relations that are so typically Canadian. As a nation we have managed to achieve a constitutional balance of forces, uneasy though it may be, and the government structure we have developed is almost federalism in microcosm. It is argued that not to recognize this in seeking new forms of government for the Capital would be somehow untrue to the reality of Canadian political life, and a deviation from the natural evolution of the Canadian governmental system.

I recognize the force of these arguments, and another parallel conclusion that is linked to them, that is, that in Canadian political circles continuation of the *status quo* or its incremental modification unusually tends to be preferred to innovation. "Better the devil you know..."

At the same time, I must reiterate my doubts. I know the democratic process is untidy, and to attack this untidiness is to court the charge of attacking the system itself. Yet Mr. Henry Kissinger operates within a democratic framework, and seems to have made considerably more progress in relieving international tension than a dozen open assemblies of the United Nations. I suppose my main concern about the usefulness of the consultative process in the Capital has been the growth in the number of governments involved—from the effective two governments in 1968 to four tiers of government (or even five tiers if the community associations are included), and with a number of governments in several of the tiers. If all interested federal departments are added in, the amount of consultation required is awe-inspiring. Consider one aspect of this, the time it takes.

Consultation Is Time-Consuming

Persons who have watched federal-provincial conferences in action will have an idea of what is involved in the consultative process. Each year the meetings become more frequent and take up more time, but the results bear little relation to the frequency or length of the discussions. Inside each government the same process is going on, with more and more departments and persons involved in most issues. Every provincial or federal minister I have met complains about the increasing drain on time posed by cabinet or committee meetings, and the less time each has to administer his or her department. All very democratic, of course, but hardly conducive to the efficient carrying on of the nation's business, (and one other reason why our bureaucracies are growing so fast).

The difficulty increases when more governments participate. I remember once trying to arrange a meeting involving federal, Ontario and Québec ministers. It took us three months to find a date when the three ministers concerned could be in one city on the one day. At lower levels of government, time may not be quite so precious, but at the NCC we often had considerable trouble in finding a date for a meeting that was equally convenient to two or three mayors or reeves. And how do we fit the need for more intergovernment discussions on Capital issues into the increasingly tight schedules of our political leaders?

Declining Appeal of Municipal Office

A related problem is that of attracting good people into local politics. The diffusion and dispersal of power, particularly when it is accompanied by ever-increasing demands on time and by growing frustration, discourages many from seeking municipal office. The problem is accentuated because so many of the potential candidates in the Capital are full-time government employees. This leaves the field even more open than usual to professionals, principally lawyers, whose working hours are more flexible and whose practices may eventually benefit.

But even for such persons as are available, higher pay appears to provide an inadequate incentive. One reporter noted in a column:

> ...my ten-year-old span on Ottawa's municipal beat has not been accompanied by the advent of a new era of better government. It has, in fact, seen the opposite with increased cost to boot. Ten years ago, the city was entering the last nine months of the Charlotte Whitton regime and municipal politics was at its colorful best in the nation's capital. Board of control meetings were edged with drama. Decisions were made and sometimes rescinded. But no matter what happened, civic politics had flair and still managed to attract key businessmen and professionals. Today, board of control generally boils down to an exercise in boredom, long-winded discussions and few significant decisions. People still want leadership but they are experiencing increasing difficulty in finding it.[12]

He neglected to point out that ten years ago the post of Mayor of Ottawa carried with it considerably more power and status than it does to-day—and one main reason for it has been the advent of regional government, and the consequent loss of some City independence. If the public is having difficulty in finding leaders as the report suggests, then it is this latter factor which has been significant.

Conclusion

I may be overstating all these difficulties, and understating the growing appreciation by politicians and officials that the present system of government in the Capital will not work without a much greater degree of cooperation than we have seen to date. Politicians may be persuaded to forego the satisfactions and glory that comes from news releases that scoop other governments, and choose instead to share the publicity. Who knows, even the threat of a new system of government may have the merit of inducing everyone to get together to face the common enemy.

Yet I remain a sceptic about the consultative process itself. It seems to me that it has too many inherent flaws to provide the basis of a good government for the Region. One such flaw is that it tends to give legitimacy to the existing levels and numbers of government, and in this way may interfere with needed structural reform. "The people are tired of being overadministered", the Hon. Oswald Parent noted in his April 10th letter to Outaouais mayors. "It is evident to all citizens and public administrators that the excessive number of municipalities is beginning to interfere with the harmonious development of the region"...[13] The same need has been felt on the Ontario side, and led to the reduction in the number of municipalities in January 1, 1974. This process must be allowed to continue in response to public demand for a simpler and less costly municipal government.

The consultative approach has other failings. The fragmentation of authority leads to delay in reaching decisions and uncertainty in implementing them. Too often, when meetings of different levels of government reach a consensus after long deliberations, everyone assumes that action will follow, but often no one participant has the authority to follow up and act—or at least without further consultation and meetings. I have watched this process at work within the federal government itself. I hesitate to enunciate a "law" to cover it, but there is no doubt at all that the more departments there are involved in any particular project, the longer the time it takes to reach a decision, and the even longer time it takes from the moment of decision to its implementation. And, of course, the more people there are that are needed to service the machine The sharp rise in the number of municipal employees in the NCR since Regional government came into being, and the doubling or more of municipal expenditures, is clear evidence of the process at work.

Time and money, of course, seldom have as high a priority with officials as the delicious satisfactions of endlessly sitting around tables discussing problems with their peers. I am sure that a paradise designed by bureaucrats would make provision for continuous, 24-hour, multi-level—and of course top-level—meetings and conferences, with the whole population of this paradise harnessed to the task of drafting, typing, editing, correcting, revising and translating the stream of memoranda that would provide the only diet needed for the elite group around the table.

Any democratic society requires extensive consultation to settle problems; that is what the political process is all about. What it does not need and cannot afford much longer is the continuing development of massive structures and empires which appear to exist mainly to justify and perpetuate the bureaucratic species. The public are growing tired of this travesty of democracy. Consultation, yes, but within a simplified framework and with more meaning, Officials, elected or appointed, who spend their days locked in meetings with their colleagues generally have little time for the consultation that really matters, that with the public.

Footnotes

1. One incident, back in the late 1920's, illustrates this. A Hull member in the Québec legislature complained that Hull had not been shown on a new provincial map of Québec. Another member replied in the assembly that it was not surprising, since Hull was "le trou de cul" (anus) of the province. Another version suggests that the member's reply alluded to Hull being shown on the map of Québec in the area where the first letter of the name "Québec" was printed—therefore in the "Q" (pronounced as "cul") of the province.

2. *Joint Committee of the Senate and the House of Commons on the Federal District Commission* (1956), p. 475.

3. See Chapter Three: first reference p. 31-2, second p. 26.

4. See Chapter Two, page 14-15.

5. *Ottawa Journal*, February 26, 1974, article by Henry Heald.

6. *Statutes of Canada*, 1899, 62-63 Victoria, Chapt. 10 (Reprinted in Appendix A).

7. Ibid., 1927, 17 George V, Chapt. 55.

8. Ibid., 1946, 10 George VI, Chapt. 51.

9. Last autumn the editor of *Le Droit*, Marcel Gingras, resigned, explaining his position in a signed article in the Ottawa Citizen, "*Why I Quit Le Droit*". *Inter alia* he said "Being a federalist is now a crime at Le Droit. Separatists only can express themselves. This is so true that the publisher himself, Jean-Robert Belanger, had to give in, on Oct. 19, when the reporters' union ordered him to withdraw from the editorial page an article I had written at his own request about the integration of Hull federal civil servants into the public service of a sovereign Québec..." "Six days later, to prove that he still retains some form of control over the paper, Mr. Belanger wrote a front-page editorial in favor of federalism. Not to hurt the separatist militants from the newsroom, Mr. Belanger was careful to say that the independence option was undesirable at present. The statement left the door open to another option for the future, even if separation of Québec from Confederation should result in the death of the Franco-Ontarians and that of other French-speaking Canadians living outside Québec."

10. Gallant, E. *Notes for a speech to Ottawa Kiwanis Club*, January 18, 1974.

11. Gallant, E. *Notes for Remarks to the Commercial and Industrial Development Corporation of Ottawa-Carleton*, April 18, 1974.

12. *Ottawa Journal*, "Clingen at City Hall", April 5, 1974.

13. Parent, The Hon. Oswald, *Letter to Mayors of Municipalities* in the Outaouais Regional Community, April 10, 1974.

Chapter Nine

The Lack of a Coordinated Federal Approach to the Capital

My terms of reference included the following area of study:

"...the role of the National Capital Commission and its relation to other bodies concerned with the governing of the Capital Region, and the coordination of those federal activities which bear upon the development of the Region as a national capital." As I noted earlier, this Study originated out of my concern about growing jurisdictional problems in the Region, including those within the federal government itself. With the overwhelming economic dominance of the federal government in the Capital, it would be surprising if conflicts had not developed among the many departments and agencies from overlapping or competing operations. In some respects each department sees itself as an independant state or principality, and is quick not only to defend its territory but occasionally to mount raiding forays into that of others.

In pursuing these questions, I faced a number of difficulties. One was my former occupation, which exposes me to a charge of bias in favour of the NCC; as a somewhat scarred veteran of four years of federal infighting it would be difficult for me not to be affected by it. And poking into government operations will be regarded by some as washing federal dirty linen, an exercise any government prefers to have done behind closed doors rather than in public. These hazards led me to restrict my investigations, but there is enough material available to illustrate the problems arising from lack of clear definition of departmental boundaries, and the need for more of an improved federal understanding of the unity of the Capital and for a better coordination of the federal role in it.

I. «Intégrité de la capitale».—A Matter of Identity

The Dorion Report[1] made much of the wholeness or integrity of Québec's territory, and condensed its view into the phrase, "integrité du territoire", which was to become the slogan of that Report. What the federal government has failed to do is to generate within its own ranks a similar attitude towards the Capital. Federal policy has for more than half a century been devoted to widening the definition of the Capital's boundaries beyond the narrow concept of the City of Ottawa. Its many moves in this direction, notably the National Capital Act, the creation of the National Capital Region, the development of Gatineau Park, the construction of federal office buildings in Hull, and the expansion in NCC expenditures on the Québec side, have been recounted elsewhere in this Report. But somehow the idea that Ottawa, *and Ottawa only*, is the capital, remains to this day strongly held throughout the federal public service—and to some extent in Parliament (see discussion in Chapter Two, page 18-19). Whatever the reasons for this view—chauvinism, bilingual backlash, anti-Québec prejudice, attempts to score political points, or a belief in the sacredness of the constitutional definition—it is beyond my understanding how anyone who stands at the back of Parliament Hill and looks out at Hull scarcely a stone's throw away, can fail to see the essential unity or oneness of the two cities.

At the core of the problem within the federal government may be the divergence between the public service's different images of the cities of Ottawa and Hull. To the extent that federal employees see Hull as meaner, run-down, foreign, remote, they will resent the inclusion of it as part of the Capital, even if they are shifted to an office across the River. This resistance may erode as new federal buildings go up in Hull, as improvements are made in the services and amenities of Hull and its environs, and as more and more Ottawans find out that Hull as a place to work may have some advantages over, say, Tunney's Pasture, Confederation Heights, or even downtown Ottawa. But this process will take time, and prejudices die hard; more internal federal emphasis on the unity of the Region—on the "intégrité de la capitale" if you like—would ease this difficult transition period.

The Ottawa versus Hull issue keeps coming up in many interesting ways, such as the argument over the siting of the proposed new National Gallery. Because the Gallery has always been in Ottawa ("the Capital"), Ottawans regard it as theirs, and view the proposal that it might be placed in Hull almost as sacrilegious. We don't propose to join in this particular controversy, except to note that the site proposed by Gréber in 1950 might not be exactly right for the Capital of the 1980's and 1990's, but the real issue remains the widespread lack of acceptance of Hull as being part of the Capital. Here is an example of such a parochial point of view, contained in a letter to the *Ottawa Citizen* on January 18, 1974:

> Various articles in the Citizen indicate our politicians are having extreme difficulty in locating a "National Gallery" in the nation's capital. From some of the locations suggested, it would appear they are also having difficulty locating the capital.
>
> May I suggest that if the prime minister would write to the "Canada Party" at Box 5548, Station F, Ottawa, he would be advised of the exact location of the nation's capital in short order.

What can the federal government do to change attitudes in the Capital? Many things, some of them relatively simple. The Government's mailing address for example is still "Ottawa, Ontario"—except for that of at least one Crown agency, the NCC; my successor was daring enough to adopt the address "Ottawa-Hull, Canada". Why not Ottawa-Hull for all government departments, regardless of their location in the Region? Or better still why not Ottawa-Hull, N.C.R., Canada? (Incidentally, the E.B. Eddy Company, the factories of which lie in both Ottawa and Hull, uses the double-barrelled address). Why not use Ottawa-Hull for all mail addressed to the Capital, including residential? Why has the Post Office kept its local Ottawa and Hull branches as separate operating entities, with one directed from Toronto and the other from Montreal? And why has the postal code for Ottawa the prefix "K", and that of Hull "J"? We understand that changes in this are being considered; we hope so because a new federal postal address, and coordinated Capital post-office operations, could go a long way towards unifying the Region.

One example, if a simple one, of the type of change I am seeking, occurred on the cover of the Government Telephone Directory. For several years "Ottawa" was the only address shown and I asked the deputy minister of Communications Dept., why? He replied that he had never thought about it, and in the next issue "National Capital Region" replaced Ottawa. Many similar instances occur because nobody had been compelled to think about it. Another such may be the "Ottawa International Airport". Why not Ottawa-Hull (as it is described in Air Canada's domestic schedule)? Or better still "National Capital Airport"?

Fortunately, changes are appearing. The radio and TV stations increasingly refer to "National Capital weather" and promote their station as covering the "Capital Region". Widespread circulation of the NCC's map of the Region has helped give residents the conciousness of the size and boundaries of the area; the existence and growing attractiveness of Gatineau Park further helps to increase the acceptance of the larger two-province Capital.

The address is one thing; designation of department operations in the Capital another. For Manpower and Immigration, there are three Canada Manpower Centres in Ottawa, and one Centre in Hull; there is an "Ottawa District Immigration Office" and a "Canada Immigration Centre—Hull" (the latter with no name and only one phone number listed). One can understand offices in a variety of locations in the Capital, if dictated for reasons of efficiency or even of language concentration—but why not Capital Region etc. etc.? Some departments have organized themselves on this basis. The Department of Public Works functions locally are combined into a "Capital Region" office, as are those of Supply and Services, and Health and Welfare has its operations in the Capital appropriately described under "National Capital Zone". This is a rather tiresome recital of telephone listings, but it does illustrate the lack of a consistent federal policy for local operations as distinct from national, and the great emphasis on "Ottawa" as the shorthand word for Capital than the phrase "National Capital" itself.

In some instances, a split between the Ontario and Québec sides of the Region appears to be dictated by an organizational structure which divides operations by province, but is this beyond the power of a department to adjust? We have noted the difficulty in assembling statistics data on an "NCR" basis; could Statistics Canada not establish a new geographical category for the Region? It does assemble some data now for the Ottawa-Hull metropolitan area, and this is very useful, but the regular publication of statistics on the NCR basis could have tremendous psychological impact. Grants for the Opportunities for Youth and the Local Initiatives Programmes for the Region were handled from Montreal and Toronto. We won't labour the point further except to note that when federal departments and agencies organize their Capital operations to reflect the existence of the NCR, not only will their employees become more aware of the unity of the Region but so will the world outside.

II. Jurisdictional Problems: the NCC and Public Works

In the discussion in Chapter Four about the respective roles of the NCC and the DPW in the Capital I referred to some areas of overlap. During my tenure as NCC Chairman, the single issue which aroused most concern among my NCC colleagues was the fear of the gradual loss of NCC's property function to the DPW, and along with it some of the NCC responsibilities for urban planning and development in the Capital. As events have developed, these fears appear to have some basis in fact.

Until recently, the NCC was clearly the principal federal agent for real estate transactions in the National Capital Region, initially through the purchase and expropriation of land for the Greenbelt, for bridgeheads, for Gatineau Park, for other parks, and for the parkway system. In 1967, however, the NCC expropriated the Kent-Sparks-Bank-Queen block in central Ottawa, and in 1969, fifteen acres in central Hull; both properties were to be used mainly for the construction of federal office buildings. DPW's activities in the field of property operations (as distinct from construction) had been largely leasing of office space from private developers, the purchase of a number of buildings for federal use, and the acquisition of land from the NCC, from other departments or from the private sector for the construction of federal buildings. The line drawn between the two agencies was thus never very precise, but the NCC was the main agent for land acquisition in large amounts, and particularly where expropriation was required. The magnitude of the NCC operations are cited in Chapter Four: 124,000 acres of land acquired in over 3000 separate property transactions. Of these, 119 reached litigation. These realty operations were not only securely based on the National Capital Act, and on a series of legal decisions, notably Munro, but they gave the NCC staff considerable expertise in the property business. This knowledge of land and property values in turn contributed importantly to NCC planning decisions, with such decisions of course reinforced by the power derived from land ownership.

We have noted that between 1957 and 1968, the NCC reported to Parliament through the Minister of Public Works; in the later years the Minister was the Honourable (now Senator) George McIlraith, who lived in Ottawa and had a particular interest in and insight into the work of the NCC. The shifting of the agency to another department[2], however justified for other reasons, did remove an important mechanism for reconciling NCC-DPW conflicts at a level below that of the Cabinet. How effective this process might have been in later years is difficult to say, because a Minister less sympathetic to the NCC might well have supported his department at the NCC's expense, but at least the NCC would have had an easier time making its case.

We have also referred in Chapter Four to the growing role of the DPW in federal land operations in recent years—the transfer to it of the land inventory, of Transport's property division, of exclusive powers of expropriation for the federal government. As noted in the DPW's 1970-71 Annual Report,

> these various activities were related to the ultimate destiny of Public Works becoming the federal government's designated agent in the areas of land acquisition and disposal, development of Crown-owned lands, and design and construction. Public Works would, in fact, become Canada's largest construction and property management 'firm'.

Various attempts were made beginning late in 1969 to reconcile this responsibility, along with DPW's economic "highest and best use" approach for land, with other federal objectives or urban planning and environmental policy. Insofar as the Capital Region was concerned, one proposed solution, involving joint NCC-DPW management of federal land, was acceptable to NCC but was not followed up by DPW.

Rather than attempting a step-by-step story of DPW's expanding property role in the Capital, I will cite only one example. In 1969 there remained four private holdings of property on the south side of Wellington Street, between Elgin and Bank Streets, including the U.S. Embassy; the remainder was owned by the federal government. Rumours began to appear in the press about the Government interest in acquiring these properties, and indeed by 1970 three of the four owners had approached me to find out if the NCC had alternative sites available for them; they were ready to go along with a phased sale to the Government, and assumed that the NCC would be the federal agent. I tried to obtain ministerial approval to follow these matters up: the NCC core plan, which had been approved by the Government, clearly involved the eventual acquisition of all four properties, but I met with no success.

By the spring of 1972, however, the DPW had been authorized to purchase by negotiation one of the buildings, that of the Metropolitan Life, (which occupied half of one block) as "accommodation" for Parliament. It had also received preliminary Cabinet approval to expropriate not only all private buildings on the south side of Wellington (excluding the U.S. Embassy), but the remainder of three full blocks in question (Wellington-Elgin-Sparks-Bank). The NCC was not consulted, and indeed was not even informed that Cabinet was considering the matter. I protested the decision for a number of reasons I won't go into here; the matter was later reopened but the decision stood. The expropriation took place in July 1973, and the DPW is now in charge of the planning of the three-block area as part of the parliamentary precinct; the NCC, I understand, will be involved to some degree in the planning process.

Well, apart from the adverse impact on NCC morale, what is wrong with DPW becoming the principal federal agent in land transactions in the Capital? Several things, one of the most important being the case law built up around expropriations under the National Capital Act; federal expropriations under a different authority have no Munro case to fall back upon and may face tougher court battles and higher costs. Another problem is the power associated with land ownership by a federal department; the NCC has generally had much greater difficulty in exercising its responsibility as a planner on federal land it does not own. On the three Wellington/Sparks blocks, it will be the DPW which hires the outside planners and controls the direction of their work, in this central area of the Capital. The DPW is fast developing, in fact, a planning operation paralleling that of NCC.

Another aspect of the expanding property role of the DPW is that it appears to ignore the essential link between planning, control of land, and doing things with the land. The National Capital Act was created in 1958 to bring these functions together for the Capital under one body, the NCC. We have emphasized many times in this Study that the NCC is more of a developer than it is a planner; it has been the acquisition of land, and the use of that land to meet the objectives of government and of good urban policy, which has been the main thrust of NCC activities for the past 15 years.

Why then has the NCC failed to make its case better known to the Government? I don't know for sure, but I have a few theories. One is that the Commission has been for decades a relatively unknown agency. The favourable publicity the NCC generated from such "people" things as the skating on the Rideau Canal may have made it more popular, but they added little to the bureaucratic understanding of the NCC and how it operates. A second possible NCC liability is the continuing emphasis on its role as a planner. The Gréber "plan" casts a long shadow, even if it was less a land-use plan in to-day's sense of the term than an amalgamation of four or five major and practical development proposals. Thus people tend to think of the NCC as containing a large group of planners who sit in a back room preparing complex drawings of future road networks and zoning regulations which can then be bound into a volume and labelled "master plan". As we have noted, the reality is considerably different. I suspect it is the view of NCC as a planner which in the past has dominated the thinking at the DPW, and possibly elsewhere in the government, and which may explain the restricted role often assigned to the NCC.

Another cause of weakness in the NCC's position may simply be the power game as it is played at the Cabinet level. The Minister of Public Works has only that one department's interests at stake in negotiations with his colleagues; moreover he is a dispenser of new structures in Member's constituencies such as wharves or buildings, and provides office space to departments. This gives him considerable clout. For the Minister of State for Urban Affairs, the NCC ranks third in importance to his own department and to Central Mortgage and Housing. This naturally limits the time he has available for NCC matters, and his bargaining power is diffused.

I know that as Chairman of the NCC, I faced an added handicap which arose from the NCC remoteness from the Minister's office—the almost total denial of access to Cabinet agenda or documents. The knowledge of what is going up to Cabinet, and what Cabinet committees are discussing, is a vital part of the federal government information network at the senior level. I found it particularly aggravating when documents were circulated which affected us, and meetings held, both of which we only found out about later (Wellington Street was a case in point). Management at the DPW suffers no such handicap.

In summing up, I think it is important to note that the main issue is not really the protection of the NCC from a DPW invasion; it is that two arms of the federal government are charged with overlapping responsibilities, and have been competing rather than cooperating in trying to resolve the problem. If the balance of power continues to reside with the DPW, then the resolution of this problem will inevitably involve a declining role for the NCC. This might be a satisfactory solution in some respects, but it has risks in others; the NCC has had a special responsibility in the Capital and special legal powers to back it up.

The Building Heights Fiasco

If the DPW has been moving in on NCC's property function, there is one area of DPW's operations that could have gained from more input from NCC. I refer to government leasing policy, which we touched on briefly in Chapter Four (pp. 44 and 45). As we noted, in 1963 the new government leasing policy took effect. Although all federal buildings were subject to design review by the NCC under the 1958 Act, no provision had been made in the Act for a similar screening of leased buildings. No control has been exercised by the government on the design of such buildings; the federal policy of not giving speculative builders any formal leasing commitment in advance of construction, and rental price competition, in fact ensured a total abdication of federal design control of any kind.

The first result was a burst of second rate but lowrise (up to ten story) buildings in the central area, built speculatively by the private sector, thrown up as cheaply as possible to provide on a competitive basis low cost rental accommodation for the government. However, in 1964 the new City Bylaw AZ64 raised the buildings heights ceiling from 110 feet to 150 feet above grade, with provision that it could be pierced "on merit", and the high-rise race was on. There is no single planning issue that has aroused more concern among residents, public officials and parliamentarians, all of whom fear the dwarfing of the Peace Tower as it is gradually fenced in by high rise office buildings. The Right Honourable John G. Diefenbaker, in referring to his first visit to Ottawa, said in the House of Commons on March 26, 1973:

I saw the grandeur of Parliament Hill, the majestic location. Nowhere in the world is there the equal of it. I hope I do not speak out of turn when I say that I am concerned over the fact that more and more as high buildings are going up this magnificent structure is becoming a pygmy, of it I could invent a word, is being pygmatized. Let us do something now before it is too late.

Some hon. Members: Hear, hear!

Let this House catch something of the tremendous inspiration of Mackenzie King when, having secured the appointment of Jacques Gréber, a plan was made that this place would not only exemplify the greatness of freedom but would stand out magnificently.

I walked up Parliament Hill this morning and the thought came to me, how changed it is in more than three decades! I do hope that some action will be taken by parliament before it is too late and that agreement will be reached as a result of the setting up of a committee not only of the Senate and the House of Commons but of the mayor and city of Ottawa to the end that we do not allow this trend that is taking place to continue. If we do, the day will not be far distant when the greatness of the location that Champlain saw will have been obliterated by modern economic change...

Because of this wide interest in the subject, I am documenting this story of the battle over building heights with some care. I will quote first from an internal NCC memorandum, prepared in 1970 by a senior staff member who had been actively involved in the issue:

Although the Federal Government itself did first exceed the original 110′ maximum height for buildings throughout Ottawa, none of these exceptions has in any way caused visual or aesthetic harm to the Parliamentary group of buildings. For example, the Lorne Building (National Gallery) is well below sight line from the base of the Peace Tower and does not interfere with the silhouette of the Parliament Buildings from the Quebec side. Similarily neither does the Brooke-Claxton Building at Tunney's Pasture which is far removed from Parliament Hill and is built at a lower ground elevation. Moreover, the Federal Government has never made the case for a blanket building height limitation over the whole of Ottawa but limited its concern to a practical application of building height control directly related to the preservation of the visual integrity of the Federal Buildings on Parliament Hill in the core area.

In the Federal sense, the economic consequences on private developers of building height control has not been ignored. A case of economic rationale was prepared for the Commission and made available to the City of Ottawa by Dr. Wilbur Thompson, showing there was no justification for buildings to be built in the central area higher than the Commission was recommending in order to protect Parliament Hill. In this the Floor Space Index was the economic determinant, not height.

Briefly the history of building height control in Ottawa is this: at the request of the Federal Government height regulations were first imposed by the City of Ottawa in 1910 and redefined in 1914. The overall height control was

110′ above grade everywhere in Ottawa. Not until 1963 was this changed, when Bylaw 68-63 set a height of 500′ above sea level. This was changed to read 150′ above grade in the AZ-64 Zoning Bylaw. Provision was, however, made for exceeding the 150′ height "on merit" and the Building Appearance Committee (of the city of Ottawa) had criteria on which to evaluate the "merit", (of buildings over 150′) including the effect of height on the Parliament Buildings. To this point the situation was under control but with this obvious weakness; the Board of Control could upset the Building Appearance Committee recommendations.

At the beginning of 1968 seven applications for Bylaw amendment to exceed the 150′ height limit in the proximity of Parliament Hill were submitted to the City. The largest and the significant test case was Place de Ville Phase II. The first proposals to the Building Appearance Committee showed a building height approximately twice that of the first stage of Place de Ville. The Commission representatives on the Building Appearance Committee recognized the environmental danger implicit in this submission, and as a result the Commission promptly made representation to the City urging a study of building height control in the core area relative to protecting the visual significance of the National Parliament buildings and the Parliament Square. In view of the urgency of the situation the City of Ottawa and the Commission joined forces and appointed a special Technical NCC—City Task Team. . . . (Roderick Clack and Peter Korwin were NCC appointees).

In February 1968 the NCC—City Task Team submitted its recommendation for a sloping height plane building height control regulation for the central area of the City. (The validity of this concept was supported at subsequent Ontario Municipal Board Hearing for the necessary relaxation from the overall 150′ permitted building height).

The Technical NCC—City Task Team was required to report back to both the Board of Control and the National Capital Commission. The Commission, through its staff and Design Advisory Committee endorsed the recommendations made by the Task Team. On the other hand, the Board of Control was not prepared to endorse the recommendations without further study toward anticipated change. This encouraged the Place de Ville project to proceed with less opposition and the Commission could not stop it.

Because the City was supporting the developers' proposals for the Place de Ville Phase II project, the Commission made representation through its Minister requesting "Federal Government support in whatever way might be most appropriate to prevent the construction of these buildings which it deemed would detract from the nature, character and significance of the seat of Government of Canada". Amendments to the National Capital Act to empower the Commission to control such matters as building height within a designated area as being in the national interest, were suggested. At this point the divergence of viewpoint between the Commission and the Board of Control became a public issue.

Acting on a recommendation of the NCC—City Task Team, the Central Area Consultant Study was undertaken jointly by the Commission, the City and the Department of Highways Ontario. The terms of reference required Hammer, Greene, Siler Associates to review the building height problem. In making its recommendations on this subject there was, unfortunately, a lack of liaison between the various Consultants involved in preparing the report and two conflicting recommendations concerning building heights were included. The Consultants report however did accept the principle of a sloping height plane earlier advanced by the City—NCC Technical Task Team but the Consultants report was unnecessarily complicated and in some cases far too lenient on building heights control.

The Commission agreed that the Central Area Study was too lenient with respect to building heights. The Board of Control, taking the opposite view, was prepared to take the recommendations contained in the Consultants report as the basis for City support before the Ontario Municipal Board of the application to amend the building heights bylaw for Place de Ville Phase II. Although the original submission which would have seen a building height twice that of Place de Ville I was considerably reduced, the amendment allowed a building height far in excess of the original recommendations of the NCC—City Task Team. To make matters worse, a City bylaw interpretation allowed a penthouse to exceed the nominal building height whereas the NCC—City Task Team had recommended absolute heights.

A number of other applications for amendment to bylaw AZ-64 for increased height above the 150′ established limit have occured since the Place de Ville Phase II Project. In these cases the City of Ottawa has used the Central Area Consultants Report as its guideline in supporing applications before the Ontario Municipal Board. In most cases the buildings in these applications have not been located where their height would be detrimental to the Federal Parliament Buildings. However, there have been notable exceptions. Again, the discrepancy and conflict in the Central Area Study Report supported by the City of Ottawa, has permitted exccssive height in such buildings as the Bell Canada Tower on Elgin Street and the Lord Elgin Plaza, Office Building on Slater Street.

Probably the most damaging effect from lack of suitable height control regulations is La Promenade[3] on the Sparks Street Mall. This building is actually within the 150′ height limit and did not need bylaw exception yet it exceeds by about 50′ the height recommended by the NCC—City Task Team which Board of Control did not agree to adopt under the sloping plane principle for that portion of Sparks Street. The sloping plane line was based upon a control line along Wellington Street which took into account the scale and proportion of Parliament Square and the height of Langevin and other buildings facing Parliament Hill.

The serious effect of the permitted height of La Promenade on Parliament Square was recognized by the Commission and some efforts were made to investigate what steps could be taken to reduce its height to that recommended by the original NCC—City Task Team. These efforts were without success.

Let me quote another version of the Place de Ville II story, which appeared in the press:

> One of the most famous occasions where city council ran counter to the advice of its planners was Campeau Corporation's Place de Ville.
>
> After selling land to Campeau for the bargain price of $851,000 in 1965, council turned around and raised the floor space index by a third, thus making a gift to the company of about $250,000. It was on this land and one other small parcel that Campeau built the Skyline Hotel and Phase I of Place de Ville.
>
> In January of 1968, just after the completion of Phase I, Campeau announced Phase II on the block immediately to the north. He said he was building two 450-foot towers on the site when the necessary zoning didn't exist.
>
> Mr. Campeau's confidence was apparently justified because city council agreed to increase the floor space index on the land to eight from the existing five, and extend the height limit to 450 feet despite the vigorous opposition of its planning staff and the NCC.
>
> Even planning board had decided that a height limit of 325 feet was to apply.
>
> When the Ontario Municipal Board postponed decision on the development to allow time for completion of the Hammer report—which was to study building heights in the Centre Town area—then mayor Don Reid appealed to the Ontario cabinet to force the OMB to make its decision.
>
> Cabinet refused to act on the request, but the buildings were subsequently built to a height of 342 feet on the recommendation of the Hammer report. The company retained the floor space index of eight.[4]

This has been a complicated story of how the battle to control building heights in the vicinity of Parliament was lost; essentially it reflected the fact that the City (subject to the Ontario Municipal Board) had final control over by-laws, zoning, and building appearances. Yet the federal government, which subsequently leased part or all of every speculative office building put up, could have exercised its own form of control. Had the government, when it adopted the new leasing policy in 1963, announced to the prospective office builders that "no building will be rented that does not conform to building height ceilings set by NCC", this sad story could have been avoided, as could the costly expropriation of the three Wellington-Sparks blocks. No builder hoping for the federal government as a tenant—and I know no speculative office builder in the Capital in the past decade who has not had such a hope—would have risked being so cast into outer darkness. The benefit of hindsight notwithstanding, I suspect that if NCC had been involved, and a coordinated federal approach adopted, the preeminence of the Peace Tower would not now be so compromised.

Other NCC/DPW Issues

Some other sources of friction between NCC and DPW have been touched on already and we will simply list them briefly here:

(i) *Construction*—DPW believes that it should be the NCC's agent in all construction matters. NCC, having been for most of its history active in construction, particularly earth-moving and parkway building, does not contemplate the loss of this capability with much enthusiasm.

(ii) *Landscaping*—The responsibility for original design and construction of landscaping on all government building sites in the Capital rests with the DPW. Normally the NCC carries this out on a contractual basis; after the first year, the NCC takes over responsibility for ongoing maintenance. The NCC charges the DPW with short-sighted economies on initial costs, which add to the expense of maintenance, and suggests that there is an inherent conflict in the division of responsibility: DPW's concern with the lowest possible costs to meet basic needs, and NCC's concern with developing landscaping appropriate to the Capital, but also with a view to reducing maintenance expenditures.

(iii) *Building Design*—DPW architects and consultants design federal buildings, but subject to design approval by the NCC. On the one hand, NCC Design people argue that often they are brought in too late to allow desirable changes to be made; on the other hand, DPW management suggests that the NCC experts are too slow to reach decisions, too fussy about minor details, and not enough concerned about the factor of time and the cost of delays.

(iv) *Competing for Property*—There is not enough liaison between the two property departments. On at least two occasions the DPW and the NCC were competing to buy the same property, without the other being aware of it. The main problem here appears to be a lack of sharing of knowledge and expertise, arising in part from the NCC fear of DPW's expansionary policy. I understand that consultative machinery has now been established.

(v) *Land-use Objectives*—The DPW may want NCC land for purposes which do not conform to NCC planning objectives, or which may lead to overly dense construction of office buildings. The NCC may make plans for DPW (or other departmental) land, which are not acceptable because of conflicting departmental objectives.

III. The NCC and the DPW—Each States its Position

On February 12th, 1974, I received a letter from Mr. John A. MacDonald, the Deputy Minister of the DPW, outlining his department's views on the future of the Capital and the appropriate roles for the DPW and the NCC as the principal federal bodies involved. He sent a copy of his letter to Mr. Edgar Gallant, the Chairman of the NCC, who replied directly to Mr. MacDonald on March 20th, with a copy to me. Since the subject matter is so central to the purposes of this Study, I am publishing both letters, with permission.

Letter of John A. MacDonald, Deputy Minister of Public Works, to Douglas H. Fullerton, Special Study on the National Capital, February 11, 1974.

In rather belated response to the invitation contained in your letter to me of June 21, 1973, I welcome the opportunity afforded by it and the broad terms of reference of your Special Study to transmit to you an account of our developing thinking on the future of the National Capital Region.

Let me begin with our conclusion that the present configuration of federal institutions and distribution of administrative responsibilities looks very much, from a pragmatic and political point of view, like the optimal solution. But I want to retrace the steps which lead us to that conclusion, for therein lies the logic that leads us, as well, to our view of the directions in which the existing responsibilities of federal, regional and municipal institutions ought to develop.

The pragmatic solution arrived at lies somewhere between two pure models, between the model of a Federal District on the one hand, and the model of a metropolitan conglomerate on the other hand, wholly typical but for its domination by one major employer and landholder. On both extremes, the relationships between the federal government and the municipality are clear. The urban design and growth of a Federal District is legitimately the concern of the federal government, and legitimately a responsibility of its realty function. In the pure model that is the other extreme, there is no legitimate place for an agency of the dominant employer and landlord charged with responsibility for development of the metropolitan conglomerate as a 'company town'. Its legitimate role in the development of property within the metropolitan area begins and ends with its concern for its own realty needs, and its realty function is everywhere subject to the municipal responsibility for urban design and growth.

These are both pure, and consequently extreme, models. Neither, we feel, describes reality or prescribes a desirable course of action. The tension between them does describe the reality, and in the tension lies a logic that leads us to a view of a preferred course of action.

Beyond the constitutional constraints which would have to be overcome to create a Federal District, we are inclined to think that there are sound political reasons for not advancing in the direction of the first model.

It would be to misunderstand the nature of Canadian federalism, as it has developed and is developing, and the relationship between the federal government and its constituency, to advocate the creation of a Federal District as a physically realized, geographically identified, national capital, set against its constituency and the other levels of government. Indeed, its constituency is exactly co-extensive with the sum of the constituencies of the other levels of government, differing from them in the interests it takes in the affairs of the constituency. There is not among the Canadian federal institutions a body such as the U.S. Senate from which it could be argued that the Provinces, as individual entities, are constituents of the federal government. Canadian federalism is a more subtle creature, and more subtle yet by reason of the cultural, linguistic and regional diversities within its constituency. Nor are these diversities identifiable by interests that are fixed and determined for all time. We have seen them shift within a decade, a community of interest on one issue fractured by conflicting interests on another.

The federal government's presence should be felt *from within* its constituency. Consequently, it would seem unfitting that it should reside outside it in a geographically distinct Federal District. It is also desirable that its presence be felt *throughout* its constituency, marrying its cultural, linguistic and regional diversities with one another in a community of national interests. The current interest in decentralization expresses this objective. And it is the consequence of this consideration too that a fixed and determined physical realization of a national capital within a Federal District seems undesirable as reducing the flexibility of federal response to shifting divergences of interest.

However, to raise objections to a course of action directed towards creation of a Federal District is not to advocate a course of action directed toward the pure model at the other extreme. The Ottawa-Hull metropolitan area is historically, and in fact, not a wholly typical municipal conglomerate, dominated as it is by one major employer and landlord. That one major employer is the federal government and its dominance is profound. It is the historical seat of the federal government and will always be despite decentralization, the nerve centre of the federal government, the seat of Parliament and the repository of much of the history of Confederation. Internationally, it is the primary face of the national image and the national interest. Consequently, the federal government has a special responsibility in the Ottawa-Hull metropolitan area to create for its political constituency the primary face of federal government, and to do so with sensitivity to the host municipalities.

Wherever, throughout Canada, the federal government shows its face, it has a special responsibility to show the best possible face and to do so with particular sensitivity to its host municipality. For there it must, as everywhere, marry the diversities within its constituency with the commonality of the national interest, and to do so in the context of the provincial and municipal institutions that represent those divergent interests within a constituency co-extensive with that of the federal government. The tension is between interests, not between constituencies. It is in that tension that the quite particular appropriateness of present jurisdictional arrangements lies. In the National Capital Region, the federal government lives with its constituency in the diversity of linguistic and cultural distinctions. Here lies the opportunity to demonstrate the marriage of that richness with the national interest in the context of provincial and municipal institutions. That is everywhere the context of Canadian federalism. It is a fitting context for the primary seat of the federal government.

However, the acceptance of that role for the federal government within the Ottawa–Hull metropolitan area, as well as throughout its constituency, commits one to the implications of the second model. For that model is the context within which the primary image of the federal government must be achieved. The mechanism for achieving that end, the National Capital Commission, has been laid, as it were, over the reality of a one-industry town. That reality defines the Commission's role as a *coordinator* of the interests and responsibilities of all the various jurisdictions within the National Capital Region to the end that *an integrated plan* is developed for a National Capital that reflects the fundamental values of, and is worthy of the aspirations of, the people of Canada. The same reality defines the limits of the federal government's realty function in the National Capital Region. The legitimate federal role in the development of property and its administration begins and ends with its own realty function, principally in the Department of Public Works.

The federal perception of its own realty function is responding currently to a new sensitivity to the effect of federal land use on the interests of host communities. The implications of the new sensitivity are everywhere a more directly participatory role in the design and management of urban Canada. We have cited good reason to support the view that the federal government's role ought to be even more directly participatory in the Ottawa–Hull conglomerate. However, and by the same token, it is a role that must be played out with even greater sensitivity to the host municipalities. This is a sensitivity that is achieved through the agency of the NCC.

Consequently, we see the relationship between the National Capital Commission and the realty function of the federal government continuing to develop in the following directions:

National Capital Commission

(1) Continue to promote inter-governmental liaison on plans and programs affecting the National Capital, and to lead the federal government's participation in the discussions/negotiations flowing from this liaison;

(2) Develop, and keep current, a general plan for the National Capital area;

(3) Refine, and keep current and flexible, existing forums and discussion and coordination of the specific decisions, plans and programs of the various jurisdictions, including DPW.

Federal Realty Function, principally, the Department of Public Works

(1) Continue to develop, and keep current, operating plans and programs for the federal government's real property requirements (within the general plan developed by the NCC, and in close coordination with the Commission's planning components);

(2) Continue to implement approved operational plans and programs:

(3) Continue to carry out present responsibilities for federal government real property operations.

The last several months have seen the relationships among the various federal jurisdictions involved in the National Capital Region, particularly among the NCC, DPW and CMHC, begin to mature in this direction. We are optimistic that the NCC's role as coordinator of federal interests in the NCR is taking even firmer shape.

The NCC's coordinating role at the inter-governmental level is complicated, we realize, by the intricate structure of provincial and municipal governments. It is obviously desirable that municipal planning authority be concentrated in as small a number of institutions as possible, and there may be some hope that the emergence of regional governments on both sides of the river may be advancing us in that direction. It is our perception that the Regional Municipality of Ottawa-Carleton is developing a strong planning capacity and authority. New planning legislation currently under consideration by the Government of Quebec may provide the Communité Regional d'Outaouais with similarly centralized planning authority.

I trust that the general account of our perceptions will be of some use to you.

Letter of Edgar Gallant, Chairman of NCC to John A. MacDonald, Deputy Minister of Public Works, March 20, 1974.

"Thank you for sending me a copy of your letter of February 11th to Doug Fullerton setting forth your views on the respective roles of the Department of Public Works and the National Capital Commission insofar as the National Capital Region is concerned.

The role of the National Capital and the interests and responsibilities of the federal government in fulfilling this role will undoubtedly be the subject of extensive discussions in the months ahead. It is obviously a matter concerning which there exists a wide range of opinions and we all look forward to Doug Fullerton's report for a comprehensive analysis of the many points of view which have been expressed and of the various considerations to be taken into account.

After reading your letter I concluded that we should meet soon to pursue our discussion of this important matter with a view to clarifying further the perception of our respective organizations in this regard. With this in mind I am writing to put forward the essence of the NCC thinking. If you agree we could arrange a special meeting of our permanent co-ordinating committee to consider this matter.

The role of the federal government in the National Capital Region is unquestionably and fundamentally different from the federal role in any other Canadian municipality or group of municipalities. In the National Capital the federal government pursues three main objectives or sets of objectives which may be generally described as follows:

(i) to ensure the development of a Capital which appropriately fulfils its role as the seat of the Government of Canada and to ensure that the accommodation requirements for national government services are adequately met;

(ii) to promote the development of the Capital area as a symbol of the Canadian society and as a model urban community for Canadians; and

(iii) to ensure that the range of urban services required for federal activities in the NCR are provided in a manner which best meets the needs and aspirations of the people living in the Region as reflected by their local and provincial authorities.

Such objectives, rather than the quantitative importance of the federal government as employer and landlord, distinguish the federal role in the NCR from that which it may be called upon to play in any other community. Furthermore, it is because of its role in the life of the nation as the Capital of the country that this urban area is fundamentally different from any other.

The NCC interprets its responsibilities under the National Capital Act to include the following main tasks:

(*a*) to develop a basic approach to planning for the NCR in order to best meet federal objectives for the Capital;

(*b*) to identify the principal planning policy implications of this approach for the programme activities of the various federal agencies operating in the NCR;

(*c*) to reconcile federal planning and development objectives for the NCR with those of the other jurisdictions engaged in planning and development in the Region;

(*d*) to develop and keep current the urban planning context for federal programme activities in the NCR whether these be undertaken by the federal government acting alone or jointly with other jurisdictions; and

(*e*) to carry out on behalf of the federal government the many programme activities which it is best suited to undertake by virtue of its exclusive concern for the National Capital Region (e.g., open-space development for conservation and recreation, matters concerning regional transportation services and regional urban infrastructure in general).

Given the present legal context we see the relationship between the NCC and other federal agencies such as the Department of Public Works and the Central Mortgage and Housing Corporation continuing to develop along the following lines:

A—*The NCC* (1) as the agency of the federal government responsible for planning for the whole of the NCR: to make recommendations for the use of federal lands in the Region including the location of the various forms of accommodation on such lands and joint responsibility with the government agency concerned for site plan and building design;

(2) as the principal agency for federal interest in open-space and urban infrastructure development in the NCR: to be mainly responsible for federal land acquisition in advance of need in the Region.

B—*The DPW* (1) as the agency responsible for the provision of federal government accommodation services: to be the lead agent for developing and keeping current operating plans and programmes for meeting federal accommodation requirements in the NCR (for administrative, cultural and commercial space);

(2) to implement approved operational plans in a manner consistent with A (1) and (2) above.

C—*The CMHC* (1) as the federal agency responsible for residential construction: to be the lead agent for developing and keeping current plans and programmes for federal involvement in residential construction in the NCR;

(2) to implement approved programmes in a manner consistent with A (1) and (2) above.

In the above paragraphs I have attempted to portray in concise form the essence of the NCC thinking concerning its major role and responsibilities under the National Capital Act. Like others we are searching for what seems to us to be the most effective approach for the orderly and effective planning and development of the National Capital Region. I feel that we have come a long way in improving the situation through regular interdepartmental and intergovernmental consultations. I am optimistic that the continuation of this process will lead to general agreement on the respective roles and responsibilities of the many jurisdictions engaged in activities which are shaping Canada's Capital, and on procedures for better co-ordination of the activities of all concerned.

I shall look forward to our forthcoming discussion of these complex issues.

IV. Jurisdictional Problems: The NCC and Other Departments

Parking

Jurisdictional conflict between NCC and other departments are not very common, and I will refer only to one: parking. Government parking policy is set by Treasury Board as part of its staff relations function. Its main characteristic is the absence of a consistently planned policy; it just developed as the public service grew. If there is a common thread it is that in older areas, such as centre town, parking is provided to departments to the extent that space is available; each department then applies its own priorities to equate the number of permits with the space available. These priorities include distance to work, physical disability, the need for a car during working hours (or unusual working hours), and seniority, which has a fairly high rating. In newer federal building areas, some distance from centre-town, the space provided when the offices were built was based on the generous provision of the City by-law: one space for each 500 square feet of office space. Many of these buildings are not adequately served by public transit, and parking is provided free.

I understand that changes are under review which will tighten up on the existing arrangements, and lead to more public servants being charged a fee for their parking space. I don't propose to discuss the policy here, except to note the irrationality of the government giving a tax-free and valuable benefit to one group of its employees, when those who don't receive a permit, and take the bus, walk, cycle, or drive in car-pools to work, or who have to put their car in commercial parking, get no such benefit. The real issue, however, is that parking policy in the centre of any city is an integral part of the planning process. The availability of parking spaces, and their cost, is one of the main determinants of whether or not people choose to drive their cars to work. In many world cities, policies are being adopted to cut down on parking in city centres, and increase its cost through scarcity and in some instances taxation.

In the Capital, the generous federal parking policy has been a powerful factor shaping growth; by encouraging the use of the car for commuting, it has helped push the suburbs farther and farther out (and particularly towards the west end). These tendencies have been reinforced, I am afraid, by the NCC parkways and by federal assistance in the construction of other arteries such as the Queensway and the new highway network being built on the Québec side. Paralleling all this has been the damage done to the development of good public transit. Buses have always had a difficult time giving good service when forced to compete with private cars for available road space, but when the private car driver has a free berth at his office, the problems of weaning him away from his car and into the bus become almost insuperable.

During my years at the NCC we kept urging Treasury Board to give more thought to the urban planning aspects of its parking policy, and less to its preoccupation with the fear that a tougher policy would disturb staff relations and hurt the wage bargaining process. We pointed out the unfairness in the present parking subsidy inherent in the giving of parking permits free to a selected group, leaving the larger group unsubsidized. We even made a film about it: it showed the visual damage to downtown caused by the sea of parked cars of government employees—spilling over many acres of land acquired at great expense to beautify the Capital—and the other planning and environment consequences of the policy.

I wish I could report progress, but if policy changes have been made they have not been publicly revealed at the time this is written. One problem was the frequent changes in Treasury Board staff dealing with the problem; no sooner had we at the NCC persuaded one group of the need for action,they were moved on to something else, and we had to start the education process again. We were not helped by the fact that the issue is not one about which Ministers might normally be expected to become excited, particularly when each of them was subject to departmental pressures to obtain even more spaces for employees. I could go on, but will simply point to parking as another instance where there was a policy clash between NCC and a department, and NCC was outgunned all along the way—despite, in my opinion, having every argument of logic and equity on its side.

V. A Coordinated Federal Posture

The NCC under its Act is certainly intended to be the coordinator of those federal plans and programmes which affect the Capital, and which involve relations with local municipalities. Section 10(2)e authorizes NCC to "cooperate or engage in joint projects with, or make grants to, local municipalities or other authorities for the improvement, development or maintenance of property;" and its other powers and responsibilities in the carrying out of its planning function clearly involves it in consultation with other levels of government in the Region. NCC's role in this intergovernmental liaison is generally accepted within the federal government and by the municipalities.

However, there are some interesting exceptions or deviations from this general policy. One such exception is the application of the Municipal Grants Act to local municipalities. This grant is administered by the Department of Finance, and negotiations with the municipalities are carried out by that Department as part of its responsibility under the Act. Since this issue is discussed in detail in the next chapter, we won't pursue it here except to note that it is a classic example of how the federal government, by splitting its approach to Capital municipalities into different compartments, has allowed itself to be outmanoeuvered and continually placed in a defensive position.

The municipalities, in fact, are quick to try to seize any opportunity they can to exploit divided federal departmental responsibilities; some of their manoeuvering is simply to snub the NCC, or to avoid having to deal with it at a time of other negotiations with the NCC; sometimes they hope it will mean more money in their pocket. Often the federal department is not even aware that the NCC should be involved. For example, in December last federal representatives (reportedly from Privy Council Office) met with Ontario Government people to discuss parking policy—and no one from the NCC was invited. The Chairman of the RMOC has gone directly to the President of Treasury Board to talk about parking policy or staggered hours for public servants. None of these matters is earthshaking in nature, but they reveal on the federal side a lack of awareness of the need for federal coordination in terms of consistency in policy and a combined negotiating position.

Sometimes the municipal efforts to bypass the NCC are not without humour. One such instance concerned a proposed federal grant to provide a new bus loop between Ottawa and Hull and to cover removal of the then existing double fares. In 1972 the NCC tried to persuade the Ottawa and Hull public transit systems to work together to improve bus service crossing the Ottawa River; discussions were held at that level of officials, tentative agreement reached, and an NCC submission proposing grants went to Treasury Board. It was turned down as being too generous, and the NCC was instructed to negotiate again. About this time the NCC plan was leaked to the local French paper, *Le Droit*, apparently by a Québec transit official. The English papers came to the NCC for corroboration, but the story came out in rather garbled form, implying that the loop would have special "NCC" buses on it. This stirred up the local politicians, and negotiations broke down.

Then in late autumn 1972 the chairmen of the two public transit systems submitted a combined proposal to the Minister of State for Urban Affairs. The proposal did not once refer to the NCC, but sought a special federal transportation subsidy for a plan identical to that the NCC had proposed earlier, with the identical original subsidy which the Treasury Board had already turned down, but with all references to federal participation removed! The reply drafted for the Minister's signature directed them to go back and talk to the NCC, the negotiations were resumed, agreement was reached, and endorsed at all levels, and the new system came into effect in the autumn of 1973—a year later than planned.

One problem faced by the NCC is the continual efforts by elected municipal officers to go over its head on the grounds that they are "politicians", with a right to deal directly with other "politicians", i.e. federal cabinet ministers. The NCC Chairman and staff are bureaucrats, a lesser breed. I had some sympathy for their position, but felt compelled to point out occasionally that most Ministers lean on their bureaucrats for advice, that as Ministers were busy people an approach to them could often by very time-consuming, and that usually the fastest way into the federal government was often to persuade the responsible official, however recalcitrant he might appear to be, of the merits of the case.

However, as we have noted elsewhere, the lack of political status for the NCC Chairman is a weakness in the federal system, one which could really only be overcome by a clear indication, from all levels of the federal government, that the NCC is the primary channel by which intergovernmental relations on matters affecting the Capital are to be carried out. Such a recognition is only likely to occur when the federal ministers and departments become more aware of the need for a unified approach. One method to achieve this is discussed in the next section.

VI. The Need for a Better Internal Coordinating Mechanism

One difficulty for the NCC in its role of coordinator has been the lack of any permanent mechanism for reconciling different federal points of view. Particular proposals could be dealt with at the Cabinet Committee concerned with the rather broad field of government operations, but internal jurisdictional issues do not have a high priority, and Cabinet Ministers and senior officials do not particularly enjoy arbitrating jurisdictional boundary lines between departments. In any event little time is ever provided for a discussion of general issues. Following the end of the Tripartite discussion, the federal committee of officials continued for a period to deal with certain National Capital issues, but it too tended to become involved with immediate ad hoc problems. I believe that in 1972 it met only once. As a result, it is perhaps not surprising that the Government has tended to view the NCC's role more in terms of the series of the specific proposals of varying merit that it puts forward to be processed by the Cabinet assembly line, than in terms of its coordinating role in the Capital and the problems it faces in trying to carry out its responsibilities for this.

Another factor limiting the NCC's ability to act as a true federal coordinator in the Capital may stem from the diffused bargaining power of its Minister. Any department or agency with responsibilities which at times cut across or conflict with other departments needs particularly solid backing at the Cabinet table if it is to perform these duties effectively. Ideally its spokesman should be the Prime Minister, the person best able to adjudicate problems of inter-departmental jurisdiction. The existing burdens on the Prime Minister may preclude him from speaking personally for all departments or agencies of the NCC type, but there would seem to be many sound reasons why the NCC should be responsible through either of the two bodies charged with particular responsibility for departmental coordination, Treasury Board or the Privy Council office. We will have a recommendation on this in the final chapter.

Footnotes

1. *Rapport de la Commission d'étude sur l'intégrité du territoire du Québec, Les problèmes de la région de la capitale canadienne*, Quebec City, May 22, 1968. (Dorion Report).
2. To the Department of Regional Economic Expansion (Hon. Jean Marchand) July 1968.
3. Expropriated in the Autumn of 1973 by the Federal Department of Public Works.
4. *Ottawa Journal*, June 2, 1973, story by John Ferguson.

Chapter Ten

"The Federal Government Doesn't Pay its Way!"— Or Does It?

One of the oldest traditions in Ottawa, as we suggested earlier, is the periodic charge by city fathers that the federal government doesn't pay a fair share of the cost of running the city. Colonel Gray forecast this continuing complaint at the time of Confederation.[1] By 1877 the government was paying the city a fee for water, and in 1883 the City Corporation "made representations to the federal government that it should receive compensation for the loss of tax revenue from the expansion of government property across Wellington Street into the heart of the commercial area, and to reimburse it for the additional burden laid on it in maintaining civil services because of Ottawa being the seat of government".[2]

The federal government kept responding in rather niggardly fashion to City appeals, and in the period from Confederation to 1943, the total amount of grants over the 76 years was only $2.5 million.[3] A special joint Committee of Parliament was set up in 1944 "mainly to examine claims by the corporation of the City of Ottawa for 'better fiscal terms' from the federal government".[4] Grants at that time were $100,000 a year plus payments for a number of specific services. At the hearings of the Committee, the predictable arguments were put forward by city spokesmen—loss of taxes on highly taxed commercial property acquired by the federal government, damage to neighbouring business by "government blight", higher costs of such services as police and fire protection, and water. Compensating federal expenditures, on the other hand, were rejected as "strictly a matter of Federal policy of beautifying the capital of Canada—all costs of such schemes should be borne by the Federal Government.... It is exceedingly unfair to ask the taxpayers of Ottawa to supply services necessitating large expenditures of money and suggest that this outlay should be offset by a park, a driveway or other developments that are considered by the Government proper for a Capital city. It is obvious that under ordinary municipal policies these extensive improvements would be uneconomical and considered a luxury".[4]

As a result of the Parliamentary Committee's recommendations, the grant was raised to $300,000 a year. In 1950 the Municipal Grants programme came into being, applicable to federal property across the county, but limited until 1957 to municipalities with above-average concentration of federal property. The Municipal Grants Act itself dates from 1951, with amendments in 1955 and 1957. Payments under the Act to Ottawa have increased steadily over the years—largely as a result of federal building construction and increases in City tax rates. Thus, these "grants-in-lieu-of-taxes" increased from $762,392 in 1950 (under an Order-in-Council) to $2.8 million in 1955, $4.9 million in 1960, $6.7 million in 1965 and $11.7 million in 1970.

The estimated payment under the Act for 1973 is $12.5 million. If grants in respect of redevelopment charges and payments for diplomatic properties are added, the City of Ottawa total for 1973 comes to about $13.1 million. Similar federal grants to other municipalities in the Region amounted to $1.3 million for the Ontario side, and $.7 million for the Québec side. Thus the City of Ottawa receives 86% of the $15.1 million total for the Region. In addition are the grants-in-lieu paid in the Region by the NCC in 1973, a further $1.5 million, and paid by other crown agencies, approximately $2.0 million. In summary, current grants paid by departments and agencies in the National Capital Region are $18.6 million.

The Debate

Clearly federal grants until the 1950's were inadequate; the municipalities had not been getting a fair deal. What about to-day? In June 1973 Mayor Benoit of Ottawa returned to the attack, arguing that the grants received by the City fell some $16 million short of what they should be. His arguments were a refinement of those of his predecessors over the preceding century, having no doubt been honed by the continuing debate back and forth over the preceding decade between the City and the federal Department of Finance, responsible for negotiating the grants. In summary he based his case on two main points, that the federal government:

> (*a*) exempts substantial property holdings from municipal taxation of any kind;
>
> (*b*) refuses to pay what is generally known as "the business tax" which is an integral part of the total property tax base of a municipality in Ontario.
>
> At the same time, the Federal Government further aggravates the situation by unilaterally charging back to a municipality, by deduction from the total Federal grants-in-lieu, a portion of Federal expenditures which the Federal Government deems to be of a municipal nature. It also, unilaterally, further reduces the grant payments by an amount that is supposed to recognize the cost of municipal "type" services to certain Federal establishments where the Federal Government has provided its own services that parallel the municipal services.[5]

With respect to (*a*) above it was argued in the City's submission[6] that such property as the Parliament Buildings, National Arts Centre and other cultural properties such as museums, park lands, and federal engineering structures, should be fully taxable. The business tax argument is more complex. Essentially the City case is that the business tax is an integral part of the overall property tax structure in Ontario and simply one means of increasing the weight of the real property tax upon commercial and industrial property. The City argument implies that government is a business like any other and should be similarly taxed. Existing deductions for NCC parks, parkways, and police (RCMP) protective services are challenged mainly on the grounds that (*a*) federal parks are often on land that would otherwise be taxable, (*b*) federal provision of its own services is "opting out", not allowed for other taxpayers—payment should be for "services available" rather than "services received", and (*c*) "The Federal Government *must not determine priorities* for the people of Ottawa through projects funded with monies arbitrarily withheld from the total grant".[6]

We shall have a number of comments on the City's position, and on the general approach, but before doing so, we would like to summarize as briefly as possible the basis used by the Department of Finance in calculating the grants.

The first point, of course, is that federal property is not taxable under Section 125 of the BNA Act—"no Lands or Property belonging to Canada or any Province shall be liable to Taxation". However, the Municipal Grants Act was a recognition that there is a legitimate need for the national government to assume some sort of role as a local taxpayer, particularly since property taxes are such an important source of municipal revenue in Canada. In reviewing the relevance of the various principles used to establish a basis for taxing, "ability to pay" has limited applicably to governments because of their theoretically unlimited resources. Hence the effective criteria for the federal government in establishing a policy has tended to become a blend of first, "benefits received", and second "equality of treatment", that is paying the same property taxes as others. These principles are subject to a number of qualifications including the reciprocal benefits conferred on the municipality, services the federal government provides itself, the high proportion of federal property in some municipalities, and the granting to local government of certain important exemptions from federal sales tax. We do not feel competent to push this analysis further,beyond stating that the simple argument that "the federal government, to be a good citizen of a municipality, should pay the same taxes as anyone else" does not really stand close scrutiny. We will be making the further argument that the National Capital is indeed a very special case, requiring a different conceptual approach than that covered in the philosophical guide lines which currently establish the federal municipal grants policy.

Specific Basis of Federal Grants in National Capital Region

Under the authority of the Municipal Grants Act, the federal Department of Finance follows certain principles and regulations in determining grants to Ottawa and to other municipalities in the National Capital Region. The basic federal grant is the "accepted value" of federal property, multiplied by the "effective rate" of tax. Both value and tax-rate are those agreed to by the federal government, after consultation with local officials and provincial officers responsible for assessing property in Ontario. A special grant, about one-third of normal, is paid on the Houses of Parliament based on a "worker-occupant" and a "fire-protection" component. In addition there are "service deductions" amounting to about $1 million, covering services the federal government provides for itself (elementary schooling, police and fire protection—chiefly at defence bases) and services which it provides for others (parks and arterial roads).

If the City arguments for more money are predictable, and based on a well established and traditional position, so too is the federal stance. In summary it is that a great many special factors bear on the calculation of the federal grant for the Capital. This includes the contribution to the Capital of the federal presence, the special recreational and cultural facilities federally provided, the expenditures by NCC, the level of property taxes in the Capital compared to other Canadian cities, the lack of logic in applying a business tax to federal operations which produce no taxable income, and the need to offset grants by the cost of services provided by the federal government. The federal government case is buttressed by evidence that apparently the provinces, which under the BNA Act have a special relationship with the municipalities, adopt a grants-in-lieu posture considerably less generous than that of the federal government, in spite of operating some very business-like establishments like liquor stores.

While we are on this question of the City's claim, there are two of its points in particular which merit specific comment. One is the suggestion that the federal government should pay business tax. The federal reply is that it is not an income earning business, has no income against which to charge such a tax and that the provinces do not pay the tax. (It might also argue that since business tax is a corporate deduction from income for tax purposes, the municipalities are being subsidized by the federal and provincial governments in the amount of income taxes foregone). A second City point was that when a building such as the Metropolitan Life is sold to and occupied by the federal government, the City loses the business tax, in this case $311,000. Since the former owner is merely moving a block away, and will be subject to both realty and business taxes in its new location, this is a difficult argument to follow. In fact the City *gains* the amount of the realty tax of $485,000, presumably payable as a federal grant-in-lieu!

However, the case of the City has always been superficially plausible, and certainly has been widely accepted in the Capital. Understandably, local taxpayers have a tendency to support anything which might reduce their property taxes. I confess to having held the popular view myself, and in a column I wrote about the Capital in 1968 I suggested that the federal grant was inadequate. My experience since I joined the NCC in 1969 has forced me to change my mind. For a wide variety of reasons, I now conclude that the citizens of this Capital do very well out of the federal treasury. Let me outline these reasons, which centre around three issues, (i) the level of property taxes compared to those in other cities, (ii) special federal expenditures in the Capital, and (iii) the special amenities received by the people of the Capital from current and earlier federal expenditures.

Level of Property Taxes in the Capital

Various attempts have been made to compare taxes in Ottawa with those in other Canadian cities, but these comparisons tend to suffer from several defects. One is the method of valuing the property, particularly in a period of rapidly rising real estate prices, another differing components in the property tax, and still another the varying amounts of provincial subsidy to home-owners. Several years ago the Department of Finance did a study which suggested that Ottawa property tax rates were among the lowest of Ontario cities.

In 1972 two professors at the University of British Columbia did a study "The Real Property Tax in British Columbia"[7] in which they collected data on 1971 taxes and sales price for 9 cities across Canada (Victoria, Great Vancouver, Ottawa, Winnipeg, Calgary, Edmonton, Saskatoon, Montreal and Toronto). Except for Vancouver the data are from multiple listing boards. The taxes are net of any homeowner grants and expressed as a percentage of sale price. The results are given in the following table, reprinted with permission:

TABLE 10–1

NET PROPERTY TAXES AS A PERCENTAGE OF SALES PRICE FOR SINGLE FAMILY HOUSES IN 9 CANADIAN CITIES*

City	Number of Sales	Median Percent
A	148	3.20
B	315	2.51
C	151	2.21
D (Ottawa)	150	1.85
E	152	1.68
F	150	1.52
G (Toronto)	144	1.49
Greater Vancouver	626	1.20
Victoria/Saanich	194	1.11

* Net property taxes include school, hospital and general taxes exclusive of any homeowner grant or other tax rebate applicable in respect of single family houses.

At 1.85% Ottawa is in the middle of the range, but above the Toronto figure of 1.49%. House prices have gone up sharply since 1971, however, and despite rising municipal costs and taxes, the above percentages have undoubtedly fallen across the country. In order to provide a check we did our own survey by asking those employees of NCC who owned homes to give us in confidence (anonymously) two figures, first, what they thought their home was worth, and second, what they paid in property taxes in 1973; they were also asked to name the municipality in which they lived.

We had a good response, although we have no way of checking how complete was the coverage. There were 114 replies, 70 from Ontario and 44 from the Québec side of the Region. For the City of Ottawa, the average tax was 1.54%. For other municipalities on the Ontario side (Nepean, Gloucester etc.) average tax was 1.28%. For the Québec side the average was 1.43%, although the small sample (7 respondents) from the City of Hull provided a surprising 2.25%. Overall average for the National Capital Region was 1.43%.

These figures are gross and should be reduced to the extent that the homeowner benefits from any provincial concession on realty taxes. In the case of Ontario there is such a benefit, which takes the form of a reduction in income tax that is available to all owners and renters of residential property. This tax reduction is on a sliding scale, and disappears at an income level of about $25,000. For owners and occupants of residential property in Ottawa we understand the average reduction would be in the order of about $75-80, on an average gross property tax per household of about $425. This would bring the 1.54% for Ottawa down to about 1.25%.

Obviously, inter-city comparisons of this sort must be interpreted with considerable caution, particularly in the light of the rise of at least 25% in Ottawa house prices in 1973, and the subjective quality of the basis of measuring "value". Still it suggests that the Capital is very comfortably below the 2% figure referred to by Professors White and Patterson as a "rough and ready" rule of thumb, but cited in the Report of the Michener Commission in 1964 as follows:

> The Government of Canada, which studies municipal assessments and rates of realty taxes for the purpose of settling its grants to municipalities in lieu of taxes on federal properties, regards taxation as being very high when it exceeds two per cent of capital value. The New Brunswick Royal Commission on Finance and Municipal Taxation recommends the reduction of the tax on residential and non-business property to two per cent of current capital value and the payment by the Province of equalization grants to municipalities which cannot perform their limited services on their share of this rate. Commissioner V. J. Pottier in his 1957 report on the taxation system in the City of Halifax expressed the view, "The area of hardship and genuine tax resistance is reached for those taxpayers who have to depend on 'fixed salaries or fixed incomes' when the tax rate reaches 2% of actual market values.[8]

Moreover, taxes as a percentage of value tend to be lowest in those cities where housing prices are increasing at the fastest rate. However much homeowners like to see their house rise in value, it doesn't ease their tax burden. Partly for this reason, the Department of Finance did a study which related real property taxes per capita in 1971 against per capita income, in eight Ontario cities with a population exceeding 100,000. Toronto showed the highest ratio of property taxes to income, 1.70%; Ottawa stood in the middle of the range at 1.45%; Thunder Bay was lowest at 1.02%.

The City of Ottawa, presumably looking for ammunition to support its case, produced in its brief a table of net long term city debt per capita which showed Ottawa at the top of eleven Ontario cities (excluding Toronto). We have no way of testing the validity of these figures or of judging how to interpret them.

However one qualifies the property tax figures, they do suggest that Ottawa's tax rate is not the lowest among Canadian cities, but is certainly in the middle range and probably on the low side of it. There is little evidence that taxpayers of the Capital have suffered unduly through the "inadequacy" of federal grants.

Federal Expenditures in the Capital

The other side of the story is federal spending which makes a special contribution to the Capital, either by relieving the municipalities of expenditures or of providing amenities to residents which are better than those available to residents of other Canadian cities without such federal assistance. In using federal spending figures, of course, it is important to exclude first those expenditures which relate to the carrying on of the government's own business operations—including costs of office buildings and the general salaries and wages bill of the public service. In addition, federal funds spent on monumentality and special embellishment of the Capital are not properly a charge against local residents, but really a national obligation to the building of a capital worthy of the country. However, to the extent that residents receive direct and tangible personal benefits from such federal spending it must be taken into account. Benefits to residents derived from all federal spending before the Municipal Grants programme came into being in 1950 can quite properly be excluded, simply on the grounds that they should be regarded as offsetting the abnormally low level of grants paid to Ottawa in the early years.

Against this background of qualifying factors, we will examine first the NCC operations since Gréber. One important contribution by NCC over the years has been its expenditures on roads, parkways, and bridges, either built by itself or through grants to municipalities. The main arterial expressway in Ottawa is the Queensway; four to six lanes in width, it cuts across the city about a mile from the Parliament Buildings. The NCC contribution to the Queensway was much of the land needed for it and in particular the land required for several miles in the central area of the city; this was valued on the NCC books at $3.2 million. Yet most of this land was obtained as a result of the railway relocation which cost the NCC about $50 million; without this total expenditure there would either have been no Queensway, or the city would have been involved in prohibitive expropriation costs of homes and businesses. What is the value of this contribution? Ask anyone from Toronto, Montreal or Vancouver what expropriation for their downtown arterials costs per mile!

The NCC scenic parkways have become one of the favourite commuter pathways to centretown. The Ottawa River Parkway cost $14.5 million a decade ago. What would the cost be to the City and Region of building an equivalent six mile arterial from the west end to city centre? $50 million? Or the Airport Parkway, costing NCC some $15 million, including land; this became necessary to provide a respectable access road for persons using the Airport. The City had allowed developers to build closely against the existing roads, overloading them with local traffic, and had also allowed building directly across the most direct route to the Airport, a link connecting McCarthy Road with Bronson Avenue. Ironically, municipal politicians feel quite aggrieved that the NCC Parkway is not opened to traffic from surrounding developments, seeking a quick route downtown, which would of course subject it to the same fate as overtook the original city roads to the Airport. Other NCC parkways provide similar access routes, yet the City appears to argue in its brief that the annual deduction from grants-in-lieu for them, presently about $560,000, should be eliminated.

Another area of direct if perhaps less measurable benefit to residents arising from NCC expenditures is the availability of federal land for municipal projects. For many years it was the custom of NCC and its predecessors to give land needed for parks, recreational purposes, bridges, road widenings, new roads, and easements for sewers, hydro lines etc., at little or no cost to the municipalities. Not only are such expenditures paid for in other cities by the taxpayers, but the large and strategically placed federal land holdings have made it possible for municipalities in the Capital to obtain most of the land needed for their purposes in recent decades without costly expropriations. One example was in the widening of Carling Avenue from Bronson to Island Park Drive. However, with the growing needs for land for variety of purposes, the NCC decided several years ago that for some purposes the market value of the land had to be taken into account. Thus when the city sought six acres of NCC land in Sandy Hill to build a semi-commercial arena on land usable for housing—and was offered the land by the NCC at about one-half its market value—the City public stance was that of outrage; it argued that it should get the land free or at a nominal price. Apparently the City believes in a double standard of equity—one for federal grants-in-lieu of taxes, and another for federal land it covets.

A further indication of the scale of the NCC contribution to the Capital is found in an examination of its current budget. A very large proportion of NCC capital expenditures are cost-sharing grants on such local projects as Québec sewers, roads, filtration plant and water mains, and for Ontario sewers, as well as direct expenditures on specific projects of its own such as the parkways and the Portage Bridge to Hull. In any other city these costs would have been borne by local municipalities and the provincial government.

Level of Cultural and Recreational Amenities

Up to now we have been discussing federal expenditures which have clearly contributed to urban services in the Capital Region and benefited municipal taxpayers. We propose to look now at some items which are more difficult to assess—the federal expenditures on recreational and cultural additions to the Capital scene, such as parks and parkland, art galleries and museums, skating on the canal, and the "Changing of the Guard" on Parliament Hill. All of these add to residents' enjoyment of life in the Capital, all attract tourists, yet all are part of the federal responsibility to build a better national capital.

Incidentally, one curious City argument is that deductions from grants-in-lieu for federal services should be reduced because the federal installations in part serve "tourists". Tourism is the second largest industry in the Capital, reportedly bringing in $100 million a year. It exists mainly because of Parliament, the federal presence, and the embellishments to the Region largely financed by the federal government. The income from this industry goes to businessmen of the Region, to employees of hotels, restaurants, taverns and so on, and to the municipalities which collect property and business taxes from them. Why should there be any difference between the value to regional municipalities of federal services to residents on the one hand, and to tourists on the other?

What are federal contributions to amenities worth to residents? A tough question to answer. One could begin by arguing, I suppose, that without them the area would not be a very attractive place to live despite its natural setting. The expenditures might then be justified or rationalized as being necessary to attract people to the Capital to work for the federal government, a kind of fringe benefit. This argument has been used to defend the Commonwealth of Australia's expenditures in Canberra. In a sense, this is the case put forward by the Mayor of Ottawa when he protests against being deluged with federal "cake", when what he feels the City needs is more "bread".

There is a measure of truth in this latter assessment of federal contributions to the Capital. At the same time, residents do benefit substantially and personally, and these benefits are paid for by the people of Canada. As such they must in some way, partially at least, be taken into account in appraising whether the federal government is "paying its fair share" in the Capital.

What are federal parks in the Capital worth to residents and tourists, and in particular, Gatineau Park, Vincent Massey Park, and federal land along both sides of the Ottawa River? One approach might be to apply "alternative use" valuation, or indeed market value. The latter figure is well over several hundred million dollars; the annual carrying charges on this would be of the order of at least $20 million. But how can one allocate this between "embellishment"—a national responsibility—and value to residents?

Another approach might be to ask what residents of Toronto, say, would pay to have a wedge shaped Gatineau Park of 130 square miles, beginning one mile from Yonge and Bloor and extending for 30 miles in a northwesterly direction? Or for a park along the Lake Ontario shoreline between the Humber and the Don? One measure of this is the fact that some of the land for the proposed new federal park along 1¼ miles of Toronto's Lake Ontario shoreline cost $35 million. What would Vancouverites pay for an enlarged Stanley Park extending for 30 miles northwards from its present site? Or Montrealers for a Mount Royal park extending as far as St. Jerome?

However difficult to measure, the direct value of these parks to residents is unquestioned. No other city in the country is similarly endowed, and the municipal and provincial contribution to the network of parkland in the Capital has been relatively small.

Culture and Entertainment

Turning to federal expenditures on cultural amenities, one must begin with the National Arts Centre. It was built in the late 1960's in Central Ottawa on land donated by the City (which however received federal land free on which to build the City Hall). Cost, including landscaping, was close to $50 million; the federal government paid for it all, together with an annual budget to cover the operating deficit. In fiscal 1973 this budgeted deficit was $4,469,000; paid attendance in 1972-73 was 675,000 and in 1973-74 is expected to be about the same. In summary, the average federal subsidy per person per performance is $6.60. If one added a modest 8% for carrying charges on the capital cost of the Arts Centre, the federal subsidy would be over $12.00 for each person attending a performance. The Centre has been a great success, and has made a tremendous contribution to the cultural life of the Capital, as well as making it an interesting and lively place. What we want to emphasize here is that no recognition is given to this sizeable federal contribution in the grants settlement with Capital municipalities.

How does the City of Ottawa view this question? One might have thought with some recognition of the extraordinarily large subsidy the people of the City are getting from the federal treasury. Instead, the City submission asks for full grants-in-lieu of tax for the Arts Centre, covering both realty and business taxes, of $1.9 million! As a longtime payer of Ottawa property taxes, I naturally welcome the efforts of City fathers to extract the maximum return from any source they can to ease my tax burden. I also understand the negotiating process, but I have great difficulty in finding a suitable phrase to describe this bare-faced attempt to squeeze more money out of a government which has already gone farther than anyone in the Capital has a right to expect. The irony is compounded by the City's decision this year, presumably to strengthen its bargaining hand, to give a grant of $100,000 to help meet the Arts Centre's deficit. (An additional $39,000 was received in grants from other local municipalities).

The Arts Centre is only part of the federal cultural endowment of the Capital. The National Gallery has an operating budget of $4 million, and other federal museums in the Capital, $6 million. In addition there are a host of other federal expenditures in the field of recreation, culture or simple entertainment. The NCC's park maintenance, flowers, bicycle paths, ski trails, canal rink etc. ($4 million), Festival Canada, each July ($100,000), Changing of the Guard ($500,000 plus), the Experimental Farm's fall chrysanthemum show ($300,000 plus), and so on.

What does this federal endowment of the Capital all add up to? I suggest that a conservative estimate, *solely* in terms of municipal expenditures saved, or direct benefits to residents and tourists increased, might be a minimum of $40 million per annum. Here's an attempt, if a rather risky one, at establishing this total by separate category:

1. (*a*) NCC part of shared cost for municipal infrastructure programmes (sewers, water, roads)	
(*b*) Direct yearly NCC expenditures on roads, parkways, bridges	$15 million
2. Savings to municipalities from earlier NCC parkways, and from the cost of land they require (reduced need for municipal roads and lower cost of land for essential purposes)	$ 5 million
3. Value of NCC parkland (taking arbitrary 25% of interest costs on estimated market value of park land—excluding Experimental Farm and Greenbelt)	$ 5 million
4. Cultural, entertainment and recreational facilities contributed by federal government (50% of estimated outlays)	$15 million
	$40 million

To the above figure should be added the federal grants-in-lieu of $18.6 million. Does this suggest that Capital municipalities are being short-changed by the federal government? It follows that I view the City of Ottawa claim for an additional $16 million in federal grants as devoid of merit (as well as being somewhat unconscionable), however much the City might argue that elements of the federal contribution are unnecessary frills or chargeable to the nation for the embellishment of the Capital. But if I reject the City claim, I must at the same time attribute at least part of the blame for it to the federal government, and to its continuing insistence that the Municipal Grants Act be applicable equally to the Capital and to municipalities across the country. In the next section I argue that the federal role in the Capital is so different from that in any other Canadian city that it must approach its financial obligation to the municipalities in the Capital in an entirely different way.

A New Approach to Federal Aid to Capital Municipalities

The argument against the use of the Municipal Grants Act approach in the Capital rests on a number of premises. The first, and most fundamental, is the special nature of the Capital: in terms of federal responsibility it is unlike any other city in the country. That fact recognized in the BNA Act, in the National Capital Act., in the operating of the NCC and its predecessors, and in the allocation over the years of vast amounts of federal money to improve the Capital. The federal claim to a seat at the governing table, which we discussed in Chapter Five, is in fact based on the special nature of the federal role, and on the special federal relationships with municipalities in the Capital.

Why then should the government feel impelled to continue to apply the same rules to grants to Ottawa as it does to say Calgary? When the Municipal Grants Act was passed in 1950 there was certainly a reasonable case for universality, particularly since the level of grants and of federal spending in the Capital had both been very low; no one could reasonably challenge supplementing grants paid to Capital municipalities with other forms of federal assistance through the Federal District Commission. But it is now 25 years later, grants-in-lieu have reached a respectable level, and federal expenditures on improving the Capital have soared. The federal government need no longer feel guilty about its past sins of omission in the Capital, and the uncritical application of the Grants Act to Capital municipalities has become increasingly less justifiable.

Perhaps more to the point is that the existence of the Municipal Grants Act, and its terms, provides a very handy bargaining lever for the City of Ottawa. The City can point to clauses that make sense where there are only isolated parcels of federal property, and can mount its case on the exclusions that apply only in Ottawa. Its position is strengthened by the relative isolation of the grants calculation process from other federal contributions, except for the few specified deductions noted earlier. I have the impression sometimes that the Act has become a strait-jacket for Department of Finance officials in their negotiations with Capital municipalities, one which the federal government itself has unwittingly fashioned.

Almost a captive of its own ingenuity, the federal government has thus continually been placed in a defensive, even apologetic, posture locally on the Grants issue. The City of Ottawa has become adept at playing the game of divide and rule, which suits its interests so well and gives it many tactical advantages. It allows City spokesmen to attack government grants "parsimony", and to use this argument to justify special price concessions on land from NCC. Special expenditures by NCC or other agencies for improving the Capital can at the same time be denigrated and be written off as being solely in the national interest. We have even seen the fascinating spectacle of an Ottawa Mayor one minute arguing how badly the City has been treated on grants-in-lieu of property taxes, and in the next criticizing the federal government for daring to put some of its office buildings across the River in Hull, thereby reducing prospective city grants![9]

In addition to these general issues, there is one specific defect in the application of the Grants Act in the Capital which must be noted. The location of federal property eligible for grants is mainly in the City of Ottawa, but government employees live in all parts of the National Capital Region. With school costs about one-half of municipal budgets, the payment of 85% of federal grants-in-lieu to the City of Ottawa discriminates against those municipalities where large numbers of federal public servants reside. Although we understand that there is an equalization formula applied through RMOC on the Ontario side, at least 15% of the public service live in Québec, where federal grants to date have been very low. The move of federal departments will improve the grants balance, but the anomaly persists.

In summary, I believe that the application of the Municipal Grants Act to capital municipalities makes little sense in the light of the special role of the federal government in the Capital and its spending programme which flow from that role. It provides another example of the divided or compartmentalized federal approach to municipalities in the Capital, which we discussed in Chapter Nine, and which has hurt the development of the Capital, and diminished the ability of the federal government to achieve many of its goals. A new and more coordinated federal approach is overdue.

Proposals

In seeking alternatives to the application of the Municipal Grants Act to NCR municipalities, I believe that any proposal must satisfy a number of criteria:

(i) It must be judged fair to the municipalities, both in terms of federal treatment of other Canadian cities, but also as to the allocation among the various Capital municipalities.

(ii) It must give the federal government the right to take into account the totality of its special contributions to the Capital—and the equivalent right of the municipalities to challenge any item in the federal list.

(iii) It must allow for continuity from the existing Grants Act approach, which means for practical purposes no reduction from present grants.

(iv) It must provide for possible changes in local government structure in the Capital which are discussed later in this study.

One interesting approach to this problem is given in the present US "District of Columbia Self-Government and Governmental Reorganization Act," signed by President Nixon on December 24, 1973, which provides for a substantial measure of self rule to residents of Washington[10]. Sections 501 and 502 are directly germane to the Canadian situation, and are quoted below in full:

> TITLE V—FEDERAL PAYMENT
>
> Duties of the Mayor, Council and Federal Office of Management and Budget
>
> Sec. 501. (*a*) It shall be the duty of the Mayor in preparing an annual budget for the government of the District to develop meaningful intercity expenditure and revenue comparisons based on data supplied by the Bureau of the Census, and to identify elements of cost and benefits to the District which result from the unusual role of the District as the Nation's Capital. The

results of the studies conducted by the Mayor under this subsection shall be made available to the Council and to the Federal Office of Management and Budget for their use in reviewing and revising the Mayor's request with respect to the level of the appropriation for the annual Federal payment to the District. Such Federal payment should operate to encourage efforts on the part of the government of the District to maintain and increase its level of revenues and to seek such efficiencies and economies in the management of its programs as are possible.

(*b*) The Mayor, in studying and identifying the costs and benefits to the District brought about by its role as the Nation's Capital, should to the extent feasible, among other elements, consider—

(1) revenues unobtainable because of the relative lack of taxable commercial and industrial property;

(2) revenues unobtainable because of the relative lack of taxable business income;

(3) potential revenues that would be realized if exemptions from District taxes were eliminated;

(4) net costs, if any, after considering other compensation for tax base deficiencies and direct and indirect taxes paid, of providing services to tax-exempt nonprofit organizations and corporate offices doing business only with the Federal Government;

(5) recurring and nonrecurring costs of unreimbursed services to the Federal Government;

(6) other expenditure requirements placed on the District by the Federal Government which are unique to the District;

(7) benefits of Federal grants-in-aid relative to aid given other States and local governments;

(8) recurring and nonrecurring costs of unreimbursed services rendered the District by the Federal Government; and

(9) relative tax burden on District residents compared to that of residents in other jurisdictions in the Washington, District of Columbia, metropolitan area and in other cities of comparable size.

(*c*) The Mayor shall submit his request, with respect to the amount of an annual Federal payment, to the Council. The Council shall by act approve, disapprove, or modify the Mayor's request. After the action of the Council, the Mayor shall, by December 1 of each calendar year, in accordance with the provisions in the Budget and Accounting Act, 1921 (31 U.S.C. 2), submit such request to the President for submission to the Congress. Each request regarding an annual Federal payment shall be submitted to the President seven months prior to the beginning of the fiscal year for which such request is made and shall include a request for an annual Federal payment for the next following fiscal year.

AUTHORIZATION OF APPROPRIATIONS

Sec. 502. Notwithstanding any other provision of law, there is authorized to be appropriated as the annual Federal payment to the District of Columbia for the fiscal year ending June 30, 1975, the sum of $230,000,000; for the fiscal year ending June 30, 1976, the sum of $254,000,000; for the fiscal year ending June 30, 1977, the sum of $280,000,000; for the fiscal year ending June 30, 1978, and for each fiscal year thereafter, the sum of $300,000,000.

These latter figures of course cannot be compared directly with existing grants-in-lieu in Canada's Capital. The Washington payments represent what amount to a combined federal grant to the City as a state and as a municipality (see sec. 501(*b*)7 above). The equivalent in Canada would be combined grants-in-lieu and the Capital's share of federal grants to Ontario and Québec.

There are other differences between the District of Columbia and Canada's Capital, the most notable one being that the new elected governing body of the United States Capital will be a single tier government compared to the multi-level situation here. But the principle of the American approach makes a good deal of sense, that is, rather than adhering solely to the basis of some motion of applying property taxes to federal property, *all relevant factors are taken into account.*

We are particularly attracted by Section 501(*b*)9, the relative tax burden on District residents compared to other cities in the metropolitan area and other cities of comparable size. We believe that this would be a good basis to use in setting the amount of the federal grant in our Capital, provided that some measure of the "efficiency" of local government is simultaneously adopted. One such measure might be a comparison of municipal employees on a per capita basis such as indicated in Table 7-2, page 77. In other words, it would not be enough to equate the property tax level in the Capital with that of other Canadian cities, unless operating costs were similarly weighed. Otherwise there would be no incentive towards economy.

We will be making more precise recommendations in Chapter Sixteen about changing the present approach to exclude municipalities in the National Capital Region from application of the Municipal Grants Act. The negotiation of the amount of the basic grant would be carried out directly with municipalities by the Department of Finance, in consultation with NCC, but having regard particularly to property tax levels in the Capital relative to other cities, municipal efficiency in the Capital, other benefits conferred by the federal government, and the basing of school taxes on the distribution across the Region by residence of public service employees.

Footnotes

1. *The Queen's Choice*, p. 44 et seq.
2. Ibid, p. 50, see also pp. 177-180.
3. *City of Ottawa brief* to 1956 Parliamentary Committee on FDC.
4. *The Queen's Choice*, p. 177-180.
5. Benoit, Mayor Pierre. *Letter to Honourable J. Turner*, Minister of Finance, June 27, 1972.
6. *Submission of City of Ottawa on the Federal Government Policy of Grants-in-lieu of Municipal Taxation.* May, 1973.
7. *B.C. School Trustees Association*—"*Research Report by Dean Philip White and Dr. Stanley Patterson, Faculty of Commerce and Business Administration, (April 1972)*. see page 41.
8. *Report of the Manitoba Commission on Local Government Organization and Finance*, (Queen's Printer, Winnipeg, 1964), p. 112.
9. *Inaugural speech of Mayor Fogarty of Ottawa*, Jan. 6, 1970.
10. *U.S. Public Law 93-198*, 93rd Congress S. 1435 (87 Stat. 774) "*District of Columbia Self-Government and Governmental Reorganization Act*". December 24, 1973.

Chapter Eleven

The Capital's Excessive Growth Rate — Should Federal Offices be Decentralized?

One issue came up repeatedly in the briefs, the fear of many residents that the Capital will become too large. Listen to some of the comments:

> The present population of the region is probably almost ideal... It would be far better if new government offices were dispersed throughout Canada..."
>
> The size of the Capital should be controlled—or better—a significant portion of the Government machinery should be decentralized, e.g. Fisheries split into West and East regions with a co-ordinating body central; Forestry the same, e.g. Québec and B.C.; Agriculture—etc. Again the main intent should be to make the Government visible to all of Canada, but also to hold down the costs of a mushrooming city.....
>
> Ottawa should set an example to other cities by restricting its size. In an electronic age there is no need all to huddle together. Federal Departments and Agencies located in other Provinces would greatly help national unity. And it would prevent the Civil Service becoming a 'Praetorian Guard' with vested interests, clustering around the Government.....
>
> The Federal Government should indeed assume the leadership for a better population distribution by relocating government departments and redirecting industries to establish new cities or growth centres.....
>
> ...Urban pressures of the type felt in other cities threaten many of the valuable environmental assets we enjoy in the National Capital Area.

Or the following from one perceptive public servant (the same person who is quoted in Chapter Five (p. 53):

> ...the present national capital philosophy is in part responsible for what I feel to be the insular and often removed from the real world view of the Ottawa civil servant. Bear in mind that we are the ones advising the government and it is not surprising that our policies and programs are sometimes inappropriate for the very different regions of Canada. We are too dispersed a people in too big a country to manage from Ottawa. Dispersing Federal Administration and national amenities will bring about a much more productive and imaginative federal perspective. ...If we really want to make the medium and smaller sized Canadian communities viable alternatives to Toronto, Montreal and

Vancouver, then one of the federal levers toward this end is the diffusing not only of federal administration but of national capital amenities throughout Canada.

This opposition to growth is a world-wide phenomenon, and represents a turning away from the old idea that bigger is automatically better. Most complaints centre around growing pollution, congestion, the destruction of neighbourhoods by traffic and by high-rise buildings, and the awareness that development leads to higher, not lower, taxes. If most cities appear powerless to do anything to control growth, the federal government, because of its enormous physical and economic impact on the Capital, can by its policies exert considerable influence on not only the rate of growth, but on its form and location.

The first question we faced was whether this subject, in spite of the wide interest in it, was appropriate to include in this Study. In many respects it is a planning issue—certainly a knowledge of federal plans, rate of growth, and building and rental decisions are of crucial importance to every planning body in the Region—and we have done our best to stay out of the planning field. But the issue appears much broader than that of planning alone; the form of government which evolves in the Capital will be inevitably affected by the pace of federal growth, by the location of federal buildings, and by the myriad decisions of the rapidly growing number of federal employees about where they will live.

There is an even more fundamental reason for looking at the growth issue. If the federal government decides - and is able - to slow growth in the Capital by transferring departments, agencies or branches to other parts of Canada, would this damage attempts to build up the symbolic role of the Capital as a unifying force in the country? Or would the benefit of a greater federal presence in the cities or regions to which the units are transferred, presumably slower growth areas, do more for national unity?

The rapid growth in federal employment in the Capital has caused many problems for local municipalities, and has intensified inflationary pressures, particularly in housing. This growth has also adversely affected the federal government's own limited control over the physical development of the Region. For example, the need for office space for the growing number of federal employees has forced the government not only to continue a wide-open leasing policy, but to give up any hope it had of limiting the construction of future office buildings to its own buildings in locations based on government plans. Instead the pattern of office buildings continues to derive mainly from the random land holdings and decisions of the speculative builders and developers.

In discussing decentralization, we are not referring to shifts from the centre of the Region to the suburbs. That is another issue; as we note elewhere it is a source of a considerable difference of opinion among planners in the Capital, and among politicians and governments. And if federal employment in the Region continues to grow at its present rate, nobody need worry about federal offices being solely concentrated in the core—there won't be room for all of them there.

The Size and Growth of the Federal Bureaucracy

How fast has the government been growing? One of the astonishing things about this is the difficulty of finding out. This is not to suggest that the government is consciously hiding the figures, but rather that it faces these problems: (i) defining what constitutes a government employee (e.g. permanent, casual, temporary, contract, military, RCMP etc.); (ii) pinning the figures down for a certain date and (iii) being certain that every department, agency, commission board, tribunal, centre, court, laboratory, institute, council, branch, division or secretariat is included—and their numbers are legion.

The official total of "Federal Government Employment" published by Statistics Canada,[1] showed 57,591 employees in the N.C.R. in 1970, 65,928 in 1971, and 70,293 in 1972. (Comparable figures for 1951 were 30,069 and for 1961, 46,095). These aggregates however cover only "departments and departmental corporations as designated in Schedules A & B of the Financial Administration Act." This excludes employees of agency and proprietary corporations and other agencies and corporations, such as the Armed Forces, the Bank of Canada, the Mint, etc. Other information is available from Central Personnel Records division of the Department of Supply and Services. However, many gaps remain, and the NCC carried out a survey to try to obtain as complete a list as possible, mainly for purposes of transportation planning. Although they believe their coverage is still incomplete, the survey suggests that as of late summer 1973 the total was about 94,000,[2] representing an 8% increase from the previous September. As a crosscheck we refer to the main federal estimates for 1974-75. It lists 415,000 federal man-years, and goes on to say "some 75% of the federal government's employees are located outside the National Capital Region".[3] We are therefore inclined to accept 100,000 as a good working figure for federal employment in the NCR in 1974.

The absolute figure—however well it demonstrates the importance of the federal government as the main employer in the Region—is not as important as the rate of increase. On the basis of the Statistics Canada figures quoted above, the annual rate of growth in federal employment in the NCR between 1970 and 1972 was 10.5%. For Canada as a whole the figure was 8.1%. Some government officials believe that both growth rates are inflated by the deferred results of the 1969–70 "austerity freeze". The 1962–72 rate of increase in the NCR is just over 3%, and this appears to be regarded as a more appropriate figure to use for long term extrapolation—at least by the optimists.

Another basis for calculating the growth rate is provided in the federal main estimates for 1974-75, which show that total Canadian employment ("planned continuing employees") grew from 270,904 in March 1973, to 288,506 forecast for March 1974, to a forecast 304,295 on March 31, 1975. The 1973 to 1974 increase is 6.4%, and for 1974 to 1975, 5.5%[4], although what impact the supplementary estimates have on this latter figure is difficult to predict. The percentages presumably include members of the public service and employees of federal agencies, but exclude military personnel and uniformed RCMP. Even the use of the lowest 3% figure mentioned means a doubling of federal employment in the Capital by the turn of the century.

Still another crosscheck on recent growth in employment can be derived from the office space figures of the Department of Public Works. Leased or owned space provided by DPW to departments or agencies (some crown agencies such as the Bank of Canada provide their own) increased from approximately 10 million square feet in 1969/70 to nearly 16 million square feet in 1973/74—close to a 60% increase in four years. Since the average new space allowed is 225 square feet per employee, this suggests that some 25,000 employees were added in the four year period (although some of the increase may be due to an upgrading in the quality and amount of space for employees moving from old buildings to new).

The Implications of Growth for the Region

The demand for office space has naturally meant a great many new jobs in the construction industry in the Capital. So has the boom in housing; the following table suggests that Ottawa-Hull housing starts have been growing at a pace much faster than in any other City in Canada.

TABLE 11-1

HOUSING STARTS IN MAJOR CANADIAN URBAN AREAS*

Calendar Year 1973

	1973 Housing Starts	1971 Census Population (000's)	1973 Starts per 100 population in 1971	Value $ million
Ottawa-Hull	15,511	602	2.57	273
Halifax	4,181	223	1.87	68
Hamilton	8,708	499	1.74	146
Calgary	6,981	403	1.73	115
Vancouver	17,334	1,082	1.60	344
Edmonton	7,384	496	1.48	140
Toronto	37,697	2,628	1.43	1062
Winnipeg	7,698	540	1.42	99
Montreal	30,700	2,743	1.11	406
Québec	4,648	481	.96	70
Windsor	2,033	259	.69	47

**Source:* Statistics Canada—*Housing Starts & Completions,* December 1973, *Building Permits,* December 1973, *Census of Canada, 1971*—Final Count of CMA by municipality (1971 area).

In spite of this extraordinary rate of housing construction, house prices have been climbing rapidly in the Capital. The average house price rose about 25% in 1973; many houses have doubled in price in three to four years. This may benefit those who happen to own houses but is hard on new home buyers. We suspect, however, that the rush to buy houses is not solely the pressure from new federal employees arriving in the Capital, (it is even being suggested that the scarcity and high prices of housing are hurting Government recruiting) but stems in part from the simultaneous conclusion of many people that a home provides one of the best hedges against inflation.

Construction of new housing and other buildings has of course had an impact on the needs for municipal utilities and services—more new subdivisions, more streets, more sewers, more water lines, more buses. The Québec side has been particularly affected, first because federal-provincial programmes in sewer and roads accelerated expenditures to meet long overdue needs, and, second, because the lower cost of land on that side has been an added stimulant to home building. The ability of all municipalities on both sides of the River to meet these pressures has been strained, despite federal contributions through NCC, and this may account for some of the rapid rise in municipal employment and expenditures referred to in Chapter Seven.

In summary, federal growth in the Capital is a mixed blessing, and I share the concern of the many people who want to see it controlled. But that may be the selfish point of view of a Capital resident, or Capital planner, rather than a reasoned government approach to a problem with many facets. Before we consider the broad question, however, of whether or not the government should curb its own growth in the Capital, we propose to examine some of the problems that are likely to arise if the attempt is made.

Can Federal Growth in the Capital be Curtailed?

Growth and concentration in cities is not an unnatural phenomenon, as some people seem to believe. There are good reasons why it occurs, and perhaps the most important are the economic advantages. The headquarters of any organization—business or government—has particular reasons for concentrating. Those involved find it convenient; the leaders who run the show like to have their senior people close by for support, and those who don't lead, but aspire to, wish to remain close to the centre of power. This applies all the way down the line, of course, and the agglomerative or centripetal pressures are considerable. They are reinforced by inertia—moving to another city is not most people's idea of fun. Thus if any change in current tendencies are to occur, it is only likely to be after some considerable force is applied from on high, and then only if justified by good and compelling arguments.

There are also some special factors which bear on the problems of decentralizing or deconcentrating the Canadian federal headquarters operations:

(i) *The Bilingualism Programme*—Increasing the bilinguality of the federal work force is proving to be a difficult task—expensive, slow, and full of political booby traps. Yet the Anglophone federal employee who is learning French in the Capital is exposed not only to an excellent system of language education for himself, and an improving one for his children, but all the family has a chance to practice French and to hear it on television and radio. What would happen to the hard-won French acquired by him and by his family if they are moved to say St. John's or Regina? More particularly, in a public service where the capacity to function in both languages will be an increasing requirement for promotion, what would such lost opportunities in French-learning entail? The other side of this argument of course is that it would be a good test of the alleged backlash against federal bilingual policies. Presumably those unhappy at having to learn French would not object to being shifted out to a solidly Anglo Saxon area!

(ii) *Attractiveness of the Capital*—In the last five years many people have come to think that the Capital is a good place to live and bring up families—even for Francophones—as well as being close to Montreal and Toronto. This will breed resistance to transferral to other cities as part of a federal programme. In a sense, the federal government would become a victim of its own success in building a more attractive and liveable Capital!

(iii) *Loss of Efficiency*—There is reason for concern that decentralization would lower government efficiency. For example there is the tendency of bureaucracies to build up parallel structures; move a branch to the hinterland, and headquarters will try to add a group of equal size to carry on liaison with it. Another is the availability of people with certain needed skills in the receiving municipality, on the assumption that only intermediate and senior headquarters staff is likely to move. Then there are the needs of the visiting public. The concentration of government in one place makes it easier for those doing business with it to establish contact with the variety of government people they wish to see. Finally there is the problem of communications and travel; this is a large country and the transportation service not only suffers from the climate but the connections to smaller centres leaves a good deal to be desired.

(iv) *Transferring Growth Problems*—An interesting argument against decentralization is that it might merely lead to dumping the Capital's growth problems on to other Canadian communities. One could hope that the moves would be limited to those areas in need of a growth stimulus, but there are few cities that could accept a rapid influx of several thousand public servants without severe growth pains. Given that, the opponents to the policy might well argue that at least in the Capital the government has some mechanism in place for coping with growth—through the NCC and its own projects and planning, and through grants that ease the burden imposed by growth on the municipalities. This could be overcome in some measure by similar government assistance being given to the receiving municipalities.

Experience in Other Countries

In 1969 the Swedish government launched an inquiry into the possibility of moving a quarter of the 42,000 national government employees out of Stockholm. This was to be a two stage plan, with the first stage involving some

5,500 persons to be shifted between 1972 and 1976, and about an equal number in the second stage between 1976 and 1980. There were three basic reasons for the proposed relocation, the rapid rate of growth of Stockholm, the excessive concentration of service industry there, and the need to stimulate growth in other areas. Criteria used to pick receiving areas included the size of the city—preferably of 100,000 or over—and a location outside the sphere of influence of the three principal Swedish cities of Stockholm, Göteborg and Malmö. Fifteen cities were chosen, but not all met the 100,000 minimim requirement.

Attention was paid to special needs of each agency to be moved, such as proximity to a university, its relation to other agencies, and regional politics. Financial benefits were given to people moving—including payment of removal expenses, a number of free trips to Stockholm, allowances for rent, special housing loans, etc. The costs amounted to an estimated $5,000 per employee transferred.

In principle, staff had to accept transfer, subject to certain exceptions, such as nearness to retirement age, and employment of spouse. This latter proved to be an unexpected problem. It was difficult to find satisfactory work in the new locations for working wives, many of whom having been employed in jobs found only in large urban concentrations such as Stockholm. Employees have been strongly critical of the "forced move" from Stockholm, but it is expected that about 80% will accept transfer.

Nevertheless, organized opposition has been growing in the Swedish public service. Further detailed inquiries are being made into the communications problem resulting from Stage 1. In addition, it was found that the efficiency of government was being threatened by some of the proposed moves, and the combined effect (along with increased political opposition) may impede full implementation of stage two.

The United Kingdom has had some experience in dispersal of units of the national government from London. The first effort was made during the war, and the second following a 1962 study by Sir Gilbert Flemming. Two policy decisions resulted from this latter study:

(i) Whenever a new government organization is to be set up, it should if possible be located outside London (1965).

(ii) If possible, when choosing receiving locations, preference should be given to locations in the assisted areas (1967).

In 1970 a review was commissioned, leading to the Hardman report[5] in 1973. The main conclusions were these;

(i) Costs would be offset by gains after five years.

(ii) Choice of receiving locations is influenced by two main considerations, efficiency of operations and regional policy.

(iii) Efficiency is affected by distance from London, capacity of receiving location, (in terms of office space and available staff) and attractiveness of the area to persons transferred.

(iv) Communications—face-to-face, telephone, mail etc.—pose a particularly awkward problem.

(v) Human aspects—relocation is a major and costly upheaval for civil servant and family, but these usually can be offset if adequate information is provided and if alternative choices are made available.

These conclusions were followed with specific recommendations to shift some 31,000 jobs from London, with about half to be filled by transfers, and the balance to be newly created jobs in the receiving locations.

The experience of other governments points up some of the main issues facing us in Canada, although the comparisons are impaired by differing national and geographic characteristics. For example, there would be fewer communication problems in the U.K. than in Canada because of the relative proximity of even remote receiving areas to London.

Experience of Canadian Government with Decentralization

The current efforts to shift sections of the Department of Regional Economic Expansion (DREE) to the regions it serves is something of a pilot project for the federal government. The goal is to reverse the existing 70:30 split between headquarters and the regions to a 30:70 proportion. Although it remains to be seen if this goal can be achieved, officials of the Department say that substantial progress towards it has been made already in spite of a variety of expected (and unexpected) problems encountered. There were however some side benefits that had not been foreseen. One was that the shift was welcomed by a number of employees, as it gave them a sense of independence and new purpose. Another was the fact that it is leading to more visits to the region by headquarters' staff (and not only from the DREE) to learn more about the problems first hand.

The government itself has reported favourably on the project as follows:

> The reorganization to which the Department of Regional Economic Expansion has committed itself is an example. From the time of its creation in 1969, the objective of the department has been to reduce regional economic inequalities, and it was evident that programs had to be adapted to the specific economic development needs of each region. A further decentralization of authority is now being effected in order to adapt program and procedures still more closely to regional realities. And, for the first time in the history of any department, regional centres are, as a consequence of this approach, being managed by assistant deputy ministers.[6]

As for more general progress, the government reports as follows:

> In the past few years the pace of decentralization has been accelerated and now touches key sectors of government organization. An important element in these changes is an effort to increase the decentralization of administrative authority across Canada in a way that the needs of the population will be met more quickly and efficiently. The objective is, in effect, to root decision-making in every part of Canada.[6]

The decentralization of "decision-making" may be more difficult than shifting people; all the normal instincts of the federal bureaucracy appear to run counter. In addition ministerial responsibility is a very important feature of any parliamentary system and, decentralization of decision-making to parts of the bureaucracy that are geographically distant means that the Minister concerned, and therefore the federal government, must be prepared to take some risks. These risks are delicate ones because they can create the impression that important significant decisions about the use of public funds are being made by bureaucrats without the proper control of elected representatives. The problem is compounded by the fact that the federal bureaucrats must often deal with elected representatives of other levels of government. In this kind of relationship, the potential for tension and possible misunderstanding is significant.

However, whether a substantial delegation of decision-making can be achieved or not, the government should extend such experiments as that of the DREE, and see what develops. Certainly it appears that the easiest method would be to site new agencies or branches of departments outside the Capital. Along similar lines is the interesting suggestion to induce departments to cooperate by putting a ceiling on the manpower allotted to them for the NCR, and by permitting additional manpower growth in certain other designated locations. In this way, the normal bureaucratic tendency to expand staff could be harnessed to the decentralization policy. Exceptions might be permitted in certain special cases, but if this approach were applied with some stringency it could yield worthwhile results.

I am sure that other effective suggestions will come forward if the government accepts decentralization as a firm policy, regardless of the problems which stand in its way. I can only urge the government to approach the issue with some of the same zeal it has used in its bilingual policy—a more difficult and more politically sensitive issue.

Conclusions

If the obstacles appear sizeable, the benefits of a successful dispersal of some federal employees from the centre would be substantial. One obviously would be the slowing of the rate of growth in the Capital. Another would be the acceleration of growth in areas needing stimulus; when one considers the amount spent to persuade industry to move into these areas, estimated at $5,000 per job created, the potential economic gains are measurable and large. The federal presence would be better distributed across the country. Headquarters staff might be exposed to a clearer view of the "real world" outside of the Region. And such a policy represents good politics; the move of the Mint (or part of it) to Winnipeg received a good press across the country, as did the proposals to decentralize the DREE.

In summary, if I have some doubts about the ability of the federal government to decentralize, I have no doubts at all about the desirability of slower growth in federal employment in the Capital, and a decline in the Capital's proportion of federal jobs. The government is growing at an extraordinarily rapid rate and the degree of centralization appears to be increasing. This is encouraging an unhealthy isolation of the central bureaucracy from the Canadian people, as well as contributing to the growth problems of the Capital which we have noted above.

I realize that this has been rather a superficial analysis of a very complicated problem, but I assert that the case for federal decentralization is sustainable on its merits, and that the issue is important. I can only urge the federal government to give it increasing study from the points of view of the interests of the Capital, of national unity, and its own efficiency and effectiveness.

Footnotes

1. Statistics Canada, *Federal Government Employment* (Catalogue 72-205).
2. Gallant, E. *Notes for Remarks to the Commercial and Industrial Development Corporation of Ottawa-Carleton,* April 18, 1974.
3. As cited in Treasury Board's "*How your Tax Dollar is Spent*", February 1974, pp. 11-13.
4. Federal Government *Main Estimates* ("Blue Book"), 1974-75, pp. 1-98, 99.
5. United Kingdom Government "*The Dispersal of Government Work from London*", Cmnd. 5322.
6. Treasury Board "*How your Tax Dollar is Spent*", February 1974, p. 14.

Chapter Twelve

The English and French Languages in the Capital

The question of bilingualism, like that of excessive growth, is a subject that does not fit entirely comfortably within my mandate. I have thought it appropriate for study, however, for a number of reasons. One is that it was referred to in many of the briefs, and touched on by most of the people we interviewed. If the interest in language is greater on the Québec side, because of Francophone fear of assimilation, it has surfaced in other ways in Ontario. The essential problem is that the depth of feeling about this issue is such that it could well be an impediment to the acceptance of measures to simplify government structures. It follows that any steps which can be taken to allay these concerns would contribute to the objectives of this Study.

But how far into this question should our examination be pursued? If bilingualism is clearly a local issue of major significance, it is not easily divorced from the larger national picture. If the federal public service in the Capital is to remain representative of the people of Canada, the government must continue to draw its employees from the length and breadth of the country. At the same time the language capability of migrants to the Capital is a factor which may well affect both their career and their adjustment here. Thus, while only Ontario and Québec are directly involved in the governing of the Capital, they and the other eight provinces are involved in a different way. Many of their sons and daughters will be working for the largest employer in Canada, the federal government, and in the course of their careers may well be living in the Capital.

Because of the importance I attach to this subject, I asked Mr. James Weld to prepare a special paper on it. His paper is attached in Appendix B-2, along with a companion piece by Professor Kenneth McRae dealing specifically with related educational issues in the National Capital Region. In this chapter I shall set out certain ideas deriving from these papers, from the briefs we have received, and from my own thoughts on the subject.

Before moving on to a detailed look at bilingualism, however, I must refer briefly to one related topic—multiculturalism. I received one impassioned but well reasoned brief that deplored the emphasis on the two language groups, when one-third of Canada's population is of neither British nor French origin. "What do you propose to do about this forgotten third?" the brief asked. A good question, and my only reply was that although the argument made sense in terms of the cultural needs of the Capital, it did not appear to have much of a bearing on problems relating to its government. The issue of bilingualism, however, has all kinds of implications for the development of a new structure of government, and for the political atmosphere in which changes will be considered.

1. Bilingualism Problems—Assimilation and Backlash

On the surface there are two problems. The Francophone fears assimilation and seeks an atmosphere (ambiance) where he can live in his own language. The Anglophone, on the other hand, is aware of his linguistic vulnerability in the competition for those jobs where both languages are required, and he therefore tends to look upon bilingualism with a somewhat jaundiced eye. Let us look at the assimilation problem first.

The Société nationale des Québécois de l'Outaouais, through its President J. B. Bouchard, expressed concern to the Study about the assimilation taking place in the National Capital Region. Table 12–1[1] is taken from his brief.

TABLE 12–1

POPULATION ACCORDING TO MOTHER-TONGUE AND LANGUAGE MOST OFTEN USED, OTTAWA-HULL REGION

	French Mother Tongue	French Most Often Used	English Mother Tongue	English Most Often Used	Total
City of Ottawa	62,235	51,700	210,460	232,235	302,435
Ottawa-Hull Region (Ontario side)	96,895	82,115	317,415	348,610	453,290
City of Hull	56,825	56,380	5,190	6,060	63,565
Ottawa-Hull Region (Québec side)	123,435	121,480	22,830	26,070	149,265
Ottawa-Hull Region (complete)	220,330	203,595	340,240	374,680	602,555

It will be noted from this table that although some net assimilation of Francophones appears to have taken place in the Capital Region (fewer French "used at home" than "mother-tongue"), it is nevertheless difficult to estimate the trend at the present time. Some persons of French mother-tongue may have come to the Capital from the Maritimes or the West and spoken English when they arrived here as adults. Others may have been born in the region but have grown up at a time when there were no French high schools in Ontario, except private schools for parents with means, and may thus have drifted into English to continue their education. Still others may have joined the public service at a time at which it was largely an English-speaking preserve, and became more accustomed as a result of work situation to speak English rather than French—even at home. There is also the factor that as little as ten years ago a pressure towards social conformity encouraged the use of English. It was the language one heard on the street, the language one used to ask for tickets on the bus or to complain to City Hall about the garbage collection. This pressure to English conformity has probably weakened, and it will be interesting to see in the 1981 census whether the new "bilingual" atmosphere will not have encouraged more and more of the young Francophone families now forming to preserve their language.

Using Census of Canada figures, Professors D.C. Rowat and K.D. McRae of Carleton University, in consultation with Mr. J. Kralt of Statistics Canada, prepared the percentage comparison given below on language characteristics of the National Capital area as between 1961 and 1971.

TABLE 12–2

POPULATION HAVING FRENCH AS ETHNIC ORIGIN, MOTHER-TONGUE, HOME LANGUAGE, AND OFFICIAL LANGUAGE, AS PERCENTAGE OF TOTAL POPULATION, OTTAWA AND HULL CENSUS METROPOLITAN AREAS, 1961 AND 1971*

	Ottawa CMA		Hull CMA		Ottawa–Hull CMA	
	1961	1971	1961	1971	1961	1971
Ethnic Group	23.1%	25.5%	82.9%	82.3%	41.6%	39.6%
Mother-Tongue	24.2	21.4	82.8	82.7	38.6	36.6
Home Language**		18.1		81.4		33.8
Speak Both French and English	26.3	27.4	45.2	28.5	31.0	32.7
Speak French Only	4.6	4.0	42.5	40.5	14.0	13.1

* The 1971 census metropolitan area is used for purposes of comparing 1961 and 1971 percentages.

** New category in 1971.

Anyone attempting to appraise the significance of these figures should pay particular attention to the pitfalls that lie in his way. The Weld paper warns about the need for caution in using statistics dealing with social characteristics. The census measurements with regard to language have been refined and altered over the years (ethnicity, mother-tongue, language spoken in the home), making many types of comparisons between different decades statistically unsupportable. Many census districts have been changed as urban areas grew. Immigration and the entry of Newfoundland into Confederation have had a distorting effect on the natural trend of English/French demographic statistics.

The effect of migration within Canada makes positive statements on assimilation very risky. Some situations are manifestly impossible to classify. (What is the language of the home of a family where both languages are spoken?) Finally, there is no blinking the fact that demographic statistics which suggest assimilation are political ammunition for those who advocate the break up of Canadian Confederation; as such their use must be viewed with particular care.

In summary, the French population of the National Capital Region, while experiencing a slight decline relative to the English, has been increasing in absolute numbers. Between 1941 and 1971, the Francophone population more than doubled. The statistics quoted here and the more detailed tables in Appendix B-2 suggest that language characteristics are slow to change and that the subject should be approached with steady persistence rather than alarm. As the Hon. Gerard Pelletier has remarked,[2] "At least once in every generation since 1760 there have been prophets of doom predicting the imminent demise of the French adventure in North America... It is history that has made them lie." Nevertheless, the assimilation problem brings me to a central point. If, as the Weld paper argues, it is accepted that Frenchness is a vital part of our Canadian identity, and that this Frenchness is, if not threatened, at least vulnerable, then we must also recognize the limited means at our disposal to preserve it. We must use our limited resources effectively.

II. The Limited Hiving Principle

One approach to preservation of a language or culture is the principle of "territoriality". By this is meant that within certain geographical and administrative boundaries one language will predominate, and that predominance will help it to survive. Switzerland, Belgium and other multilingual countries operate on this principle. The Royal Commission on Bilingualism and Biculturalism, following the example of Finland, tried to combine the principle of territoriality with the principle of personal choice. This implied that, as all Canadians share this country, their languages should share it too. These should be honoured throughout the country insofar as this is administratively feasible by means of public services in the two official languages in the Capital and in bilingual districts, in public transportation services, and in minority language schools.

This is a noble ideal, but it is legitimate to ask whether it flies in the face of reality in some of its applications. The Weld paper contains extracts from a book by Richard Joy which points to the steady assimilation of Francophones outside a line drawn from Sault Ste-Marie to Moncton (the so-called Soo-Moncton Line). Another analysis in *Le Droit*[3] by Yvan Allaire and Jean-Marie Toulouse examined the position of the Franco-Ontarians, and provides a handy guide relating Francophone concentration to resistance to assimilation. In refining the philosophic structure of the Royal Commission on Bilingualism and Biculturalism, I offer a new concept: the "Limited Hiving Principle", or LHP. In essence, it means encouraging the grouping together of Francophones on a territorial basis, but within the limits of practicality. Superficially, LHP may seem unattractive because it conjures up the idea of a French-Canadian ghetto; because it somehow seems to build walls rather than tearing them down. To these charges I would reply that intercultural understanding can be built up only when both parties are secure in their own identity; that it is only when a culture no longer feels threatened that it reaches out; and that hiving or concentration is the best method in sight to prevent assimilation.

I would like, however, to comment on the word "Limited" in Limited Hiving Principle. The Study received at least two briefs from French Canadians which were moving cries from the heart. If there was no questioning the genuineness of their Canadianism, there was also no doubt about the depth of their feelings about the threatened loss of their culture. They suggested that the Québec side of the Capital be kept all French and the Ontario side, English: the territorial principle with a vengeance. Although I favour hiving, the beautiful simplicity of the above proposal is not a manageable goal, as I shall illustrate later.

A very good example of LHP is the City of Vanier. According to the 1971 census,[4] French is the language spoken at home by slightly more than 62% of the population, while the Municipal Council is solidly Francophone and the City has traditionally offered a full range of bilingual services to its citizens. When we asked the Mayor of Vanier how he justified that City's existence as a separate entity, completely surrounded as it is by the City of Ottawa, he replied that it was a home for French-speakers on the Ontario side of the Capital. Further, the French Canadian Association of Ontario (ACFO), as strong an anti-separatist group as it is possible to imagine, presented me with a well-thought-out brief expounding on the advantages of concentration, and proposed Francophone areas or boroughs in any municipal restructuring of the Ontario side of the Capital.

If LHP can be justified because it corresponds to historical fact (Joy, Allaire & Toulouse, European experience, Vanier) and because it is wanted (ACFO), it may also be seen as a hope for the future. One of the main problems of attracting Québec Francophones to Ottawa has traditionally been the lack of French schools, the strange feeling of living in an English neighbourhood, the lack of cultural amenities and the like. Application of the LHP notion would at once answer such a complaint and would eliminate a host of problems, such as the fact that many children have a long drive by bus to French schools.

In its simplest sense, LHP rests on the belief that, while some people like adventure, most prefer to live in familiar surroundings where things are comfortable and known. I believe that this principle is true for both Anglophones and Francophones and can be applied on both sides of the Ottawa River. I shall refer to this notion again in a later chapter.

III. *English Backlash*

If we start from the assumptions that the public service of any country traditionally attracts people looking for security, and that any one objects to a whittling down of privilege, it is easy to understand the root cause of Anglophone backlash in the federal public service. The shock for a firmly entrenched and competent public servant suddenly finding himself vulnerable because of an inadequate knowledge of French is intensified if he believes, as many have believed, that things were fine as they were. The vagueness and confusion attached to the first attempts to implement the new bilingual policies added fuel to the fire. Although the current programme is certainly less vague, is spread out over a longer period, and contains provisions to prevent hardship and injustice, it would be blind not to admit that resentment lingers. In fact, the Study received comments from some Anglophones which were almost identical in their own way to those of some Francophones concerned about assimilation. "Let the French enjoy their culture and way of life in Québec, but Ottawa (not Ottawa-Hull) is the Capital". On the other hand, the majority of briefs from both English- and French-speakers argued that the Capital must reflect faithfully both linguistic communities. In dealing in the next section with bilingualism at work, an attempt is made to take account of both Anglophone and Francophone concerns.

IV. *Bilingualism at Work*

At the outset of the examination of the language problem at work, I would like to make two points. First, as the federal government is by far and away the main employer in the area, and as almost all other employers service the federal government or its employees, it is federal policy in the matter of language which is going to be the determining factor. If bilingualism in the federal government service becomes a reality, there will be bilingualism at City Hall, in the restaurant, the corner store, the pool hall and the barber shop—in Ottawa as well as in Hull. The role of both provincial governments, of local governments and of the private sector can be extremely helpful (or damaging as the case may be) in bilingual development, but will necessarily be complementary to the federal government's success or failure.

My second point is that there is a limit to the extent to which the federal government alone can cope with the problem. Save for the native peoples and a few other exceptions, we are all rather recent immigrants who came to this land and stayed here as a matter of choice. Freedom to choose is a most precious part of our heritage, even if this choice is to give up one's culture. The role of the state, as I see it, is to assure that this choice is a free one. Let me give two examples. One is the federal decision to build offices in Hull; I do not think that that city will ever be the same again. But the federal programme should assure, insofar as is humanly possible, that Francophones in Hull are not forced to give up their language and culture as a result of the metamorphosis although some, possibly for economic advantage, may freely choose to do so. Another example is the provision of simultaneous interpretation facilities at assemblies in the Capital. The state can assure that representatives of both language communities have an opportunity to speak in their own language and to be understood. But there is no way of forcing the Francophone to speak French if he chooses otherwise as many do.

The federal government's present policy with respect to bilingualism in the public service has the advantage of having been backed by an overwhelming vote in the House of Commons to which all party leaders gave their support. Only 15 private members voted against it. The approved formula, which involves the identification and designation of bilingual positions, is the classic Canadian compromise approach, in that it is one which makes no one really happy but where the distress level is not sufficiently acute to cause revolt. The Francophone may be inclined to think the Anglophone is mollycoddled, being given time off with pay to learn a language, when he (the Francophone) had to learn English the hard way. The Anglophone may resent having to take so much time for what seems to him a marginal requirement in a technical job.

In Appendix B-2 an attempt is made to assess the progress achieved to-date. How well the current approach will succeed or whether new modifications will have to be introduced will depend on a whole host of factors, psychological as well as political which are beyond the compass of this report to forecast. It would seem clear to me, however, that within the context of the Canada of today, a functionally bilingual federal public service is indispensible, and that quiet and persistent effort is the way to achieve it. The high profile of the Royal Commission on Bilingualism and Biculturalism was appropriate in its time, but the depoliticization of this question now is likely to yield better results. Both the Public Service Alliance and the Professional Institute of the Public Service as well as almost all the Members of Parliament in the National Capital area have expressed satisfaction with the new government approach and have been cooperating to make it work. I hope that the comments which follow will commend themselves as practical and unprovocative.

V. The FLU Concept

The first recommendation of the Royal Commission on Bilingualism and Biculturalism with respect of the federal public service concerned the establishment of French Language Units. The basic idea of the FLU is that work can be ordered in such a way that a group of Francophones can work together entirely in French save for communications with interacting units. The FLU notion is new. It was brought to the Bilingualism and Biculturalism Commission by some of its academic advisers, and was accepted experimentally by the government. Most of the 450 FLUs in the federal service today are in Québec. While the idea can thus be seen to be surviving, it has without doubt raised some false hopes. FLUs can be especially useful in bringing together a "critical mass" of Francophones who can thus work effectively in French. The FLU notion indeed can be regarded as a working level version of my Limited Hiving Principle enunciated earlier. The Francophone Institutions Division of the Department of External Affairs, the Québec Planning Branch of the National Capital Commission, or the French Manuscripts Division of Public Archives are obvious examples of ready-made FLUs in Ottawa. But *most* divisions and branches are structured to serve all of Canada, or all of a department (if an internal service is involved), and consequently cannot enjoy the luxury of working in only one language.

It can also be judged from the above example how impractical it would be to try to bunch together a number of FLUs from different departments. They would have nothing in common except for the fact that they speak French. Yet this has been seriously suggested by several Francophones who submitted briefs and a number of the mayors and councillors whom we visited. To me it seems obvious that there would not be enough FLUs in the Capital to fill half of any one of the major government buildings in Hull, and even if there were more FLUs in the Capital it would be administratively inefficient to cut off one section from the rest of the departments. As a result of the government building programme of the last 20 years, most departments are now consolidated and enjoy easy communication within one building. It is hard to see ministers or deputy heads being willing to accept a new fragmentation.

A similar idea, however, which I shall raise again in the concluding chapters, is much more practical. It is that more careful consideration be given to the transfer of departments to the Québec side of the Capital and that, with a view of maintaining the French character of Hull insofar as possible, transfers of departments be related to their Francophone population. If the Department of Secretary of State rather than the Department of Environment had been the first to transfer to Hull, the complaints about the invasion of Anglophones might well have been more muted.

VI. Passive Bilingualism: Attitudes

My own experience in working in French supports Mr. Weld's conclusion that the primary goal of language training should be to give the public servant a "passive" knowledge of the second language, that is the ability to read it and to understand it when it is spoken at conversational speeds. Time and again I have been told in Francophone groups that all they want is to be able to present their arguments in their own language, and that they vastly prefer the Anglophone to talk English rather than to garble his own arguments by being forced to use his own indifferent French. But the often-heard Anglophone refrain "I don't speak French", which forces the Francophone to speak English, is what the latter finds hard to take as a steady diet. I also think that the teaching of languages in the public service may have focussed too much attention on speaking and writing at the expense of improvement in comprehension; I agree that they all go together, but for many Anglophones at least, their real hang-up is fear of appearing a fool in oral expression.

While I count myself among those who believe that the bilingualism battle must ultimately be won in our schools, I can also see no substitute for the continuation of government language schools in the foreseeable future. In this area, while the state can be expected to provide a high level of teaching, it is the attitude, positive thinking, sense of perspective and of humour of the student which will win the day. This is inherently a personal matter, and fundamentally an Anglophone matter, since English speakers are in the vast majority in language school. A great disservice is done, in my view, by political leaders who, for partisan gain, denigrate directly or indirectly the efforts by public servants to master a second language, the better to serve their country. While the system should, and I believe does, provide safeguards to prevent injustices, the role of leadership must be steady and positive over a long pull. The exhileration of the language students who have "broken through and made it" is a joy to behold. Their example must be held high.

VII. Provinces and Municipalities

Premiers Robarts and Davis of Ontario set new guidelines for the Province in the matter of bilingualism. Ontario policy which, to a great extent, rests with individual ministries has to date been applied unevenly as far as the Capital region is concerned. Only the Vanier motor vehicle license bureau appears to operate effectively in both English and French and driving permits are still unilingual. My experience at the National Capital Commission was that the Ontario Ministry of Transport and Communications was reluctant to do much for the Capital in the matter of bilingual road signs, except when the question was raised as a special issue, but I understand that progress is now being made in this area. No visible advance has yet been made with respect to Mr. Davis' wish "to explore ways of permitting the use of French in the courts of Ontario, beginning in the Lower Courts".[5] The Weld paper refers to material we received suggesting that the Ontario Provincial Police have been strongly unilingual but the recent report of the Ontario Task Force on Policing[6] has recommended that police services in Ottawa-Carleton be bilingual and that this be accomplished through the hiring of Francophone recruits or candidates willing to acquire a working knowledge of the second language. Hopefully these recommendations will be implemented. Generally speaking, Québec provincial services in the Outaouais area are bilingual, although we did hear from Anglophones from English-speaking townships that regulations and instructions relating to various acts of the Québec legislature were usually received in French only.

The City of Ottawa has made considerable efforts to expand its bilingual capabilities in the last three years. By and large, municipalities in the National Capital Region are conscious of the ideal of service to citizens in both official languages, although the smaller, more distant and more unilingual municipalities have very limited bilingual capabilities or none at all. As the National Capital Region is presently structured, with over forty municipalities, I do not think any linguistic hardship is created by small unilingual municipalities. But if through restructuring the small unilingual islands are united, it will be essential that a full range of bilingual services be assured.

It may be significant in this latter connection that there is no simultaneous interpretation at meetings of either the Regional Municipality of Ottawa-Carleton or the Communauté régionale de l'Outaouais. Bearing in mind that both these regional governments embrace communities of the minority language, they might be more conscious of the responsibility to project to Canada and to the world the image of the capital of a bilingual country. The Ottawa Roman Catholic and Ottawa Boards of Education have better understood this role, and their interpretation services encourage participation and interest by members of both language communities at their meetings. While a fair degree of bilingual service is offered at the regional level, there may still be room for forward-looking leadership in this area.

VIII. Education at the National Level

The multilingual countries where language is not a major political issue usually have two built-in advantages. First, the school system provides adequate language training to equip its future citizens to take their places in the working world without extraordinary or heroic measures such as a government language school. Also they tend to have conscription in the armed services, which usually exposes their young men to immersion training away from home.

In the past, the English-speaking majority in Canada has been guilty of depressingly low second-language standards so that French, like Latin, became a book language but not one to be used to communicate with a compatriot. The situation is somewhat different today. I wrote to the nine deputy ministers of Education in the English-speaking provinces, pointing out the importance of the federal government as an employer, as well as the increasing necessity of bilingual capability in the Capital. I invited their views on the question of the language preparation of the future public servants of their country. Replies were received from seven provinces, and these showed a genuine concern for the problem of second-language learning.

"Potential" bilingualism, it seems to me, should be the federal government's objective for Canada outside the National Capital Region. Within the region, and from other bilingual areas like Montreal or Moncton, the federal government may legitimately hope to recruit fully-fledged bilinguals off the vine. For recruiting from other areas, a period of intensive government language school will no doubt be required. But the task will be incomparably easier if the individual has had basic language training. If he has none, the road will indeed be arduous. Current experience at government language school shows that the student without any foundation has a good chance of failing.

My mandate is really with the governing of the Capital, and to stray too far into educational issues may be construed as unnecessary invasion of someone else's responsibility—a vice I have deplored in the discussion of jurisdictional problems in the Capital! However, I am convinced that an important part of the problem of building the Capital into a national symbol will be to find public servants from all across the country with the training or potential to perform in an increasingly bilingual public service. If funds for bilingualism are limited, as they must be, it would seem to me that they could best be devoted to specific provincial projects to raise the level of bilingualism. By this I have in mind using federal funds to extend the second-language teaching of French or English down to the earliest grades of elementary school, and measures of a similar kind. The federal government, in my view, should not be afraid to pursue its own direct interest strongly, and should be on guard against a mere subsidization of the status quo. The annual reviews or evaluations of the use of federal funds in the area should be quite rigorous, bearing in mind that second-language teaching is a normal part of provincial educational responsibilities.

In any consideration by the federal and provincial governments of policies and proposals to meet these emerging needs, I would hope that the unique status of the National Capital area will be remembered, as well as the agreed conclusion of the eleven first ministers at the Constitutional Conference of February 1969:

> .... steps must be taken so that the two official languages and the cultural values common to all Canadians are recognized by all governments concerned in these two cities (Ottawa–Hull) and in the Capital Region in general, so that all Canadians may have a feeling of pride and participation in, and attachment to their Capital.

Footnotes

1. Mr. Bouchard cites Statistics Canada, *1971 Census of Canada Bulletins*, Catalogue nos. 92-725 and 92-726, of May 3, 1973 and August 27, 1973.
2. Speech to the Montreal Chamber of Commerce, February 19, 1974.
3. Les coulisses de l'actualité, Le Droit, November 13, 1973.
4. Derived from Statistics Canada, *1971 Census of Canada Bulletin*, Catalogue no. 92-726, August 1973.
5. Statement in Ontario Legislature, Debates, 4th Session of the Twenty-Eighth Legislature nos. 26 and 27, May 3, 1971.
6. Report of the Task Force on Policing—The Queen's Printer Toronto, 1974.

Chapter Thirteen

Problems of Living and Working in a Divided Capital— More Than Turning Right or Not on a Red Light!

I have asserted frequently in this Study that the National Capital Region is one single economic unit, in which residents share essentially the same concerns, and in which the federal government is the principal employer and the dominant economic force. But it is still a region divided between two provincial jurisdictions, and this division—and to a lesser degree that among the various municipalities—has a considerable impact on the daily lives of many of those who live and work in the Region. In this chapter we attempt to document some of the problems for Capital residents to which these jurisdictional divisions give rise, and to explain how these problems in turn tend to discriminate against certain sections of the Regional community, accentuating the political and geographical divisions. It is a situation for which there is no parallel within Canada, and few in the world, possibly excepting those urban concentrations which straddle international boundaries.

The differences which exist in the NCR are much more than a simple question of whether or not to turn right on a red traffic light—forbidden in Québec and permitted in Ontario. If less visible, too, than the colour of the licence plates, which are different on each side of the River, they cut across a surprising variety of activities—health care, professional services, union activity, educational opportunities, insurance costs and levels of pay. We have not attempted a detailed examination of all these issues, since it would form a study in itself, but the examples below show that the political boundaries which divide the capital make life more difficult for many residents, add to their cost of living, and may well be a factor of enough importance to encourage them to support a move towards a simplified governmental structure.

Labour and the Professions

Since legislation affecting labour and professions is within the competence of the provinces, it is not surprising that within the Ottawa-Hull metropolitan area we find disparities in this field. The practice of certain professions is limited to a single province, either Ontario or Québec. Lawyers, for example, must establish their practice according to the nature of their training, either in Québec civil law or English common law, (although there are a few lawyers authorized to practice in both provinces). In other fields, the situation is comparable; Ottawa real estate brokers can do business only in Ontario, Hull brokers only in Québec. Yet the mobility of the population back and forth across the provincial boundary is so great that common sense would dictate that all real estate firms in the Capital should have access to both markets.

Consider the position of a resident of Ottawa who decides to sell his house and move to Hull. He must first put his house up for sale on the Ontario market, if necessary using the services of an Ontario real estate broker. He then makes his purchase through a Québec real estate firm. To finalize the transaction he needs the services of a Québec notary, even though he has an Ontario lawyer working for him on the sale of his house. The reverse is true for a Hull resident who wants to buy property in Ottawa.

As for the teaching profession, many people reminded us that Ontario—and this holds true in the NCR—suffers from a shortage of competent teachers of French. In Québec, on the other hand, there is an oversupply of teachers, many of whom are unable to find employment; there also appears at the same time to be inadequacies in the teaching of English. And yet, because of differences in teacher certification on either side of the provincial boundary, and in qualifications in a number of subjects, exchanges which could meet the needs of both the Ontario and Québec educational system occur only very rarely. This is referred to in Mr. Weld's report in Appendix B-2.

In the different trades, and especially in the construction industry, the job mobility situation is very complex. We will not attempt to deal with it in great detail, but rather to point out the problems which are most obvious, even to a casual observer. The first point is that the trade groups in the construction industry are affiliated with various international, Canadian and Québec unions, and conditions of employment in both provinces are affected by this fact. The situation of trades in the construction industry in the Region is further complicated by the fact that labour legislation is within the competence of the provinces. Thus, for example, the Ottawa-Hull Building and Construction Trades Council is obliged to maintain offices in both Ottawa and Hull, even though the representatives of the member international unions are the same for both cities.

The hourly pay scales for nearly all trades are different in each province; wages in Ontario are generally higher, depending on the area and the particular contract signed between the contractor and the union. In Québec, wage rates are established by provincial decree[1] for each region and for each trade; they are not so determined in Ontario. In some cases—and this holds true in the Ottawa-Hull area—the difference can be as great as $2.00 per hour for a skilled worker.

Labour relations in the Ottawa-Hull area are also influenced by various inter-union and interprovincial tensions, according to testimony before the Ontario Royal Commission on Certain Sections of the Building Industry during its hearings in Ottawa in February 1974.[2] A number of unionized construction workers who live in either Ottawa or Hull, but who have steady employment on the Ontario side of the river, consider that there is a most unjust situation in the NCR which seriously damages interprovincial manpower mobility in the building trades. In a brief submitted to the Ontario Construction Industry Review Panel Board in 1973, the Provincial Building and Construction Trades Council of Ontario stated that about 80 per cent of the construction workers from around Hull were working on the Ontario side of the Ottawa River, and asked for government help in improving manpower mobility in the industry.[3]

According to an Ottawa union spokesman, it was Québec's adoption of Bill 290[4] and the Manpower Vocational Training and Qualification Act[5] that damaged the position not only of Ontario construction workers but also of those Québec construction workers who had always worked on the Ontario side of the Region. After this legislation went into effect, Québec construction workers were required to possess a work permit, and a certificate of qualification or competency, in order to practice their trade in Québec. It appears that a number of Québec workers who had always worked in Ontario were unable to obtain either this work permit, necessary if they were to return to Québec to work, or their certificate of qualification from the Construction Industry Commission. This development caused some Ottawa labour union members to complain that Québec had erected a wall around its territory. In order to show their dissatisfaction with this situation and draw public attention to it, Ontario and Québec unionized workers, who had been affected by these Québec government measures, considered on several occasions the possibility of using their cars as a barrier to block peak-hour traffic on the local bridges linking Québec and Ontario.

Québecers maintain that these legislative measures are designed to provide as much employment as possible for those permanently employed in Québec's construction industry. It also assures preference for Québec workers at the time of hiring. If there are no Québec workers in a given trade available for a certain job, the provincial government will agree to grant a certificate of qualification to an Ontario worker if he can prove his competency, and a work permit if he is able to furnish evidence that an employer is in need of his services. However, this legislation differs from other provincial labour regulations in the Ottawa-Hull region: even though it was created with the best of intentions, to protect Québec jobs and to improve the quality of work, it has caused serious problems for the parties directly affected and has added to the burden on Canadian taxpayers generally. Let me explain.

In 1969, the federal government embarked on a programme to build a number of new office buildings in Hull. The result has been that, because of the Québec government's labour legislation, construction contractors for these new buildings have been forced to import skilled labour from Montreal and elsewhere in Québec, while many local workers could obtain employment only in Ottawa. The effect is that the contractors must pay for the weekly room and board for these employees in addition to their wages. This increases the construction costs of these buildings; once again, it is the Canadian taxpayer who pays the bill.

For unskilled workers and day labourers, job mobility and freedom of movement between the provinces is not a problem, as this category of workers is not required to have a work permit in order to work in Québec. But these workers are usually hired through the Québec Department of Manpower, which gives priority in its job placements to Québec residents.

For their part, Québec residents of the Region who work in construction in Ontario also have grievances against the "system". They must, for example, pay a virtually compulsory membership fee of $160.00 to join an international union, if they wish to find a construction job in Ottawa or elsewhere in Ontario, even if they are already members of another union in Québec. Québec workers have long been accustomed to doing this because, for many years, all major construction in the Ottawa-Hull region was carried out in Ottawa. Most spokesmen for the construction workers that we interviewed, believe that the Québec and Ontario governments should conclude an agreement that would permit manpower mobility across provincial boundaries, not only in Ottawa-Hull, but also in the Cornwall-Valleyfield area, where the same situation prevails. Since the labour field remains within provincial competence, the federal government can only draw attention to the problem and urge the two Provincial governments concerned to resolve them.

To show the absurdity of this complex situation which besets the construction industry in the Ottawa-Hull region, we will end our comments with two illustrations:

(i) In January 1974, the federal government opened the Portage Bridge linking the core area of Hull to that of Ottawa. The short structural stretch of the Bridge lies partly in Québec and partly in Ontario. In its construction, different labour legislation applied on each side of the river, and it was necessary to respect the prevailing industrial wage scales for each province. For the Québec side, the contractors paid their employees according to the hourly rates for construction in effect in Québec under the decree respecting the Construction Industry. For their labour on the Ontario side of the bridge, the same workers were paid according to hourly rates negotiated between their unions and the contractors; for certain trades, these rates exceeded the ones in effect in Québec by $2.00 per hour.

(ii) Another bridge story involves the periodic repainting of the old Alexandra Bridge, a federally-owned structure connecting Ottawa to Laurier Street in Hull. The contract is given to one company. First, a crew from Québec assembles on the Hull side, puts up its scaffolding and gradually works its way toward the centre of the bridge. At the border, work ceases, the crew takes down the scaffolding and heads back to Hull. The next day, or sometimes even the same day, a crew of painters from Ottawa arrives at the centre of the bridge, sets up its own scaffolding and resumes the work, moving toward Ottawa.

Health and Welfare

In the field of welfare and public health, standards and services provided on either side of the Ottawa River vary greatly. On each side of the River there are provincial health insurance plans, but the Outaouais region has long had a serious shortage of hospital beds. Québecers in the NCR are often obliged to seek medical care in Ontario hospitals, and the provincial governments have agreements that provide for mutual reimbursement. Thus, in theory, people in Hull and Ottawa receive equal treatment in terms of health care. In practice, however, there are several differences between the Ontario and Québec Health insurance plans, which work to the disadvantage of inhabitants of either one province or the other, depending on circumstances.

(i) *Contributions*—In general the Québecer is less aware than the Ontario resident of the cost to him of hospital and medical services. The provincial treasury pays his hospital bills. If he works within the Province of Québec, health contributions are deducted from his pay cheque. If he works outside the province, e.g., for the federal government in Ottawa, the Québecer pays his contribution on filing his income tax return. For those earning up to $\frac{3}{4}$ of their income from salary, the maximum yearly fee for medicare is \$125; the rate is \$8 per \$1,000 of net income. For non-salaried persons the rate can rise to more than \$200 a year. Those with incomes of \$4,000 or less pay nothing.

The Ontario resident is more aware of the cost of hospital and medical care insurance than his Québec neighbour. A family of two or more persons pays \$22.00 monthly in contributions; an individual pays \$11.00. The cost of hospital insurance is \$2.00 more per month for a family of two or more for semi-private accommodation. But since January 1972, coverage for Ontario residents aged 65 or over has been free.

(ii) *Health Services Availability*—The City of Ottawa has four major general hospitals, two of which are teaching hospitals affiliated with the University of Ottawa. Hull has one large general hospital—Sacred Heart. In 1965 and 1971, it had sought without success to affiliate itself with the University of Ottawa and the University of Montreal. In the first case, language, and in the second, distance, had stood in the way of the proposed affiliations. Two smaller hospitals also serve Québec communities in the capital region. Teaching hospitals, having interns and specialists attracted by their university connection, generally provide better diagnostic and treatment services than other hospitals. A teaching hospital ordinarily receives funds and equipment for research and clinical investigation not available to other hospitals, precisely because of its university affiliation. Thus the two teaching hospitals in Ottawa have more resources to draw on than the major general hospital in Hull.

It would be misleading to conclude from this that the residents of the Outaouais area are necessarily at a disadvantage. In fact they are admitted to Ottawa hospitals. However, the latter are further away and, for most Québec residents, harder to reach quickly than the major hospital in Hull. In 1967, the Dorion Commission reported that 20% or more of Outaouais area patients used the services of Ottawa hospitals and that the Québec government spent $3.6 million in hospital insurance payments on their behalf in 1966. In 1972, it was believed that the Québec government paid something in the neighbourhood of $7.5 million[6] to the Ottawa General Hospital, the Ottawa Civic Hospital and to the St. Louis de Montfort Hospital for services to patients from the Outaouais and Western Québec area.

In order to draw attention to the health situation in the Québec part of the NCR, doctors at Sacred Heart Hospital in Hull submitted a brief to the Dorion Commission in 1967. Speaking before the *Commission d'étude sur l'intégrité du territoire du Québec* (the Dorion Commission), the doctors stated,

> Since opening in 1958, Hull's present hospital has gradually become a regional centre, receiving patients from the surrounding counties for diagnosis and treatment. And yet its facilities are barely sufficient for the needs of the city of Hull itself. In fact, the 350 beds that we possess cannot satisfy the needs of the approximately 100,000 residents of Hull and the districts immediately surrounding it. . . . For the purposes of your commission, this is perhaps the time to draw attention to an important economic factor for the region. Because of the shortage of hospital beds in the Outaouais, the provincial government pays more than $2,000,000 per year to Ottawa for hospital care which should be provided here. Of these payments, about 72 per cent should be going into salaries in the city of Hull, for it is a fact that about 72 to 75 per cent of a hospital budget is paid in salaries.[7]

In 1972, Sacred Heart Hospital was still swamped with patients and the population of the Outaouais region continues to grow rapidly. Recently, a citizens' movement called *L'Outaouais à l'urgence* (the Outaouais in emergency) was formed with the support of officials at Sacred Heart Hospital, and began a campaign to make both the public and the government of Québec aware of the urgent problem of hospital care in the region. In December 1972, after two members of the board of directors of Sacred Heart Hospital threatened to resign, "*L'Outaouais à l'urgence*" launched a campaign to obtain additional funds from the provincial government for the construction of another general hospital in Hull. After several months of studies and meetings, the roughly twenty-five organizations participating in "*L'Outaouais à l'urgence*" received a visit from Québec's Minister of Social Affairs, Hon. Claude Castonguay, who promised that funds totalling $19.5 million would be granted for the following purposes: general improvement of services at Sacred Heart Hospital, Pierre Janet Hospital and the Hôpital de la Pieta; 400 additional beds for old people by 1976; and the establishment of nine local community service centres. Mr. Castonguay also let it be known that the government was anxious to orient Sacred Heart Hospital toward university research.

Finally, because of the ease with which health services and medical and hospital care can be obtained across provincial boundaries, certain Ottawa doctors who receive many patients from Québec have decided to sidestep provincial government bureaucracy by sending directly to Québec their statements of account for services dispensed to patients residing in Québec. This was made possible because they use a post office box in Hull as a mailing address for communications with Québec City. This short-circuits (if somewhat illegally) the normal practice of submitting their Québec accounts to the Ontario Ministry of Health, which would then send them on to Québec City.

Ambulance services on the Ontario side of the National Capital Region have been integrated into other ambulance services throughout the province, and are now managed and financed by the Ontario government under its health insurance plan. Therefore, travelling by ambulance in the Ontario sector of the Ottawa-Hull area costs only 20 per cent of the total cost of service. On the Québec side of the National Capital Region, ambulance service is still the responsibility of private enterprise, just as it was in Ontario until several years ago. This means that ambulance users, whether they are injured, handicapped, victims of traffic accidents or the chronically ill, must pay the total cost for their transportation by ambulance ($25 to $35 in the urban area) without any financial aid from the Québec government. Moreover, the quality of service is left to the discretion of the ambulance companies, and thus may be subordinated to profit considerations. We have also heard stories about certain serious cases that required immediate medical care and emergency hospitalization, such as those of accident victims suffering from skull fractures, who, after receiving first aid in Hull, have been taken by ambulance to Montreal rather than to one of Ottawa's large hospitals. This seems to make little sense—but again it underlines the problem of the boundary for Québec residents.

The Sales Tax

This thorny question has been around for a long time. The basic problem arises from the fact that the Québec and Ontario governments have for some time had different rates of sales tax, with the Québec rate the higher. Between March 1967 and April 1973, the difference between them was three per cent; before 1967, it had been two per cent. Since April 1973, however, the difference between the two provincial sales tax rates has been only one per cent, due to the fact that the Ontario government raised its rate from five to seven per cent, while the Québec rate remained at eight per cent.

Until recently, the difference in sales tax had a tendency to brake economic expansion in Hull. It deterred entrepreneurs from establishing new businesses in the Outaouais area, and deprived municipalities on the north shore of the Ottawa River of tax sources they needed desperately. However, times have changed and this situation has been corrected by the opening of new shopping centres in Hull, where Outaouais residents now do most of their shopping, instead of crossing the river to shop in Ottawa's large department stores as they did before.

There are other aspects of this question which have affected the flow of business interprovincially. When the Johnson administration in Québec first raised the provincial sales tax to 8 per cent, Québecers buying expensive goods in Ottawa contrived to avoid both Ontario and Québec sales taxes by having them delivered tax-free. Ontario shoppers did likewise, but to a much lesser degree, because most of the large stores were in Ottawa. This loophole has been partly closed, since Ontario and Québec authorities required merchants on either side of the river to inform them of such untaxed sales. If the shopper does not volunteer to pay the tax, he runs the risk of being liable to a charge of evasion. But few appear to have been caught, and the game of tax evasion is still going on.

Residents of the Region are generally aware of the differences in the laws and regulations that apply on each side of the River, and even between the Ontario municipalities. In Ontario, beer can be bought only in brewers' retail stores or liquor stores, operated by or under the control of the provincial government, whereas in Québec, it can be purchased at any licensed grocery store. Bars and night clubs are closed on Sunday in Ontario, but this is of no consequence for persistent Ontario habitués, since they have only to cross the River to have a drink in Hull, where tavern keepers do a booming business. The Québec Liquor Corporation sells imported wines which are not available or are more expensive in Ontario; even though it is illegal to transport alcoholic beverages from one province to the other, many Ottawans buy their wine in Hull and take it back home.

Most Ottawa service stations are closed after 7:00 in the evening, but service stations in Hull are open day and night (and in Vanier as well). Stores in Ottawa and Hull close at 6:00 pm on Monday, Tuesday, Wednesday and Saturday, and at 9:00 pm on Thursday and Friday, but there are large department stores that stay open until 10:00 pm in the municipalities of Gloucester and Nepean, only a few minutes by car from Ottawa and Hull. This has been a very contentious issue between the City of Ottawa and the suburban municipalities.

Transportation

It was only in October 1973 that the two public transit systems serving Hull and Ottawa agreed to accept transfers from each other's customers; this policy was initiated by the NCC and subsidized with federal funds. Previously, a person who wanted to travel from one region into the other by bus was required to pay two fares, because neither public transit system accepted transfers from the other.

The elimination of double fares between the Ottawa and Hull areas was especially welcome to Outaouais residents, who cross the provincial boundary on a daily basis in much greater numbers than Ontario residents to reach their jobs in Ottawa. However, elimination of double fares was greeted with a certain scepticism by Québecers, since it came about precisely at the time when thousands of federal employees residing in the Ottawa area, mostly Anglophones, began to cross daily into Hull to work in the new government office buildings there. There was some suspicion in Hull that federal officials had intervened in the region's public transit system only to accommodate Ottawa Anglophones; for more than 30 years, federal employees residing in Hull, most of them Francophones, had been paying a double fare every day in order to get to their jobs in Ottawa. While this did look rather suspicious, before 1972 the Outaouais buses were privately owned and integration and subsidization of service would have been very difficult. It was only after the creation of the publicly-owned Outaouais Regional Community Transit Commission that the situation could be corrected.

The differences between Ontario and Québec legislation on automobile safety contribute to the fact that Québec has one of the highest traffic accident rates in the country. One reason is that Ontario has in the past several years developed stricter standards for used cars offered for sale, and the Ottawa-Hull area has become one of the ports of entry into Québec for used cars that do not meet the Ontario government's safety standards. These used cars, having been rejected by Ontario road safety inspectors, are sold to used car dealers who unload them in Hull or elsewhere in the Québec market, where they can be driven without first undergoing safety inspections.

This leads us to the question of differing rates or premiums for automobile and other types of insurance between the Québec and Ontario sectors of the NCR. It has always been recognized that automobile insurance rates along the Québec-Ontario border are, with few exceptions, considerably higher in Québec than in Ontario. According to the major insurance companies, the reason for this difference is that accident risks are much higher in Québec than in Ontario, and that therefore the companies must spend greater sums for the payment of claims in Québec. Thus, automobile insurance costs more for a driver residing in Hull than for one residing in Ottawa, despite the fact that driver mobility between the two cities—and provinces—is very great. We need only consider the many thousands of government employees who live in one province and drive to work in the other.

A comparison illustrates the considerable difference in insurance premiums paid by drivers residing on either side of the river. Consider the typical case of a married man, over 25 years of age, accident-free for five years, and who owns a medium-sized North American-type car with a six cylinder engine. For basically the same protection ($100,000 third party liability, personal coverage, collision and all perils)[8], the Outaouais driver pays about 50% more in insurance premiums. In actual figures, for an automobile insurance policy like the one mentioned here, with $100 deductible, costs $166 for the Ontario driver and $257 for the Québec driver; with $250 deductible, the respective costs are $146 and $218.

For property and real estate insurance, the difference is less marked than for automobile insurance, but is still to the advantage of Ontario residents. For example, it costs about $144 for a Hull resident to insure a home worth $35,000, and the personal belongings that he keeps there, compared to an equivalent $106 per year in Ottawa.[9]

We should mention one other disadvantage for Outaouais residents in the transportation field. Those who travel by train or airplane generally are forced to travel, on average, a greater distance between their home and the railway station or the Airport, both located in Ottawa. In practical terms, this means that taxi fares or gasoline costs tend to be much higher for Outaouais residents who regularly travel by air or train, than for their Ontario counterparts.

General

In terms of services generally, another source of division is that each side is frequently subordinate to one of the two major centres of economic activity, Montreal and Toronto. Often services in the Hull region are provided by Montreal administrative structures, and those in the Ottawa region are provided from a Toronto base. In the communications field, for example, even though the CBC's local English-language and French language radio and television stations are answerable to local administrators, their programming is under the direction of the English and French networks which have their head offices respectively in Toronto and Montreal. And at the local level, while the same technical services are used in the production of local programmes, there is little co-operation between the French and English sectors in terms of creation of programmes, documentation or production. As for news services, it is often the practice for a reporter from each sector to cover the same event without co-operating or sharing information with the other. Each works independently, with the result that the CBC's two listening audiences in the Ottawa-Hull area often receive two different versions of the same event. (This of course may also be a product of the political bias we referred to in Chapter Eight, page 97).

Subsidized housing provides another revealing example of the differences that exist among municipalities in the Region. As Hull and Ottawa are as yet the only two municipalities in the region that offer any appreciable amount of subsidized housing to low-income families or to senior citizens, those outside the two cities who hope to take advantage of such housing do not hesitate to move to either city to qualify for it. In Ottawa, for example, only one year of residence in the city is required for eligibility, (although this does not guarantee a unit), and the number of families on the waiting list is growing. Thus we find that a part of the subsidized housing in Ottawa is occupied by families who came originally from Maniwaki, Pointe-Gatineau, Vanier and elsewhere, but who obtained priority because they lived for at least one year in a building marked for demolition, in Lower Town or elsewhere in Ottawa.

In recent years, the growing shift of federal government employees to Hull has forced the federal Civil Service Cooperative Credit Society to attempt to make all its services available to members working or living there. However the Society has no authority to make mortgage loans in Québec, and must restrict its business transactions to Ontario where it is incorporated under a provincial charter. This also means that the Society cannot comply with the requests from its members who work in Place du Portage in Hull by opening a branch close to their place of employment. Officials of the Society have met with Ontario and Québec government officials, seeking a formula which would allow the Society to make all its services available to all of its members in the NCR. As yet no decisions have been taken, but we were told that a meeting between officials of the two provinces would be held late in May (1974) to consider the problem.

Conclusions

In listing some of the more obvious problems we are aware that to some extent they may simply reflect the essential division—Québec-Ontario, French-English—that exists between the two sides of the River. Some may argue in fact that these differences provide a desirable reinforcement of Québec's battle for cultural survival in the face of the economic impact of the strongly Anglophone Ottawa and federal government. Affiliation with a Québec union, for example, may well improve a Hull worker's adherence to his cultural roots, as well as making it easier for him to function in his own language.

These points have some validity, but division has an economic price. As we have seen above it appears to be borne largely by the Québec residents in the Region. We believe that it is possible to reduce this economic disparity without seriously compromising the natural desire of Québecers in the Region to retain their traditional links with the rest of the province. But the problem of bringing about needed change in laws and practices is one which rests essentially with the two provinces concerned, not with the federal government. In the final chapter we shall be putting forward several recommendations for action by Ontario and Québec.

Footnotes

1. *Decree respecting the construction industry in the Province of Quebec*, Order in Council No. 3984-73, October 31, 1973. Regulation No. 73-552, November 5, 1973, Quebec Official Gazette, November 14, 1973, 105th year, No. 32, page 5837.
2. *The Globe and Mail*, Toronto, February 26, 1974, page 9.
3. *Brief to the Construction Industry Review Panel Board*, from the Ottawa–Hull Building and Construction Trades Council and the Provincial Building and Construction Trades Council of Ontario, April 9, 1973.
4. Statutes of Quebec, 1968, chapter 45.
5. Statutes of Quebec, 1969, chapter 51.
6. Files compiled by *L'Outaouais à l'urgence*, Hull, 1973.
7. *Commission d'étude sur l'intégrité du territoire du Québec, Rapport, Volume III*, Mémoires soumis à la CEITQ, (Brief submitted to the Dorion Commission by the doctors of Sacred Heart Hospital in Hull, pp. 223-224.).
8. $5,000 insurance for medical expenses and a weekly allowance of $70 for a maximum period of two years are not available in Quebec. Rather, insurance for medical expenses reimburses a maximum of $2,000, and the weekly allowance available amounts to $35 for a maximum period of two years. However, the cost of an insurance premium is the same in both cases: $11. This amount is included in the overall premium.
9. Automobile and owner-occupant insurance rates utilized by 90 per cent of the insurance companies in the Ottawa–Hull area. They are a function of type of construction of the dwelling, and of fire protection services available.

Chapter Fourteen

What Do the People and the Politicians Think?

Vox populi, vox Dei, but if the voice of the people is the voice of God, it is often difficult to know what the public are saying. Most local politicians have views on the subject of the governing of the Capital, and freely profess to speak for their constituents, but we suspect that their judgments reflect in some degree their own strong instinct to preserve their piece of the power structure. The briefs and letters we received provide us with another cross-section of opinion, but we have no way of knowing how representative a sample it is.

I. A Scientific Perspective on Public Opinion

How then to find out more about the view of the people on matters which concern us in this Study? The modern method is the public opinion survey, and we were at first reluctant to consider this approach. Our reluctance arose mainly from the unsatisfactory and unscientific nature of most of the earlier local polls on such issues as a federal district, and from the vagueness and confusion in people's minds about the terminology used in the questioning.

Our doubts were reinforced by the fear that the results—whatever they showed—would be open to political attack, and that this could prejudice the more important part of the report, the analysis of the current problems of governing the Capital. However, Professor Rowat suggested that the Carleton Department of Political Science was looking for a subject for an opinion poll, mainly as training for students, and he thought their interests and ours might coincide if a topic concerning the restructuring of local government in the Capital were selected. This made some sense, and we met with Professor Falcone, who would be involved in the survey, and reached an agreement on the kind of information we wanted, and on cost-sharing.

In order to ensure that the work was totally independent of our Study, we laid down several conditions:

(i) Questions were to be drawn up by Professors Falcone and Van Loon and their associates, without reference to us except initially in terms of the general direction of our interests.

(ii) The survey was to be as rigourously scientific as possible, given the means available, and publicly defensible.

(iii) Although no special publicity was to be given to the involvement of this Study in the survey, (to avoid possible bias on the part of respondents) we had no objection to our participation being made public.

(iv) The results and opinions presented in the report would be those of the authors, again without reference to us.

These conditions were accepted, and the survey was carried out in the late fall and early winter. Most of the interviewing was done by Carleton students with some help from those at the University of Ottawa. The collation and interpretation was carried out by Professors Falcone and Van Loon, and their assistants and graduate students, with extensive use made of the Carleton computer. Their survey was submitted to us early in 1974, and is attached in Appendix B.

The method used to achieve randomness in the sample is described in the survey.[1] However, as the survey notes,

> It can be stated categorically that there never has been a piece of social science research that could not be attacked on some grounds as being unscientific. Thus the crucial issue in evaluating a study's methodology is not whether the canons of science have been adhered to, but rather whether departures from the ideal damage the conclusions. In this regard, we would contend that, unlike the methodological shortcomings of most previous attempts to determine public opinion about a federal territory in the NCR, those in the present study have not worked to preordain our conclusions.
>
> The findings reported in this survey are based on a systematic random sample of 269 persons 18 years old or older whose household telephone numbers are listed in "Section 1" of the December 1972, *Ottawa-Hull Telephone Directory*. This universe includes over 95% of the Region's population. A list of the municipalities it encompasses can be found on pp. 20-21 of the 1973 *Directory*.

An original 750 names had been selected from this telephone book. This number was reduced to 600, since 150 had moved, and these were subdivided by regions. Names were then given out on a random basis to student interviewers. The area covered in Ontario was bounded by Carp, Richmond and Orleans, and in Québec by Templeton, Templeton West and Aylmer. Ambiguous questions were deleted from the final questionnaire by pretesting. Each respondent was interviewed in the first language he or she used; several were interviewed in Italian.

We do not intend to give the results of the survey in detail, because they are best interpreted in the light of the context in which they are presented. However, a number of the survey's conclusions have a direct bearing on our own findings and recommendations, and they are summarized here.

Support For Federal Territory

The first and main conclusion of the survey is about the extent of public support for a "federal territory". As the authors stated:

> We have attempted to measure public opinion regarding the replacement of the present governmental system in the Region with a hypothetical federal territory (or federal district) and to find out what representational form of government likely would be most acceptable, assuming that some sort of government for the territory were to be created.

The results are given in Table 1 of the survey along with the authors' analysis. It shows percentage distributions of responses when interviewees were asked, "which of the following (statements) best reflects your views" on the question of whether the Region should become a federal territory.

Table 1: Percentage Distribution of Responses to Referendum Question on a Federal Territory for the National Capital Region

	%
1. The National Capital Region definitely should become a federal territory	31.5
2. It seems like a good idea but I have some doubts about it	22.5
3. It is difficult to say one way or the other	9.9
4. There seems very little reason to change the present set-up	7.9
5. The National Capital Region definitely should not become a federal territory	20.2
6. I have no opinion	7.9

(n = 275)

> Labelling item 1 and 2 "favourable", 3 and 6 "neutral", and 4 and 5, "unfavourable", the respective percentages in each category are, approximately; 54, 18, and 28. The fact that the modal category (1) is the most favourable statement and that the ratio of favourable to unfavourable replies is almost 2 to 1, clearly indicate respondent's endorsement of some concept of a federal territory. Furthermore, although the number of persons who selected statement 5 does not permit us to describe the distribution as an ideal J-shaped curve,[2] rarely do opinions on anything other than banalities so nearly approximate the classic conception of consensus.

One surprising finding in the response to this question was that opinion on the Québec side is even more in favour of a federal territory than on the Ontario side (66% vs 51%). However, as the Report noted,

> paradoxically, our French respondents appear to favour the idea slightly less than our English respondents. At first glance this seems to indicate an over-

whelming acceptance of the idea by English-speaking Quebecers, considerable support among French-speaking Quebecers, and a comparatively lukewarm endorsement by Franco-Ontarians. However, a further breakdown of opinion, by province and first language... reveals that among Franco-Ontarians, the favourable to unfavourable ratio is over two to one. The fact that a majority does not endorse the proposition obviously is owing to the large number of persons in this sub group with neutral opinions (44%) rather than to their antipathy to the idea.

In summary, says the Report:

We find that about twice as many residents favour the idea as oppose it, that support comes from all of the segments of the community that we have delineated, and that Quebecers tend to favour the idea more than Ontarians... There is also a strong positive relationship between social class and endorsement of the idea (using income to define class).

"Salience" of Different Levels of Government

Another interesting group of conclusions concerned the prominence of the different levels of government in the minds of residents. Those interviewed on the Ontario side were asked: "as a private citizen, which do you generally feel closest to, the federal government, the Ontario government, the Ottawa-Carleton regional government or the (name of municipality) municipal government"? For those on the Québec side, Québec and Outaouais government were substituted. Of those who replied, 62% said "federal", 10% "provincial", 5% "regional" and 25% "local".

As one might expect, Quebec residents are considerably more likely than Ontarians to feel closest to the provincial government. Over three times as many of our Quebec respondents identify the provincial level as that to which they feel closest, but, even for this group, a majority (52%) of respondents feel closest to the federal level.

Structure of Territorial Government

The questions asked were:

1. Should there continue to be local municipal governments something like we have now?
2. Should there also be regional governments something like we have now?

The results are given in Tables 5 and 6 of the Survey. They suggest that 61% favour local (municipal) government continuing, with opinion split evenly on continuing regional government. The Survey comments: "What does this mean? It suggests that, to achieve maximum public acceptance, any scheme for federal territorial government in the Region should include provision for local municipal government, but that the continuation of the regional governments is not as crucial."

General

A number of general findings were of interest. For example,

> We find that there is very slight agreement with the statement 'Ottawa (Hull) should remain under provincial jurisdiction' (question a) while there is quite strong agreement that the provincial governments are neglecting the region (question p). Moreover, the provincial governments get the most negative rating among various governments active in the region (question r). Yet, a second thought about these apparent inconsistencies will suggest that it is possible for people to rate the provincial governments relatively low without wishing to eliminate their influence altogether. That is, the impression we might take away from this subset of questions simply is that, in setting up a federal territory, the role of the provincial governments could be diminished, but that the public probably would not accept the complete elimination of provincial government influence in the area.

Whatever their opinions of provincial governments, respondents were not in the least willing to give up their right to elect federal members. An overwhelming majority of 90% of respondents (the highest majority for any item in the survey) stated that they wanted to continue to elect members to the federal Parliament.

Respondents were classified by income. There is considerable agreement between the sample results for family income in the National Capital Region and those which can be extrapolated from Statistics Canada data. Taking the mean of "over $30,000" in the sample as $35,000 (probably a relatively low figure), the authors of the survey estimate the mean family income for the Ontario part of the region as $15,528 and for the Québec part as $12,973. Statistics Canada said their figures for family income in the Ottawa and Hull metropolitan area were respectively $6,989 and $5,739 in 1961 and $12,412 and $9,860 in 1971[3]. Increasing these 1971 figures by 25% gives possible 1974 figures of $15,515 for Ottawa and $12,325 for Hull. The sample figures match these rather closely.

One unpublished result of the Survey is of interest to the Study, the fact that 41.5% of respondents in Ontario worked for the federal government, as did 43.3% of Québec respondents. The aggregation of these—about 42%—is a somewhat higher proportion of the labour force than suggested by the federal government's own figures for federal employment in the Region. The authors said that ambiguity was unlikely in the respondents' answers, since the interviewers were instructed to pin down employment more precisely (e.g. which department or agency worked for) of those who simply gave "federal government" as their answer. However, the percentages might be biased upwards by the over-representation of stable population in the sample and by several other technical considerations.

The final conclusions of the Survey are quoted in full:

Summary

We began this report by presenting a working definition of a permissive consensus in which the latter is conceived as a climate of public opinion, in favour of, but not necessarily demanding, a hypothetical form of government action. From our impressionistic reading of answers to open-end questions, and from our quantitative analyses of the responses to close-end items, it seems that this term admirably describes public attitudes in the National Capital Region toward the general idea of turning the Region into a federal territory. Widespread agreement in favour of a restructuring of government clearly is evident but the intensity with which opinions about government structure are held seems too low to warrant describing the consensus as "decisive", in the sense that overall public opinion in the Region is demanding such a change.

Comparisons of the opinions of significant subgroups in the sample revealed that a permissive consensus characterizes attitudes in each one of these. In general, the variations in support for a federal district territory by subgroups are politically, if not statistically, insignificant. However, there is a reasonably strong positive relationship between socioeconomic status and support for a federal territory and between the latter and the extent of participation in group activities. *In fact, among the highest income and activity groups, the consensus we have described as permissive might conceivably be termed "decisive"*. This finding is significant because, as numerous studies have shown, these are the groups forming the "attentive public" or that segment of the population with the greatest political influence.

The examination of opinions regarding whether, within a federal territory, the Region's residents should continue to elect M.P.'s, indicated an overwhelming desire to do so. There also appears to be strong support for the retention of local governments but only very lukewarm sentiment for the continuation of the regional governments as they now exist. Furthermore, the analysis suggested the advisability of representing the two provincial governments in any form of government for the Region, despite the relatively low salience of this level for our respondents.

These conclusions as well as others reached in the text obviously are only as sound as the data upon which they are based. For this reason, at the beginning of this report we discussed any factors that could affect the validity of the data, and concluded that none of them was likely to influence the results to a significant extent. In the analyses, it was pointed out that the credibility of the data is enhanced by the fact that our findings regarding classic relationships, such as that between socioeconomic status and group activity, are as expected. It was noted that our sample is not perfect. However, those groups that tend to be over-represented, i.e., the stable population and, to a lesser degree, high socioeconomic strata, are those whose opinions one might want to consider the most important in relation to the main questions posed by this survey.

Comments

We were concerned about one aspect of the Survey, the use of the phrase "federal territory" in the main question. We asked the authors if they believed that respondents found it either confusing or implying total federal control of the governmental process (e.g. as in Washington). From their discussions of this question with the interviewers, and from the response to the other detailed questions relating to the federal role or visibility, their conclusion was that respondents were, in general, aware that the question related both to the concept of some form of federal control and to the concept of some form of overall territorial government for the Region. Thus, while respondents were not asked in a separate question about the desirability of a single territorial government for the Region, the researchers believe that the pattern of their responses is consistent with, *at the least*, a tacit acceptance of this idea.

That the respondents definitely wanted either exclusive or major federal participation in this government, is shown in the answers to question 16 (*c*) to (*e*), and (*bb*) from the Report:

	Agree (somewhat to strong) %	*Disagree* (somewhat to strong) %
(*c*) The government of the NCR should be under federal jurisdiction exclusively	41	49
(*d*) The government of the NCR should include representatives from the federal and Ontario (Québec) governments	65	30
(*e*) The government of the NCR should have representation from the federal government	81	19
(*n*) Parliament should have some say in how the Ottawa–Hull area is governed	71	28
(*dd*) The Federal Government has too much to say in how the Ottawa–Hull area is run	31	69

The fact that 41% of respondents favoured exclusive federal jurisdiction, and that an overwhelming 81% favoured some federal representation in the governing process must be viewed in conjunction with their desire for representation at the municipal level, and for some continuing links with the province. Still, the survey concluded:

> ...on the whole, these results suggest that, in view of the high level of salience of the federal government in the National Capital Region, there would not be much local public disappointment should the federal government move to increase its control over local and regional affairs. In this sense, the results of this section may be viewed as corroborating the findings of the direct question on respondents' feelings about the Region becoming a federal territory.

As a corollary to these data on the image of the federal government and its role in the Region, it should be noted that the opinion of the public about the NCC is remarkably different from that of the people it elects to municipal office: 79% agreed and only 8% disagreed with the statement "Generally speaking, the NCC is doing a good job...". Moreover, only 32% of the public agreed with the statement "The NCC has too much power in National Capital Region affairs..."

Comparison of Attitudes of Politicians and General Public

Other comparisons of politicians and their constituents in the NCR that are relevant to this study can be made on the basis of research by Mrs. Margaret Kipp that utilized the Falcone-Van Loon data. She undertook a special survey of regional councillors of RMOC to see how closely their answers to the questionnaire of the opinion survey agreed with those of their economic and social counterparts in the general population. She found that by and large they did agree—except in relation to the role of the federal government in the governing of the Region:

> ... The members of the regional council were more in favour of maintaining the status quo, while members of the general public in the same (fairly high) income group were more willing to support change and governmental reorganization. This comparison revealed that at least 70% of the politicians (1) favour Ottawa remaining under provincial jurisdiction, (2) are against representation from the federal government and Ontario government in the government of the National Capital Region, and (3) agree that the federal government has too much say in how the Ottawa–Hull area is run. In direct opposition on these three issues, their counterparts in the public, at least 70% in each case, took the opposite view....
>
> Question 5d states: The government of the National Capital Region should include representatives from the federal and Ontario governments. Of the politicians who responded, only 30% agreed, while 77.5% of their non-political counterparts agreed. Question 5n states: "The Federal Government has too much say in how the Ottawa–Hull area is run". Here, 70% of the politicians agreed while only 33.6% of their counterparts agreed. It would appear that there is present among the political group a certain resentment of Federal interference which is not present among the population. Therefore, although there is a high level of agreement in attitudes between the political leadership and their constituents in Ottawa on most issues, there is a fundamental disagreement over the role of the Federal government.[4]

A second and related paper by Mrs. Kipp is also relevant[5]. She begins:

> The question that I wish to examine here concerns the theory that the members of regional council in the Regional Municipality of Ottawa–Carleton may be less willing than their non-political counterparts to welcome governmental reorganization, perhaps owing to the fact that these councillors have a vested interest in maintaining the present system.

As in her other study, the approach was to compare the results obtained from the Falcone-Van Loon survey with the responses of regional councillors to a slightly revised portion of the questionnaire sent out by mail. About half the council responded. Mrs. Kipp noted:

> ...with respect to the distribution of power among the various levels of government, the priorities of the two groups are quite different. The politicians want the municipalities to have the most power, the Federal government to be second in influence, and the provinces to be least influential. Their non-political counterparts, however, placed the Federal government first, the municipalities second, and, trailing the municipalities by a small margin, the provinces. It becomes obvious that the local politicians favour the present system with perhaps some modification, while the non-political group tends to be more receptive to change, perhaps reflecting a lack of strong personal interest in the outcome of proposed reorganization.
>
> It has been shown that the local politicians tend to favour the status quo, and disapprove of change which could possibly have consequences for their careers. Despite apparent support of a federal territory (Table IX) there is definite resistance to change among the councillors. If they appear to accept the idea on the intellectual level, there is an undercurrent of resistance which could possibly crystallize into strong opposition, given the proper political climate. There does appear, however, to be unqualified acceptance of the federal territory idea among their survey counterparts. It would appear that differences between the two groups over the federal territory idea stem from differing perceptions of what each personally stands to gain or lose as a result of governmental reorganization.[5]

II. Other Indications of the Views of Politicians

Meetings with many municipal leaders, usually on an individual basis, were held last autumn by the task force headed by Murray Jones. My own involvement was minimal, in part to lessen the possibility that my presence might steer the discussion more towards a re-fighting of old battles involving NCC than towards inducing a frank exchange of views. Whether this helped or not, the results were gratifying. The lengthy notes that were taken suggest that not only did most persons interviewed feel free to speak, but their opinions by and large were constructive and forward-looking rather than partisan.

The interviews were confidential, and we have no intention of divulging the opinions of individuals here. Rather we will try to draw some general conclusions from the diversity of opinions recorded. However, there was one common thread which ran through the discussions, and which should be noted. It is that most of the politicians tended to favour solutions which increased their own role or power-base; few of them suggested new structures that would do themselves out of a job! This is entirely understandable—the iron law of politics is survival—but it does give support to the conclusions of Mrs. Kipp.

It is difficult to see any general consensus arising from the discussions, although on some important issues opinions tend to cluster around one side or the other. We discuss these opinions below under a number of headings.

(a) *Existing Regional Governments*

General dissatisfaction was expressed with the functioning of RMOC and ORC. City of Ottawa spokesmen predictably favoured a solution in the restructuring of RMOC that involved amalgation of municipalities inside the Greenbelt into one City (Ottawa); the township representatives equally predictably favoured a solution that reorganized municipalities into boroughs, breaking up Ottawa in the process. ORC was not given very high marks by Québec municipal politicians. Although this was regarded mainly as the fault of the Province in not giving it adequate powers, the lack of effective leadership was referred to frequently as a factor. On both sides of the River there was agreement on the fundamental nature of the urban-rural division; many believed that different systems of government were needed for each. Solutions proposed included a "shrinking" of the National Capital Region into the urban area, but there were few answers as to the handling of the problems of urban spillover as the Capital grew. The concern of many rural spokesmen included the preservation of farmland and the "rural way of life" from the encroaching city—but also the preservation of the situation whereby farmers could continue to benefit from the rising land values derived from these same encroachments.

(b) *Restructuring of Local Government*

There was universal agreement as to the need for better liaison between the Ontario and Québec sides of the Region. Some supported the "committee" approach, and referred to recent progress in this. A larger proportion, however, were in favour of some form of single supervisory authority covering both sides of the River. Opinions varied as to its structure and authority, but there appeared to be agreement that (i) it should be a strong element of elected representatives, with federal and provincial input in varying degrees; (ii) some special recognition should be given in the voting to the need to protect the rights of the francophone minority; (iii) its function and powers should be broadly similar to those of the present regional governments (e.g. planning, sewers, water, public transit); but that (iv) as much government as possible should be carried out at the level of the local unit (municipality, borough, township etc.).

(c) *Role of the Federal Government and NCC*

We have touched on views regarding the roles of the federal government and the NCC many times already in the Study. Many area politicians believe that both have too much power in local municipalities, and are not accountable enough to local residents. Québec municipal spokesmen express special complaints about the province taking control of negotiations with the NCC. I have suggested that some of this anti-NCC feeling may stem from ignorance of the

NCC's role and its relative lack of freedom to act independently of cabinet. Certainly there also exists some envy of the NCC's budget and freedom from direct links between the cost of its projects and impact on local tax-payers. I am sure that another element is resentment of the power inherent in NCC's land ownership. Finally, no one likes sharing power with another body, particularly if it is regarded as a non-elected intruder.

I am not inclined to give this anti-federal attitude too much weight as a factor inhibiting structural change or federal participation in any new government which evolves. Moreover, we have already seen indications of changing attitudes towards federal participation, notably through the bilateral agreements reached on various shared-cost projects in recent years, and the establishment of new intergovernment committees. I think it is fair to say that five years ago the almost universal attitude of municipal politicians was that the federal government had no *right* to have any say in the government of the Region. That right has now largely been accepted, if somewhat grudgingly and on an ad hoc basis.

III. Role of Parliament — Views of Parliamentarians

One unsatisfactory aspect of the history of the federal role in the Capital has been the fact that Parliamentary involvement has been so intermittent. Every ten to twenty years a Parliamentary Committee is set up to review the federal operations in the Capital, but the last such review was that by a Joint Senate-Commons Committee in 1956. Another review appears to be imminent, and was referred to in the Prime Minister's statement announcing this Study. A committee of the Commons (often a different one each year) is given the job of looking at the NCC estimates, and occasionally the Public Accounts Committee examines the Auditor-General's comments on NCC expenditures. NCC staff appear before these meetings, and provides information that is useful to Commons members, but the questioning is seldom very searching or extensive.

Local members of Parliament raise issues from time to time, particularly if they are in opposition and hope to embarrass the government, and each opposition party has a spokesman who has acquired some expertise on the Capital. However, the process lacks continuity, and there have been very few significant Parliamentary debates about the Capital in recent years.

This absence of continuing Parliamentary involvement means the loss of a great opportunity to make Canadians aware of their Capital. Members of the House and Senate are a very important link to the rest of Canada; many Canadians see the Capital only through the eyes of their M.P., and from his or her reaction to life in Ottawa. If jokes are occasionally made in Parliament about the size of Ottawa's potholes, my impressions are that there is a substantial reservoir of good will towards the Capital from members of all parties, and regardless of origin. It is a shame that this reservoir has not been more effectively tapped.

In the course of the Study I met with a number of Members of Parliament and Senators, and discussed the issues with which the Study is concerned. Since most of those I spoke to had some special interest in the Capital, either because of their residence in the area, or their long involvement in its affairs, their views may not be entirely representative of those of their fellow members. However, most of them confirmed the generally benevolent feeling of Parliamentarians towards the Capital, and suggested there would be wide support in Parliament for the "federal district" concept—except of course for the partisan views—presumably raised for political purposes—which we referred to at the end of Chapter Two.

At the same time, some reservations were expressed about the parochial and inward-looking nature of the Capital and the corresponding lack of knowledge about the Capital across the country. One western Senator put forward an interesting suggestion for making the symbolic nature of the federal capital more widely known in Canada. He proposed that there be a branch of the National Capital Commission established in every Canadian city, and with roughly the same powers for embellishing and planning federal property as are given to the NCC in the Capital. This would provide feed-back both ways: NCC experiments in the Capital could be tried out in other cities, and the Commission would become more aware of urban problems across the country. Perhaps of more significance is that it would give Canadians in every city a sense of participation in the federal expenditures on its Capital, and might reduce the resentment that undoubtedly many feel when they see or visit their Capital and see what the federal government has done. This is an interesting idea, and might well have a place in current federal urban initiatives.

I have received, however, few comments from anyone as to how Parliament could participate in a regular or structured way in the governing process in the Capital. Our consultant, Mr. Poulin, suggested[6] that members of Parliament be appointed as members of a National Capital Council which he proposes as the overriding or umbrella government for the Region. This has several obvious drawbacks, not least of which is that Members of Parliament are overburdened with work now, and would have little time for a tough and continuing side assignment. Moreover, they could hardly be considered as "federal" spokesmen in the sense of being accountable to the federal government; presumably the federal government would want to have a more direct voice in the Capital's affairs and in the size of its own financial contribution.

Another possibility is the establishment of a Commons Standing Committee on the Capital. This would give Parliamentarians better continuity in their annual scrutiny of expenditures in the Capital by NCC, DPW and possibly other departments, and would give federal officials a better appreciation of parliamentary and Canadian opinion. Still another approach would be to replace members of the NCC with Members of Parliament. Both proposals probably would not be acceptable because of burdens they would impose on the time that Members have available. As NCC Commissioners, Members might also find themselves with the similar conflict of interest to those facing local mayors. Could an opposition MP on the Commission refrain from abusing his special knowledge to embarrass the government? Possibly, but I have some difficulty in seeing Members sitting as an advisory board to a government department, and then sitting in judgment later on the decision taken—either in committee or in the House.

One Senator suggested that the Senate is better equipped than the House of Commons to deal with Capital issues because of the greater flexibility in the Senate's schedule. He proposed that a standing Senate Committee be established to keep a watching brief on the federal role in the Capital's affairs. However, the Commons and the Senate have a much better idea than I do of how much they are prepared to be involved in the Capital's affairs, and this may well be an issue to be dealt with by the expected Joint Senate-Commons Committee on the Capital.

IV. What do the People Think? — Some Impressions

The public opinion sampling carried out by Professors Falcone and Van Loon is likely to provide a much more representative cross-section of opinion than we found in the 110 briefs or letters that we received. Because there is a natural tendency to draw on these latter documents to reinforce our own prejudices or preconceptions, we are reluctant to quote directly from them. However certain views did emerge which were fairly generally held, and we summarize them here:

(i) Most people believe that the area is overgoverned, and suspect that this has contributed to expanded bureaucracies and to higher taxes.

(ii) The right of the federal government to a role in the governing of the Capital was viewed much more favourably in the briefs than it was by the municipal officials and politicians interviewed.

(iii) The profile of the Ontario provincial government is low in the Capital, perhaps because so many people in it work for the federal government, and are aware of the NCC. The Québec government role is much more visible on the Hull side, for reasons we discuss below.

(iv) On bilingualism and biculturalism, two special concerns ran through the correspondence. The first was the traditional Francophone fear of being assimilated, reflecting their historic struggle for survival as a people. If the federal move to Hull was hailed because of its contribution to the economic development of the Québec side, and as a positive response to the long standing complaint about neglect, the possible anglicizing effects of the new and massive invasion of Anglophone public servants into Francophone territory is causing mounting concern. The other concern, which appears to be shared by a surprisingly large number of Anglophones in the region, is a kind of "backlash" against the government's bilingualism programme. It appears to represent a fear of domination by the Francophone minority in the region, or by an alliance between them and Francophone federal ministers. Nevertheless, apart from a few extremists on both sides of the Ottawa River who would like to see the provincial boundary more as a wall, there was general support for the idea that the Capital should be bilingual and bicultural and that it should include both sides of the Ottawa River. Several suggested "bilingual and multicultural".

(v) There was more support than we expected for a federally run federal territory. The designation of it varied—national capital, federal district, eleventh province or city state—but most suggested that it be largely divorced from provincial control. There was however some fear that an "eleventh province" would lead to a further bloating of government in the Region. Almost everyone writing in wanted to continue to elect municipal representatives; as one person put it "The Capital must provide self-government to its residents at the most responsive level—those closest to the people."

(vi) The excessive rate of current growth was widely attacked, as we noted in Chapter Eleven.

(vii) Some correspondents suggested that there was a need for the recognition by Québec and Ontario of the special status of the Capital—either by cession of powers or of land.

V. Conclusions

This brings us to the end of Part Two, the section of the Study concerned with the problems of the Capital. Since in our efforts to establish some kind of a consensus we may already have leaned too heavily on generalizations, I am reluctant to try to summarize further with the exception of noting several points which have struck me repeatedly during the course of the Study:

(*a*) The people are ahead of the local politicians in the search for solutions. The widest gap is on the Québec side, where some politicians may be inclined to tailor their pronouncements to certain press and broadcast media representatives to suggest anti-federal leanings. Other local politicians in Ontario and Québec suggest in their unguarded moments that they would go along with major changes—but their second thoughts tend to be linked to their own vested interest in the *status quo*.

(*b*) The federal influence in the Capital, and the reach of its power, is much greater than most people—and politicians—comprehend. An understanding of that at the provincial and municipal level might lead to a readier acceptance of substantial structures change. So pervasive is the federal economic influence that the boundaries which divide the Region into parts have increasingly less meaning. The passage of time itself may even impose needed solutions.

(*c*) There is a legitimate concern in the Hull area about the impact of the Anglophone invasion on its culture. The solution however is much more likely to be found in the Francophone's own will to survive, and in the federal government's efforts to encourage bilingualism in the public service and biculturalism in the Capital, than in any action the Québec government may take to protect the French language and culture. In summary, in the dispute over who controls the Québec side of the National Capital Region, the issue may already have been settled by the overwhelming economic influence of the federal government.

In the final two chapters we consider alternative forms of government, and put forward our recommendations and a summary of the conclusions on which they are based.

Footnotes

1. Falcone, D. J., and Van Loon, R. J., *Public Opinion Regarding the Restructuring of Government in the National Capital Region.* Carleton University, Ottawa. See Appendix B.
2. A J-curve is one half of a bell or normal curve. It generally fits an opinion distribution where there is an overwhelming majority taking a non-extreme position on one side of an issue, and a small minority taking an extreme position on the other.
3. Statistics Canada, Cat. 98-517 and special tabulation.
4. Kipp, Margaret, "*The Relationship Between Mass and Elite Attitudes in Ottawa-Carleton*", Carleton University unpublished paper.
5. Kipp, Margaret, "*Regional Council in Ottawa-Carleton. An Impediment to Government Reorganization*?", Carleton University unpublished paper.
6. Poulin, R., "*Proposals for Local Government in the National Capital Region*, Appendix B-4.

Part Three

Conclusions and Recommendations

Chapter Fifteen

Alternative Methods of Governing the Capital

In this Study we have reached some general conclusions about the weaknesses in the present structure of government in the Capital, and about the obstacles to change:

(i) The present form of government is inappropriate for the Capital because it neither recognizes adequately the unity of the Region nor provides for direct federal participation in the governing process.

(ii) The existing municipal structure is cumbersome, expensive and ineffective; the two regional governments have not achieved the results expected when they were set up by the provinces five years ago. Liaison among the various levels grows more complicated yearly, and consultation more time-consuming.

(iii) The obstacles to establishing a new form of government for the Capital are formidable. They not only involve the normal tendency of institutions and entrenched interests to oppose change, but are complicated by the Capital's two-province division, reinforced by federal-provincial rivalries, by Francophone efforts to protect their language and culture, and by Anglophone backlash to federal bilingual policies.

(iv) Whatever the obstacles to change, the Falcone-Van Loon public opinion survey reveals a surprising degree of "permissive" public acceptance of the idea of a federal territory for the Capital, with substantial federal involvement in the governing process but with continuing public representation through municipal elections.

(v) The problems are essentially political, and any solution proposed must be achieved through the political process itself. Ideal "text book" solutions have their place, but unless they meet the political need for pragmatism and compromise, they are unlikely to be accepted.

Delegation of Authority and Power

In the search for solutions to these difficulties there is another problem that has come up almost every time alternatives have been proposed. It is that governments are reluctant to surrender power to any other level of government, or indeed to any new body proposed to deal with areas in which there are overlapping jurisdictions. We noted in Chapter Eight that the failure of the Tripartite discussions, originally proposed by Prime Minister Pearson, was in part due to naïveté that a new agency could be created without any surrender of sovereignty by the federal government or by the Ontario and Québec governments.

Most of the proposals put forward to this Study by consultants, or interested correspondents, went to considerable lengths to attempt to devise schemes that would give the appearance of avoiding any infringement of the rights of the governments in question. One ingenious proposal was a system analagous in structure to the European Economic Community. We think that the analogy fits in some respects—questions of territoriality, language, and sovereignty are all involved—but we suspect that the complicated EEC structure, designed for the gradual integration of some 250 million people of 9 nations, is hardly suitable for a Region of 650,000. Simplicity is one of the virtues we are seeking in our search for a new and better government of the Capital, and however valuable the EEC example as a basis for meshing the economies and different objectives of the nine member nations, simple it is not.

This same fault affects several other proposals put to us. Mr. Poulin's "National Capital Council" (Appendix B-4) does represent an attempt to build a single coherent structure, and in some respects the Supra-regional Council proposed later in this chapter is not too dissimilar. But his "National Capital Council" has no clear function beyond that of a coordinating agency; the two Regional Councils have more effective power, and there is little diminution in the jurisdiction of the two provinces over their respective territories. Mr. Murray Jones' suggestion in his Report (Appendix B-3) visualizes as his second option an expansion in the federal role, and a reduction in the provincial, but proposes a "continuing consultative organization" formed of federal, Ontario and Québec ministries, again a complication rather than a simplification of structure.

All these reports are interesting, and have helped us make up our minds about acceptable alternatives to the present system. However as we note above, we find that they do not satisfy adequately the two criteria we laid down as essential: a simpler structure, and a willingness on the part of the federal government and the governments of Ontario and Québec to vest some of their present authority in the new body.

Proposals — Alternative Structures

It is against this background that we consider a number of alternative forms of government which might develop. In my opinion, these fall into three main categories, although numerous variations of each are possible:

Alternative I—A continuation of the *status quo*, with marginal changes. These could include more provision for consultation and cooperation, in particular between the two sides of the Ottawa River, and further amalgamation or regrouping of municipalities.

Alternative II—A federal territory for the Capital Region, implying a new territorial government, with provincial rights over the territory ceded or leased to the new government. Into this category fall the "eleventh-province" or "city state" proposals. A variety of alternatives are possible concerning the degree of self-government, up to and including complete control by elected representatives, and the existence or not of sub-units of government.

Alternative III—A single Supra-regional (umbrella or overarching or coordinating) council or government for the Region, with elected municipal governments below it on each side of the River. The federal government, the two provincial governments, and the municipal governments would all be represented on the Supra-regional Council. A number of variations in the municipal structure are possible, including the borough systems with substantial delegation of powers to boroughs, or city governments for the urban areas in each province.

We will consider each of these alternatives in turn:

I. Status-Quo, with Gradual Changes Occurring

One example of gradual change is found in improved procedures for intergovernmental consultation and cooperation, such as the tripartite discussions on public transportation policy begun in December 1973[1]. In addition, municipal restructuring is continuing, and may reduce the numbers of local governments.

This incremental or "band-aid" approach has a lot going for it, as Murray Jones noted in his report[2]. Consultation between levels of government now appears to be the Canadian panacea for federal-provincial problems. If the democratic process is untidy, representation and self government are more important than simplicity or efficiency; complex social realities often require complex governmental structures to deal with them. In the governing of the Capital, the consultative approach to jurisdictional difficulties raises no constitutional issues, allows politicians at all levels to maintain the illusion of power, and causes a minimum of disturbance to the present balance of forces. And when other and larger issues such as elections, inflation and energy shortages dominate government concerns, the enthusiasm of any government for launching new initiatives in the governing of the Capital is naturally restrained.

The disadvantages of slow change are less immediately visible, but none the less real. Coordination by consultation adds a new and loosely organized layer to the present four official levels of federal, provincial, regional and local governments. With liaison difficult enough as it is, the governing of the area inevitably becomes more complicated and the process more time-consuming. Rather than reduce friction, intergovernmental committees may encourage rivalries among the different levels, because they confirm the continuing existence of each layer in the governing mechanism. Power struggles won't disappear because the combatants from time to time sit around a common table.

Although the consultative approach may be favoured by those who believe that they are in a strong position (or have certain natural skills at playing the game!), the persistent losers are not likely to continue to accept it as a formula for resolving jurisdictional difficulties. Thus, even if the federal government believes it can achieve its goals in the Capital by increased consultation, the multi-jurisdictional approach has inherent weaknesses over a long period of time. It may be that a further period of struggle and attrition is required to demonstrate more fully the need for a simplified municipal structure in the Capital, but it would be a sad commentary on our inability to react only to emergencies. In summary, although I recognize the superficial appeal of *status-quo*, I do not believe it will work much longer.

I have not commented on one other possible variant of the above, that of a reorganized government structure without federal participation, achieved by agreement between Ontario and Québec. The suggestion has been put forward by those who feel that although the Capital is a company town, the federal government should have no different role in its affairs than say International Nickel does in Sudbury. Although this might be challenged on the grounds of suspicion that the unseen or partly visible hand of Inco exerts influence on the Sudbury City Council (without in the least suggesting any impropriety on the Company or Council's part), my preference is rather to challenge the argument on the grounds that for the Capital it is a retreat into the past. A century of history shows that the federal government will not be denied a say in the shaping of the future of its own Capital. If it is not given direct participation in the governing structure, then it will choose the alternative routes which we have described at length in earlier chapters. In summary, this proposal, however seriously it is put forward by those who believe that only the provinces have the right to control the municipalities, is not a feasible solution to the Capital's problems, but would rather exacerbate them.

II. A Federal Territory for the Capital

At the other extreme from the multi-level consultative approach is the proposal that the National Capital Region be established as a federal Capital territory. Throughout the years this has had considerable support, and we have seen from the Falcone-Van Loon survey that the concept is surprisingly popular with residents on both sides of the River. It may have even more support across the country. One Edmontonian (a transplanted easterner) wrote to say "What consideration has been given to making Ottawa-Hull into a district separate from provincial concerns? This might be one small way of making our Capital more of a national possession, a Capital to which all Canadians could relate."

Proposals for governing the federal territory run the gamut from total federal control to total self government; in recent years most proposals have supported a substantial measure of self-government. Common to all proposals is the cession (or "renting") of land by Ontario and Quebec, and the end of their effective jurisdiction over the territory. Variants include the "city state" or "eleventh province" concept. There is an extensive discussion of the Capital territory idea in Appendix III to Book V of the Report of the Royal Commission on Bilingualism and Biculturalism which is reproduced in Appendix A.[3] Eggleston also discusses the pros and cons at length in *The Queen's Choice*. The case for a territory was summarized in Professor Rowat's Report (Appendix "C", page 425):

(1) on grounds of principle the capital of a federal country should belong to the people of the whole nation and should not be located within the boundaries of any one province or city of that province;

(2) precedents elsewhere demonstrate the superiority of a federal capital territory;

(3) the physical redevelopment of the capital would be much easier under a federal territory; and

(4) the bilingual-bicultural nature of the national capital would be greatly improved.

I stated in the opening chapter my conviction that a federally-run district, along the lines of Canberra, was not acceptable. Local residents demand a say in the running of their municipalities. My opinion was reinforced by the Falcone-Van Loon survey, which found that 61% of respondents favoured local government continuing, and noted that "to achieve maximum public acceptance, any scheme for federal territorial government in the Region should include provision for local municipal government".[4] Thus, even if 41% of the respondents agreed, with intensity ranging from "somewhat" to "strongly", with the statement "The government of the NCR should be under federal jurisdiction exclusively", there is clearly stronger support for continuing public representation in the governing process. For these reasons, then, we reject the concept of a federal district run by the federal government.

But what about a federal territory with a large measure of self-government? As we noted in Chapter Six, a number of federal capitals around the world fall in this category. And the opinion survey reveals broad public support for the idea in the NCR. Furthermore, as we have emphasized often in this Study, the Region is one economic unit, almost totally dependent on the federal government for its continuing existence. This dependence transcends political boundaries, and the survey shows that a majority of residents of the Region feel much closer to the federal government than to all other levels of governments combined.

However, even if one were to judge that this is an idea "whose time has come", the obstacles to moving from the present form of local government to a largely self-governed federal territory appear formidable. Many of these obstacles centre around the rights of the two provinces, Ontario and Québec, and to the fact that a federal territory could only be achieved if they agreed to give up powers and control over the land in question. The issue for the provinces appears much less the practical aspects of such cession, than political and emotional considerations. The Québec government would be susceptible to the nationalist arguments about "intégrité du territoire" (the wholeness or unity of Québec territory)—although the economic case for "intégrité de la capitale" may be logically compelling. On this the views of Mr. Michel Gratton, member for Gatineau in the Québec National Assembly, are particularly interesting. He suggested in the Assembly on March 21, 1974:

> If by mischance we were to revert to the do-nothing policies of previous governments or, worse, should Quebec elect a separatist government, I confess that I myself would become one of the most fervent partisans of a federal district for our region...
>
> Mr. Speaker, as elsewhere in Quebec, we who live in the National Capital Region want to be full-fledged Quebecers. I submit, however, very humbly, that the vast majority of us entertains a further desire, and that is that we wish to contribute to an objective supported by all Canadians—to build a capital worthy of Canada. Within this National Capital, we wish to be the reflection of Quebec, with all that this signifies in the cultural, social and economic spheres.
>
> The cultural sovereignty of Quebec, within a Canadian federalist economic framework—this, I believe, Mr. Speaker, is the living symbol which we can become in the Outaouais-Quebecois.[5] (translation)

At the municipal level on both sides of the River, reaction would probably depend most on how much the proposed changes appeared to threaten individual political fortunes. The more confident a politician feels about his own prospective role in the new government, the more likely he might be to give the proposal support.

To all the prospective obstacles of a political nature should be added the one cited earlier in this chapter as a major inpediment to change, that of inertia. The strong appeal of *status-quo* is that it avoids disturbing the existing uneasy balance. In the circumstances, I have difficulty in believing that a self-governed federal territory is a short-run possibility. My conclusion is reinforced by the opinion survey, which refers to the public consensus about the desirability of a federal territory as "permissive" rather than "decisive" (although this latter word does apply to the views of the highest income and activity groups). I interpret this to mean that, although the public at large would support major proposals for change, it is not likely to be aggressive about demanding them. More vocal public support might overcome the obstacles to which we refer above, since politicians are receptive to the wishes of the people who elect them, but without a clarion call from the people the possibility of far-reaching territorial changes being made in the near future appears remote. Whether a federal territory might eventually evolve is a question I return to briefly at the end of this chapter.

III. A Single "Umbrella" Government for the NCR, With Elected Municipal Governments Below It

This is a compromise approach, which appears to have support, if largely unofficial, from some municipal leaders. It involves the creation of a single Supra-regional Council, with elected governments below it on each side of the River. There are a number of variations on this theme, both in terms of the composition and structure of each government and in the allocation of powers and responsibilities among them.

Defining Our Terms

The complexity of the present municipal structure in the NCR is reflected in the confusion that exists in the terminology used to describe the various possible types of local government levels or units. We found the confusion compounded in our efforts to be precise in describing the new forms of government which we propose, and in comparing them to those now in place. The following list of definitions is an attempt to make clear what we mean by each label:

"*Supra-regional Council*"—The senior governmental body proposed for the whole of the National Capital Region. The title was chosen to suggest that its authority extends over both existing regional governments. "Council" is meant to imply a body composed of representatives drawn in varying proportions from different levels of government: federal and provincial appointees, and elected representatives of municipal government. It would assume most of the powers of the two existing regional governments, and other powers delegated by the federal and provincial governments. In this sense it would be a "strong" government. Other phrases that might be used to describe this body are "umbrella", "overarching", or "coordinating" government. We avoid "regional" because of the possibility of confusion with the existing regional governments, and "territorial" because of the "capital territory" connotation.

"*Regional Governments*"—One on each side of the Ottawa River, similar in form to the existing two Regional governments, but with possible differences from them in composition, powers and method of election.

"*City Government*"—An alternative to Regional Government; consists of one or more centralized governments for the *urban* areas on each side of the Ottawa River. The suggested "city" governments are somewhat similar in form to the City of Ottawa, but with their powers somewhat reduced.

"*Borough*"—Proposed new sub-divisions of "Regional Government", of roughly equal population, but considerably larger in size than existing "*wards*". Their responsibility could vary inversely with those of the two regional governments above them; as a minimum they would deliver those services which can be best carried out at the neighbourhood or community level. These boroughs can also be described as "*districts*".

"*Wards*"—As now, political subdivisions of the urban "cities", which elect "aldermen".

The Supra-regional Council is common to all the alternative forms of government considered in this section. There appears to be three principal variations in the possible form of elected government below it:

(i) *Two Regional Governments*, one in Ontario, one in Québec, composed of boroughs of roughly equal size; most advocates suggest a borough size in Ontario of close to 50,000, with fewer in the Québec boroughs. Other local forms of government (townships, villages, etc.) would be abolished.

(ii) *Two City Governments*—Greater Ottawa and Greater Hull, with the boundaries widened to include the contiguous built up urban areas on each side of the River now containing close to 90% of the population of the NCR. Rural townships would continue to exist, although reduced in number, and along with the two cities, would report directly to the *Supra-regional Council.*

(iii) *More Than Two City Governments*: This envisions three urban cities of 150,000 to 200,000 on the Ontario side, and from one to three (smaller) cities on the Quebec side; it represents a compromise between the other two proposals. The cities would report directly to the *Supra-regional Council*, as would the rural townships.

Considerations Affecting the Choice

Obviously many alternatives are possible within this larger framework, and we turn now to examine a number of questions and considerations which have a bearing on the choice among these various alternatives. We leave to the last the most difficult problem, the division of powers among the different governments.

A. Boundaries of the Region

Is the National Capital Region as presently constituted appropriate? One alternative would be to increase the area to include towns and villages in close proximity such as Carleton Place, Arnprior and Rockland; another to have it coincide precisely with RMOC and ORC boundaries; still another to "shrink" the Region to the built-up areas Proposed for Greater Ottawa and Greater Hull, say inside the Greenbelt on the Ontario side and the equivalent urban area on the Québec side—Lucerne, Aylmer, Hull, Gatineau.

The arguments against change are (i) the 15 year existence of the present NCR; (ii) the difficulty of defining a new outer boundary; (iii) the continuing problem of urban spill-over into surrounding areas, and the difficult relationship between these areas and the urban city. Whether the NCC boundaries should be altered marginally to conform to county or township lines is arguable: that the present size of NCR is just about right for metropolitan planning purposes is harder to contest.

B. Composition of Supra-regional Council

The basic assumption is that it should be composed of federal, provincial and municipal representatives. But in what proportions? If the Council is to have a solid basis of accountability to residents, this would suggest that at least 50% of its members be drawn from the two elected local governments. The line of argument of this Study also suggests that the federal voice should equal that of the two provinces together. Combining these premises indicates a division of a 50% municipal, 25% federal, and 25% provincial. The federal, Ontario and Québec representatives would presumably need to be appointed directly by each of these governments, to ensure accountability or them. It would also make sense for federal appointees to be drawn from NCC or any successive agency or department. Some problems and questions which might arise include:

(i) The possible incompatibility between *appointees* of senior governments and *elected* municipal representatives. We noted earlier how the presence of Ottawa and Hull mayors on the National Capital Commission did not work out very well for this reason, although the failure may have been due in part to the Commission's own lack of authority to act independently of the federal government. And we might note that the mixed elective-appointive council works in New Delhi.

(ii) Should the chairman be appointed (say by federal-provincial agreement), elected by council members, or elected at large by vote of Region's residents? (This latter issue keeps coming up at RMOC.)

(iii) The size of the council? Preferably under 25, or otherwise it would be too unwieldy. And if the "City" alternative is chosen, how should the "elected" seats be distributed between urban and rural?

(iv) The Council's executive committee:—should it be on a full-time basis? How much power should be given to it, and what about the balance between Québec and Ontario?

C. Voting Power Balance—Québec–Ontario

One awkward problem is the interprovincial division of votes on the Supra-regional Council. Not unexpectedly, Québec municipal spokesmen are for equality, and this view is even shared by a few Ontario municipal leaders. The essential argument for equality, despite the present 3:1 population split between Ontario and Québec, is that it would be needed to protect the Quebec and Francophone minorities in the Region. Against it is the logical argument that it would stray tco far from "representation by population" to be acceptable to the Ontario majority—a group which themselves are not entirely free from fear of the other language group. In addition it would overrepresent the Francophones on the Québec side in relation to those on the Ontario side, who are almost as numerous, and would provoke the fear among Anglophones that a combination of the two Francophone groups could control the Council.

The population disparity is not as severe a disability as appears on the surface. Half of the proposed votes would be divided between (*a*) the federal government, which presumably would give equal weight to each province, and (*b*) the two provinces themselves. However, the problem could be further eased by the compromise of giving Québec municipal representatives additional votes (or members of the council) to bring the ratio from 3:1 to say 3:2. Another possible approach would be to create a strong executive committee of the Supra-regional Council, and to over-represent the Québec side, perhaps to the extent of giving equal weight to each. Since the committee would likely figure prominently in the functioning of the Council, this could provide the protection the Québec francophone group would be seeking.

Still another proposal would be to require, for certain sensitive language or cultural issues, a "double majority", that is approval by the Council as a whole, and also by the Francophone representatives. And to those who doubt that some protection is needed, we can only comment that English is not a threatened language in North America.

D. Identity—Naming the Capital

Giving a name to the larger capital is an essential element in establishing its unity. The process could also be divisive, and needs careful study. Ottawa-Hull has the advantage of the long standing existence of both cities, and might win by default. However, "Hull" is not popular with many Quebec residents, and a search has been on for some time to replace it. Outaouais, the French equivalent of Ottawa, had adjectival connotations in French, although the marriage of the two words "Ottawa-Outaouais", as the name of the Capital, appeals to many (including me).

In a search for a new name that would be acceptable to both groups, and the same in both languages, we may be almost forced back to the Indians. How about Algonquin, for the tribe that used to inhabit the region? Or Asticou, which has some support in Hull? But if this is the kind of question that could evoke as much heat as the flag debate, we suspect that residents would accommodate readily to a change, once made. Do the residents of Thunder Bay still feel very nostalgic about Fort William or Port Arthur? Or Vanier residents about Eastview?

E. Community Groups

Any government restructuring should make provision for the recognition of community groups, and their participation in some degree in the governmental process. The Winnipeg "community committee" approach is intriguing, but it has not worked out well, possibly because of the lack of delegation of real responsibility or adequate staff and funding to the committees. If the borough system were adopted, however, it should be possible to provide financial and technical help to community groups on a borough basis, and provide for regular meetings between the group leaders and the elected representatives for the borough.

There are admittedly dangers in the process—notably that of strengthening the lower level of government when we are seeking to reduce the number of tiers, and the possibility of "capture" of community groups by extremists. But there is no doubt that the neighbourhood organizations reflect local needs and are a valuable source of policy inputs, and should therefore be given some voice in municipal government. Mr. Poulin's proposed "Town Hall facility" (Appendix B-4) at the borough level would provide a useful focal point for community group activity. The degree and method of group participation will of course depend on the size of boroughs, the extent to which they have their own functioning councils, and the powers delegated to them.

F. Financial Arrangements

Logic suggests that the powers to tax and borrow be centralized at Supra-regional level, and outstanding debt assumed by that government, and also that assessment and property and industrial taxes, be equalized across the Region.

Federal and provincial contributions could be based initially on existing grants, together with costs now financed through special cost-sharing arrangements (sewers and roads), and costs of any federal operations transferred to the new body. This could be supplemented by special starting-up grants, leading eventually to a formula proposal whereby the level of property taxes in the Capital is based on those prevailing for the average of Canadian cities of about the same size (see discussion—Chapter Ten, page 130.)

There are a number of inherent problems, but the arrangements would of course have to be subject to intergovernmental negotiation at the time of the setting up of the new government.

G. The Proposed Powers of the Supra-regional Council

Designing a precise form of structure is less important than allocating powers among the new units of government. The most important decision is the extent of the responsibility given to the Supra-regional Council. Functioning as it does in two provinces and in a federally-dominated area, it will inevitably need to be a much stronger body than either of the two existing regional governments.

What powers then should it have? I suggest they will derive from four sources:

(i) Powers now held by existing regional governments, such as long term planning, public transportation, sewers, water, arterial roads, assessment.

(ii) Other municipal powers which, because of the Council's interprovincial coordinating function, will more appropriately be dealt with at the Supra-regional level. These might include industrial development, solid waste disposal, pollution control, central headquarters of both police and fire protection, ambulance service, regional parks and recreation, and control over interprovincial roads and bridges. They could also include parking, public housing, and taxicab licensing.

(iii) Powers delegated by each province to the new entity. These could include final planning authority and powers to tax and borrow. The Council would be the appropriate body to coordinate Ontario and Quebec efforts to reduce disparities between the two sides of the Region in such matters as sales tax, union jurisdictional problems, licensing of professions, interchange of health care facilities and provision of special facilities for education in the two languages.

(iv) Powers delegated by the federal government. These could include the giving up of sole federal control over federal decisions on use of its own land, on building location and design, and on federal capital planning activities, together with the delegation to the Council of servicing of and control over some federal property (e.g. parks and parkways). This would clearly involve the transfer to the new Council of a part of the NCC activities in planning and operations.

It will be noted from the above that the endowment of the Supra-regional body with substantial powers can only be achieved at the expense of all three government levels—federal, provincial and municipal. As I emphasized earlier in this chapter, this must be a central element in any new approach. There would be little point in pursuing governmental restructuring in the Capital if this basic assumption is not accepted from the beginning.

H. Powers of Lower Levels of Municipal Government

Turning to the powers of lower-level governments, it would appear that they would be doing many of the things that the city, township and other governments are doing now—but with the transfer of some responsibilities as indicated above. This would pose few problems if the "two-city" approach of an enlarged urban Ottawa and Hull is followed:

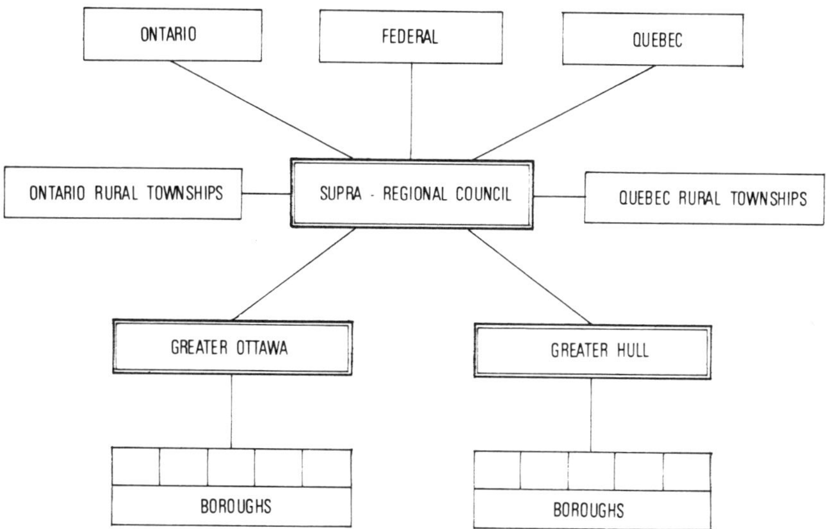

How the Regional-borough system of local government would develop is more difficult to assess. If the boroughs are given most of the residual powers, as many suggest, then the two Regional governments would have little to do, and little prospect of surviving except as a kind of provincial caucus for the boroughs. If most residual powers are given to the Regional government, then the boroughs are little more than city wards. We would then find ourselves back to something that closely resembles the "two-city" concept, but presumably with the inclusion of rural townships as well as the urban boroughs. The following chart attempts to show this difference in graphic form:

STRONG BOROUGH

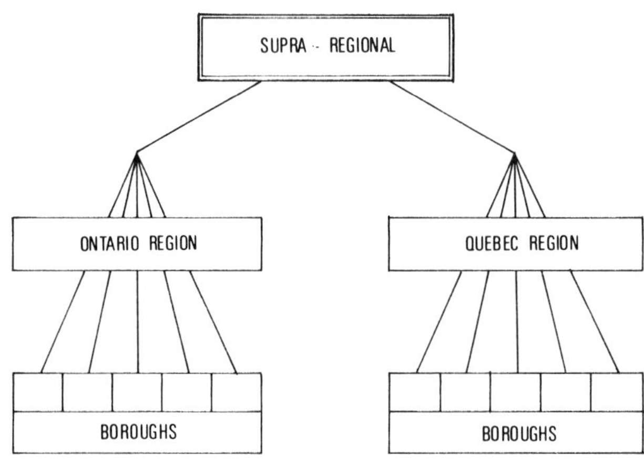

STRONG REGIONAL GOVERNMENT

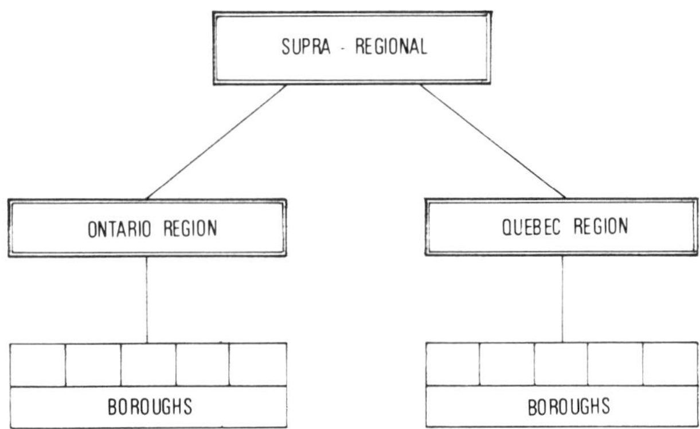

In examining these alternatives attention must be drawn to two particular considerations. The first is that the "powerful borough" approach is not too far removed from the concept of a single territorial government for the National Capital Region; provincial differences would tend to be blurred in the representation at the Supra-regional Council. The second is that the conflict in approach between the "strong borough" on the one hand, and the "strong region" or "two-city" on the other, is almost a conflict between two different philosophies of municipal government: centralization versus dispersal of power. The same inherent conflict of course exists in the allocation of powers between the Supra-regional Council and the elected governments below it, but in that case the decision is affected by other important considerations, including the two-province division and the need for participation of the federal government.

Centralized City vs. Dispersed Borough

The "City" approach is more monolithic and centralized. It assumes that the voters delegate to two small groups of elected representatives the authority to run the urban area on each side of the River—subject of course to the powers vested in the Supra-regional Council. In the Capital it has the appeal that such concentration may be necessary to offset powerful federal forces, and the somewhat less powerful provincial ones (stronger in Quebec than in Ontario). In another sense, this argument is that concentration confers economic benefits not available to smaller units.

Finally, there is the advantage of continuity. Ottawa and Hull both have established governments that have been in operation for a long period of time—despite the recent loss of some functions to the two new regional governments. Yet it must be emphasized that the stronger the Supra-regional Council becomes, the less real power there will be at the city level.

One drawback of the city approach is that this solution neglects the rural and boundary areas. As urban growth spills over into the countryside, the problems of the boundary areas, as well as rural-urban conflict, become more acute. A second problem is that the trend of the times is against centralization at City Hall, and more towards the passing down of powers to smaller local units. The most responsive government tends to be that closest to the people; the opinion survey showed that the people feel much closer to their municipal government than to their regional government. While it can be argued that the enlarged cities would be recognized as "local" municipalities, their population and the area they covered would make them appear much like the old Regional governments they replaced. One suspects that, if the two-city approach is adopted, centrifugal forces would soon be at work leading to demands for the devolution of more powers to wards, districts, or boroughs.

The borough approach also has its advantages and disadvantages. In its favour is that it provides government close to the people; residents can identify with their borough. And as Mr. Poulin notes in his study (Appendix B-4), the borough could be the "vehicle for people liaison". It could be the municipal point of contact with residents on such matters as welfare, preventive health service, licences, permits, fines etc. The borough system would seem to fit more comfortably into the *Supra-regional* structure—an enlarged City of Ottawa might well be too powerful a force in the upper government, leading to many of the same problems which arise from the City's preponderant role in RMOC.

One difficulty facing the borough system is that it means not only forming new areas from the amalgamation of smaller units, but also to some extent the carving up of existing municipalities, particularly the City of Ottawa. Few boroughs would have the historical associations and homogeneity of some existing municipalities such as Nepean Township. Thus, there might be no established political structure or geographic unity to provide continuity of government or to encourage borough loyalty by the public.

An additional problem is that of borough size. Most suggestions envisage about nine boroughs on the Ontario side, and four to six in Quebec, with an average population of up to 50,000 persons. This may be too small a population for an efficient or economic borough—at least, if it is to assume all the responsibilities not given to the Supra-regional Council. For example, the six Metro Toronto boroughs average over 300,000 persons each; the merger of the two smallest boroughs with the City of Toronto is now being considered, which would raise the average population to over 500,000. In London, England, the 32 boroughs in the Greater London Council average in size over 200,000 persons each; in West Berlin the 12 districts average close to 200,000. In the face of this, it is difficult to see how a substantial share of municipal responsibilities could be successfully decentralized to a group of relatively small boroughs; put another way, the smaller the borough the fewer the responsibilities it can carry out efficiently. Thus, the more the powers given to the Supra-regional Council, the less borough size poses a problem.

The Compromise Third Variation

This proposal envisions three urban cities on the Ontario side, and one to three on the Quebec side. It represents an attempt to compromise between the "Regional-borough" and the "two-city" approach. These cities, composed of wards, would report directly to the Supra-regional Council. Rural townships would also report directly to the Council.

The three cities in Ontario might be called Nepean, Ottawa and Gloucester, with Ottawa reduced in size to a population of about 200,000.[6] Nepean and Gloucester would each have a population of less than 150,000 but they are still growing. The rural townships and villages, reduced in number, would lie outside a rough semi-circle formed by Kanata, Glencairn, Barrhaven, the new south-east city at Carlsbad Springs, and Orleans. This restructuring meets in some degree the appeal for the "breaking-up" of Ottawa to reduce its predominance among Ontario municipalities in the Capital.

On the Québec side, there could be one urban city, Greater Hull, or the area might be divided by the Gatineau River into two cities. A third variation further divides the section east of the Gatineau into two parts.

A chart of the overall structure would look something like this:

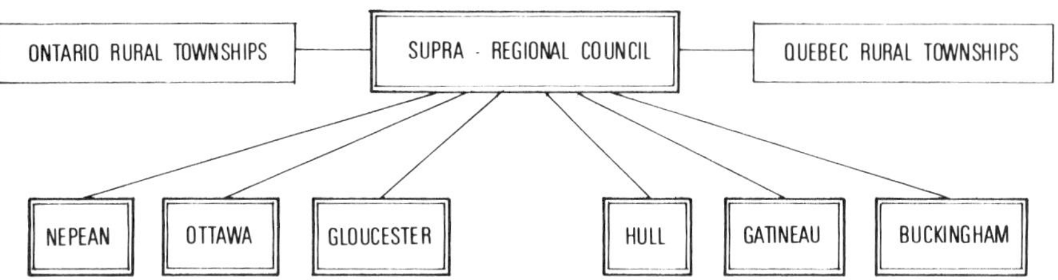

The advantages of this third compromise are:

(i) It establishes municipalities large enough to assume all responsibilities below the Supra-regional level.

(ii) It provides a better balance on the Ontario side, at the expense of the City of Ottawa.

(iii) It allows for continuity in municipal government, and for continuing public identification with an existing municipality for most of the people in the area.

(iv) On the Ontario side, it provides for healthy competition among the three municipalities in the provision of services leading to general improvement.

The disadvantages are that this approach provides little improvement in procedures for citizen contact, and fails in part to meet the desirable goal of establishing boroughs in which there are special concentrations of Francophone or Anglophone citizens and services. In other words, are the four to six units small enough to be "close" to the people?

In summing up my own conclusions about these various alternatives I would put them in this form:

(i) The crucial decision concerns the formation of the Supra-regional Council, the involvement in it of the three levels of government, and the giving to it of substantial powers by these governments. It must be a strong government, with greater powers than those of the two existing Regional governments. Anything of less stature, such as a consultative committee without a precise operational role and powers, I would regard as merely a variation of the *status quo* and unlikely to function effectively.

(ii) The structure and powers of governments below the Supra-regional level should be primarily the responsibility of local residents, their elected representatives, and the two provinces. The discussion above is merely to illustrate the various possibilities and the problems to which each might give rise.

IV. Other Considerations

Bilingualism and Education

In the preceding review of alternative structures of government for the Capital, we have omitted one special area from consideration, that of bilingualism and education; we group the two together because they are closely related. These topics have a particular sensitivity, not only in terms of provincial rights but also because of the emotional reactions which they arouse. Since they have been examined at some length in a number of places in this Study, notably in Chapter Twelve, in the studies by Mr. Weld and Professor McRae (Appendix B-2), and in Appendix III to Book V of the Report of the Royal Commission on Bilingualism and Biculturalism, which is reprinted in Appendix "A" of this Study, our comments here are therefore limited to two points. One is a statement of objectives, the second a summary of Professor McRae's conclusions on various possibilities for an educational system based on the alternative suggestions for forms of government.

The objectives might be summed up as meeting the need to protect minority languages, and the special bilingual requirements of the federal government. Measures to meet these needs might include:

(i) The guarantee of education in either language, according to choice, with the objective that all graduating high-school students be bilingual, or at the very least be able to read and comprehend both languages.

(ii) The availability of municipal services in either language to residents on demand. Such a provision would be similar to federal policy. A "grandfather" clause would be needed to protect older unilingual employees.

(iii) A conscious attempt to attract Anglophones choosing to live on the Quebec side to a particular area, following up the "limited hiving" proposal in Chapter Twelve. If a borough system is established, this might be the Aylmer-Lucerne area. Such concentration would tend to strengthen Francophone predominance in other areas on the Quebec side. A similar attempt to provide Francophone concentration on the Ontario side might be to create a predominantly Francophone borough—say, Vanier, Lower Town, Sandy Hill, and part of Gloucester Township.

With respect to changes in the structure of the educational system, Professor McRae suggests that there are three basic situations to be recognized: first, the *status quo*; a middle position (which McRae calls option 2), leaving provincial structures in place, but providing a mechanism for coordinated or interpenetrating services in the Capital; and third (his option 3), a Capital territory which would have its own legislative and administrative jurisdiction. Option 2, he suggests, could open up choices not available now to the linguistic minorities on both sides of the Ottawa River, and could offer some prospect of building a stronger and more united Francophone community from a population that is currently divided into two groups of almost equal size by the provincial boundary. Option 3, in his view, would transform the Capital region from one that consists essentially of two separate, peripheral areas, both remote from their respective provincial capitals, into a new coherent centre. It could counteract the extreme fragmentation of present education regimes in the Capital, reduce the financial disparities, and open the door to research and experimentation aimed at achieving cultural equality in a plural society.

Re-examination of educational structures from the point of view of amalgamating the denominational and public school systems must be mentioned in closing. The alleged inefficiency of two parallel educational systems has been raised in a number of briefs received by the Study. However, the philosophy behind the separate school is not based on the notion of "efficiency" in an economic sense, but rather on the cultural and religious differences between certain segments of the population. The Study will, therefore, make no comment on this aspect of the educational structure, save to say that the majority of school board trustees interviewed on both sides of the River considered that the time was not yet ripe to envisage a shift to a completely secular form of education.

Implementation

Giving birth to a new system of local government is a long-drawn out process. RMOC was nearly six years in gestation, and a municipal government of the kind suggested above, that crosses a provincial boundary and involves three levels of government, is considerably more complicated. It would be foolish to try and draw up a schedule showing step by step how the Supra-regional government could come into being. However there are certain stages required for the process:

(i) *Study* (one year)

Independently, by federal government, by the proposed Parliamentary Committee, by provinces and by local municipalities. This would lead to federal-provincial consultation to decide to follow up or not. If agreed, the next step would be:

(ii) *Task Force Review* (one to two years)

Tri-level group to consider and report on the myriad of questions involved—structure, allocation of powers, constitutional status, legislative changes needed, financing, education, municipal (borough) boundaries—leading to a report for considerations of governments. If accepted or amended, then concurrent action to bring down:

(iii) *Legislation* (one year)

Legislation required by federal, Ontario and Quebec governments to confer powers on new council. (Much longer if a constitutional amendment is required).

(iv) *Birth Problems*

Matters arising out of the setting up of a new government such as headquarters' location, absorption and reshuffling of staff from RMOC, ORC, NCC. This would require a year, but the planning of it could be carried out while legislation is pending.

Thus, if all goes well, 1978 would be the earliest date for bringing a new government into being; a more likely date would be closer to 1980.

V. Conclusion—Federal Territory

Despite the fact that a Supra-regional form of government for the Capital would not derogate from the essential jurisdiction of the provinces, some voices will no doubt proclaim that this is a backdoor way of creating a federal territory. Pushed to its limit, this argument would be summed up in the contention that the provinces would no longer be "sovereign" in their respective territories. To this, I would reply, first, that what the provinces and the federal government create by legislation, they can unmake by legislation; and, second, that insofar as powers are delegated to a supra-regional body, the delegation by the federal government would be at least as broad as that by the two provincial governments. Indeed the essence of my proposal is that to create something better, each level of government, including the local level, has to suspend the exercise of some of its actual powers and transfer these to the new body.

This proposal implies a degree of faith that the newly delegated power will not be abused. The history of responsible government has shown that at each stage when powers were to be extended, whether from an appointed council to an elected assembly, or from property owners only to all citizens, opinion was always divided between stand-pat Cassandras and those willing to experiment with new forms of political organization. Not all such experiments have led to happy results but, by the same token, unless they had been tried we would still be guided by the doctrine of the divine right of kings. I assert that the proposed Supra-regional council contains the essential elements to provide an effective balance of powers, and provides a much simpler form of government for Canada's Capital.

I know that the creation of a Supra-regional form of government would not satisfy the ardent advocates of a "federal district" or "federal capital territory", but it seems to me that it satisfies most of the basic requirements for the practical governing of the Capital, and at the same time provides a mechanism for dealing with most of the problems referred to in this Study. However, if the Supra-regional government proves acceptable and is put in place, and if it functions successfully for some years, then the time may come when Capital residents and their political leaders might wish to consider moving on to a complete territorial government of the kind described earlier as the second option. I would not expect this to occur suddenly but rather in an evolutionary manner.

The essential requirements before such a territorial government could be considered appear to be these:

(i) The elected representatives increasingly dominate the Supra-regional government, with the role of provincial and federal representatives declining.

(ii) Parliament, speaking for the people of Canada as a whole, expresses strong support for a territorial government.

(iii) The elected representatives for the Region themselves favour the move to a capital territory, and carry a substantial proportion of residents with them—preferably with the view of residents obtained by referendum.

(iv) Ontario and Quebec indicate a willingness to go along, with agreement to cede (or rent) such powers as are necessary to achieve it.

(v) A special constitution for the proposed territory is drawn up, and approved by Parliament and by the legislatures of Ontario and Quebec, covering such matters as financing, minority rights, bilingualism, special relationships with the two provinces in matters such as law and education, the form of continuing liaison with federal and provincial governments, and structure of the territorial government (bicameral or not).

One could discuss for a long time the shape such a new government might take, and the problems it would pose, but it makes more sense to wait and see what happens. The present support shown in the Falcone-Van Loon survey suggests, however, that popular support for its adoption might develop more quickly than I had originally thought.

Footnotes

1. See Chapter Seven, page 87.
2. See Appendix B-2.
3. *Royal Commission on Bilingualism and Biculturalism*, Book V *The Federal Capital*, Appendix III (see our Appendix A).
4. See Appendix B-1.
5. *Journal of Debates*, Québec National Assembly, speech by M. Gratton, p. 118/9, March 21, 1974.
6. The readjustment of boundaries to provide three cities on the Ontario side of the Region might be carried out as follows:
   (*a*) Nepean—urban part of present township, plus Carleton and Britannia wards of the City of Ottawa, plus other contiguous urban areas west of Rideau River, such as Kanata.
   (*b*) Gloucester—urban part of present township, plus Rideau Ward of the City of Ottawa, plus Vanier and Rockcliffe Park, plus other contiguous urban areas east of Rideau River, such as Orleans.

Chapter Sixteen

Recommendations

In this final chapter we submit specific recommendations, together with a brief summary of some of the conclusions on which they are based. The recommendations are directed principally to the federal government; in certain instances these involve action by Parliament, but most could be implemented by the government itself without reference to Parliament or to other governments. There are also recommendations to Ontario and Quebec, to local municipal governments, and to residents of the Region. Finally there is a particular recommendation to the Prime Minister of Canada and to his successors in office.

The recommendations below are grouped under various subject headings, with those directed to the federal government considered first. Where action by Parliament is involved it is so indicated.

I. Recommendations to Federal Government

(a) Defining the Region as Capital

Although the BNA Act declared Ottawa to be the federal "seat of government", there has been increasing recognition over the years that the *de facto* federal capital is Ottawa-Hull together with the area surrounding these two cities. The actions of successive federal governments since early in this century have clearly shown the collective desire to adopt this broader definition. These actions include the establishment of the "National Capital Region" and the entrenchment of it in federal legislation, the reference to the "Canadian Capital area" in the communiqué at the end of the second meeting of the Constitutional Conference in February 1969, and the construction and leasing of federal office buildings in Hull since 1969. We have emphasized throughout this Study that the Region is one economic entity, totally dominated by the federal government, and that this unity or integrity demands a better coordination of municipal government than now exists.

We have suggested that broad public acceptance of the larger capital has been inhibited by the apparent reluctance of the federal government itself to proclaim the Region as the Capital, and to reflect this reality in its day to day operations. We have noted further that the federal government has the power to amend Section 16 of the BNA Act to change the definition of its seat of government. This change could be effected by the passing of a simple order-in-council, by an Act of Parliament under Section 91(1) of the BNA Act, or by a compromise approach designed to reflect both the will of Parliament and executive action, which would involve a Joint Resolution of both Houses recommending executive action. We consider that the best approach would be through an Act of Parliament, reflective of the wishes of the Canadian people as a whole; this would also provide some flexibility in the formula for designating the seat of government. We are recommending below two alternatives. The first would leave with the Crown the power of designation of the "seat of government" but transfer to Parliament the power to define the National Capital Region. The second would transfer to Parliament both the designation and delineation of the Capital.

The proposals contained in this first group of recommendations would not be affected by changes in the structure of local government in the Capital. Their purpose is to focus the attention of everyone, politicians, federal employees, local residents, and Canadians generally, on the unity of the National Capital Region, and on the need for its acceptance as the Capital. Special provision is made for altering precise boundaries of the NCR, possibly to conform to the boundaries of the two existing regional governments. And if the phrase, "National Capital Region", offends in certain quarters, then we have no violent objection to calling it "Canadian Capital Region" or "Federal Capital Region". In the recommendations which follow we have limited ourselves to using "NCR", rather than suggesting alternatives each time a reference to it is made.

I recommend that the federal government:

1. ***Accept*** **the National Capital Region as its "seat of government" and as its Capital.**

2. ***Present*** **to Parliament a Bill to amend Section 16 of the BNA Act following one of the two formulae below:**

EITHER

"16(i). Until the Queen otherwise directs, the Seat of Government of Canada shall be the National Capital Region.

(ii). The National Capital Region shall include the cities of Ottawa and Hull and such surrounding areas as defined from time to time by Parliament."

OR

"16. The Seat of Government of Canada shall be the National Capital Region as defined from time to time by Parliament."

3. ***Instruct*** **federal departments and agencies to take all possible action within their power to encourage wider acceptance of the National Capital Region as the capital, including such measures as**

   (i) the changing of the government address to Ottawa-Hull, or simply to National Capital Region;

   (ii) the organization of local departmental operations in the Capital on a National Capital Region basis instead of dividing them into separate provincial compartments;

   (iii) the renaming of the Ottawa airport and other federal installations as "Ottawa-Hull" or "Capital";

   (iv) the collection of statistics on a National Capital Region basis, and their publication as a special category, but without affecting existing Ontario and Quebec statistical series.

4. ***Establish*** **an internal task force, under the direction of the Privy Council Office, to discuss with departments proposed measures arising out of recommendation (3) above, the coordination of these measures with government policy generally, and their implementation.**

(b) Parliament and the Capital

I have emphasized my conviction that Parliament should be more involved in the governing of the Capital, and to this end I have two specific recommendations. I recommend that the federal government propose to Parliament, for its consideration:

5. **The establishment immediately of a joint committee of the Senate and the House of Commons to study and report on the contents of this Study generally, but in particular on alternative forms of government for the Capital, on their impact on the future role of the NCC, and on ways of involving Parliament more actively in the governing of the Capital.**

6. **The establishment of a Standing Committee of either Senate or Commons to provide liaison between Parliament and the NCC or other body coordinating federal activities in the Capital.**

(c) Alternative Forms of Government for the Capital

I made it clear in the discussion of this in the previous chapter that in my view a continuation of the *status quo*, even with modifications, would not deal adequately with the problems of governing the Region. I said that the preferred choice involves the establishment of a Supra-regional Council, with participation of the federal government and Ontario and Québec in the governing process, with some cession of powers to this new body by these three levels of government, and with representatives from municipal government in the Region having at least a 50% vote in the Council. The responsibility for any restructuring below the Supra-regional level should reside with the two provincial governments and the municipalities.

The essence of the recommendation below is that no new form of local government will be effective unless it involves the direct participation of the three levels of government, along with some surrender of power by them to the new body. Should this not be accepted, I believe that the federal government has the necessary powers within the present system to achieve most of its goals in the Capital, but this is a poor second best to a restructuring of government.

I therefore recommend that the federal government:

7. (i) ***Study*** **the Supra-regional Council concept as a preferred alternative form of government to the present system, with special emphasis on the impact it may have on the NCC;**

(ii) ***Submit*** **this proposal for consideration and study to the Joint Parliamentary Committee of the Senate and the House of Commons when it is established;**

(iii) ***Invite*** **the views and reactions of all the provinces with respect to this proposal, and more particularly the views of Ontario and Québec.**

Should the Supra-regional concept of government for the Capital not be accepted, or be amended so as to destroy its essence (a genuine sharing of power in the governing of the Capital), I then would recommend that the federal government:

7. (iv) ***Develop*** **a more coordinated federal approach to local government in the Capital, which could involve such tactics as the tying of federal grants and the use of federal land more closely to precise federal objectives.**

(d) Federal Grants to Capital Municipalities

In our study of the application of the Municipal Grants Act to municipalities in the NCR (Chapter Ten), we concluded that a different approach was needed. The principal reason is the very important place of the federal government in the affairs of the Capital in contrast to its relatively limited role in other cities of Canada. The existence of the NCC and the large expenditures made by it, the special federal contributions to the amenities of the Capital including the National Arts Centre, the school tax problems arising out of the concentration of federal property and the regional dispersal of federal employees, all support the need for a new and distinctive approach.

These changes are required whether major changes in the local government structure, as proposed above, take place or not. I therefore recommend that the federal government:

8. ***Amend*** **the Municipal Grants Act to exclude municipalities in the NCR from receiving grants-in-lieu of taxes under its terms, but with the pro-**

vision that the present level of grants would continue until a new formula of grants for Capital municipalities is devised.

9. ***Instruct* the Department of Finance, in consultation with the NCC and Capital municipalities to develop a new grants formula which would take account of:**
   - **(i) the special needs of the Capital as the symbol of the nation;**
   - **(ii) the desirability of centralizing the grants through the two existing regional municipalities, rather than through a multitude of separate municipalities;**
   - **(iii) the factors which may affect the level and allocation of grants including other federal contributions to the Capital, the height of municipal taxes in the Capital in relation to other municipalities of comparable size in Canada, the division of school taxes on the basis of population rather than location of federal property, and the level of per capita expenditures of Capital municipal governments.**

10. ***Instruct* the Department of Finance and the NCC to study and report on the financial implications of the proposed Supra-regional Council, and in particular to consider methods of sharing costs and the tax burden among the three levels of government involved.**

(e) The National Capital Commission

My terms of reference included special instructions to consider the role of the NCC and its relations with other bodies. There has been a good deal of comment in this Study about the NCC and the problems it has been facing. However, in this aspect of the Study I have encountered two particular problems. One is that I have had no suggestions or recommendations from the NCC about its future role. If this has made my task more difficult, it is a posture which I can certainly understand, because it is linked closely to the second problem. How can anyone chart a clear course for the NCC until there are decisions taken about the future form of municipal government in the Capital? The recommendations about the NCC which follow therefore relate to the existing situation, with provision for study of the way the proposed Supra-regional Council would affect the Commission.

I recommend that the federal government:

11. ***Make* no changes at the present time in the powers and responsibilities of the Commission, or in its structure, apart from those proposed in the recommendations below, or those which the Commission itself may put forward.**

12. ***Change* the Minister through whom the Commission reports to Parliament from the Minister of State for Urban Affairs to the Prime Minister.**

13. ***Announce*** **to local municipalities and to government departments and agencies that the NCC is the coordinating agent for the federal government in the Capital on municipal matters, and that relations between these municipalities and the federal government should normally be carried out through the channel of the Commission.**

14. ***Announce*** **that the federal government will not lease privately owned office buildings, built following the date of the announcement, unless their design and height have been approved in advance by the NCC Design Committee.**

15. ***Give*** **to the NCC a right to challenge (i) existing use of federal land in the Capital, or (ii) federal policies that have a particular bearing on the planning or functioning of local government in the Capital, including such matters as parking policy.**

16. ***Instruct*** **the NCC and the Department of Public Works to form a study committee of senior officials, preferably with a neutral chairman from the Privy Council Office or Treasury Board, to consider and report on ways of resolving problems arising from overlapping jurisdiction and authority between the two bodies. Their report should consider** ***inter alia*** **the following:**

    (i) the centralizing in one or other body of the organizations of activities in the NCR now divided between them, such as property transactions, landscaping, and construction operations;

    (ii) proposals for coordinating the activities of the two organizations, including their amalgamation, or the setting up of a third and intermediate body which would encompass a number of activities of both bodies in the Capital, such as planning, property transactions, construction, architecture and design, leasing, landscaping, parks.

17. ***Instruct*** **the Commission to study and report on the implications for its future of the introduction of the proposed Supra-regional government.**

Comments

The proposal to have the NCC report directly to the Prime Minister is consistent with the difficulties faced by the NCC in carrying out its coordinating role in the Capital. These responsibilities cut across departmental boundaries, and to adjudicate the jurisdictional problems that inevitably arise, the NCC needs a minister with authority. The burden on the Prime Minister could be eased by assigning the supervisory responsibility to his Parliamentary secretary. Several recommendations are designed to remove ambiguity about the NCC's coordinating role in the Capital. The reasons for the recommendations to resolve existing jurisdictional issues between the NCC and the DPW was discussed at length in Chapter Nine, and include overlapping functions in a number of their operations. The recommendation to consider amalgation of their functions within the Region or the creation of an intermediate body, arises in part out of the Australian experience; in Canberra the federal National Capital Development Commission combines many of the present functions of the DPW and the NCC (and some of the CMHC)—planning, development, construction of office buildings and housing (municipal housekeeping functions in Canberra are the responsibility of another arm of the Australian federal government).

The final recommendation stems from the conclusion that the establishment of a Supra-regional government would require significant changes in the NCC, and possibly its disappearance in its present form. Certainly some existing planning functions of the NCC would be more appropriately dealt with by the staff of the new Council; so would responsibility for upkeep of certain federal property such as the parkway network. It follows that before any federal decisions are taken the NCC should have the opportunity to analyse the proposal thoroughly and consider its own position.

In summary, the change to the Supra-regional Council approach is not something to be considered lightly by the federal government. It means surrendering some of its present powers to a body it will not control. Yet the emphasis throughout this Study has been that little improvement in the structure of local government in the Capital can occur unless each level gives up certain of its powers. But even with a Supra-regional Council in place, there would clearly be a need for a federal agency like the NCC to carry out federal activities in the Capital which the government is either not prepared, or unable to delegate to the new Council. These might include the following responsibilities:

(i) Advising on policy relating to the new Supra-regional Council, with particular respect to planning decisions and financial grants, and to the problems of the transition period.

(ii) Carrying out liaison with other government departments in order to develop a coordinated federal position, particularly on land use and building plans and on other matters relating to the planning and development of the Capital.

(iii) Providing staff support on federal policy for federal members on Supra-regional Council.

(iv) Carrying out liaison with Supra-regional staff on federal plans.

(v) Performing various housekeeping functions such as landscaping of federal property, design control of federal buildings, and responsibility for Gatineau Park. These functions, however, could be carried out by the DPW or other federal departments, or might eventually be transferred to the new Supra-regional Council or to the municipalities under it.

(*f*) *Bilingualism*

The government has been deluged with comments, suggestions and criticism in respect of its bilingualism programme, and I will limit my recommendations to those which bear directly on the objectives of this Study. During the course of our interviews and in the letters, briefs, and comments we received, a number of fears were evident. On the Francophone side, they centred around the threat to language and culture posed by the "invasion" of the Outaouais region by large masses of Anglophones working in the new federal buildings in Hull, and by the small but rapidly growing number of Anglophones buying or renting homes on the Québec side. These fears have been reinforced by the continuing Francophone belief that progress towards bilingualism in the public service has been slow, and that a knowledge of English is still essential for Francophones working in the government.

The Anglophone concerns represent in part a backlash against the federal bilingualism programme, which is seen as seriously impeding the future of those unable to learn French or too old to make the effort worthwhile. In addition, there is a growing concern of Anglophones on the Québec side about their continuing right to educate their children in their own language, and about their minority position in a province where increasing emphasis is placed on the primacy of French.

These fears, if perhaps overblown, have a legitimate base. In my view, the more the federal government can do to allay the fears of both language groups the easier it will be to achieve a simpler, more coordinated form of government for the Capital. I therefore recommend that :

18. In moving departments or agencies to Hull, the federal government give priority to those which have a relatively high proportion of Francophones, and give particular consideration to the possibility of siting several national cultural institutions on the Québec side of the Region.

19. In its attempts to increase bilingualism in the public service, the federal government place more emphasis on the reading and comprehension of the other language, and less on the more difficult speaking and writing; this could lead more rapidly to a public service in which each group could work in its own language.

20. In any restructuring of government for the Region such as the proposed Supra-regional Council, the federal government support to the best of its ability

(i) the entrenchment of minority language rights

(ii) the provision of bilingual services within the Region at all levels of government

(iii) the right of parents to educate their children in the language of their choice

21. The federal government consult with Ontario and Quebec to consider steps which might be taken to meet the language and cultural needs of the Region, including:

(i) the measures outlined in recommendation 20 above;

(ii) **the feasibility of achieving a greater concentration of language groups in certain residential areas, to accommodate expressed needs;**

(iii) **special legislative and administrative measures for the National Capital Region to give substance to the recommendations of the Constitutional Conference of February, 1969, that the two official languages and the cultural values common to all Canadians be reflected in the area.**

(*g*) *Excessive Growth in the Capital*

The excessive recent rate of growth in federal employment in the Capital, has had serious consequences in terms of problems for the Region—sharply rising housing costs, higher municipal expenditures, and an adverse impact on planning by the government or by the municipalities. Coupled with this is the desirability of a wider display of the federal presence across the country. Despite the problems inherent in any decentralization programme, I therefore recommend that the federal government:

22. ***Accept* a policy of increased decentralization of its operations from the Capital, at least to the extent needed to bring about a marked slowing in the Capital's rate of growth, and**

23. ***Adopt* new measures to achieve decentralization, including a freeze or limits on annual expansion on manpower employed within the NCR by federal departments and agencies, accompanied by the acceptance of more rapid growth in federal employment outside the Region, but particularly in designated areas needing economic stimulus.**

(*h*) *Stimulation of Interest in the Capital*

The acceptance of the Capital as a national symbol will only grow as more Canadians learn about it from their reading, or at first hand from direct contact with it. One interesting suggestion I have adopted is designed to extend the work of NCC across the country, in order to make Canadians more aware both of the Capital and of the federal role in improving our cities. I commend it to the government for study along with several other measures. I therefore recommend that the federal government:

24. ***Subsidize* the wide distribution across Canada of books and material about the Capital and the work of Parliament, and visits to the Capital by groups of Canadians, in particular children of school-age.**

25. ***Consider* extending the work of the National Capital Commission to concentrations of federal property in major cities across Canada.**

II. *Recommendations to Governments of Ontario and Quebec*

Any restructuring of municipal government in the Capital must have the approval and support of Ontario and Quebec; my first recommendation is therefore to commend the Study to the two provinces for consideration. But whether or not a new form of Capital government emerges, there are a number of measures each province can take independently or jointly with the other, which relate to the Capital's special bilingual needs and emphasis, or which could reduce or eliminate many of the problems derived from its two-province location. These latter problems were reviewed at length in Chapter Thirteen.

(*a*) *Alternative Forms of Government for the Capital*

As emphasized throughout this Study, the National Capital Region has an essential unity, dependent on federal employment and expenditures as its economic driving force. The federal government has for a long time been involved in the Capital's affairs, and has influenced greatly its growth and development. It is unfortunate that its influence had to be exerted largely indirectly, through the planning process, the acquisition of land, and expenditures of federal funds, rather than through more direct participation in the governing process. However, with or without such participation, the federal government not only has a responsibility for ensuring that the Capital is appropriate to its national significance, but has at its disposal a considerable array of constitutional and legal authority and power to do what it believes necessary to meet this responsibility. In addition, our opinion survey has shown that there is a broad measure of support, from residents on both sides of the River, for federal involvement in the governing process.

I am fully aware of the support that both provinces have given to the development of a worthy national capital, but I must emphasize that the continuing ability of the Capital to develop as such a symbol will depend increasingly on the efficiency and effectiveness of its local government. In my judgment, this will require the three levels of government to participate in a single governing body for the Region. It is therefore in the interests of the two provinces and the local municipalities that the federal government be invited to share in the governing process: failure to do this will mean a continuation of the old system which has proved unsatisfactory in many ways.

I therefore recommend that Ontario and Québec

26. *Consider* both the analysis and recommendations contained in this Study, and discuss their conclusions with local municipalities and with the federal government. In these discussions emphasis should be given to the question of municipal amalgamation, and to the impact of the proposed Supra-regional Council on existing structures of local government.

(b) *National Capital Region — Recognition as Special Area*

I recommended that the federal government recognize the NCR as the Capital, and I propose similar action by the two provinces; they may wish to propose certain modifications in its boundaries.

I therefore recommend that Ontario and Québec:

27. *Recognize* the National Capital Region, with existing or modified boundaries, as the Capital of Canada, as a special area with national symbolic significance, and as such deserving of special consideration in terms of the applicability of provincial laws, policies and expenditures.

28. *Consider* such measures as might be taken independently or jointly to meet the special needs of the Capital, or to resolve the special problems of residents of a metropolis area divided by a provincial boundary, including:

(i) special facilities to provide education in the language of choice, the provision of bilingual services and signs across the Region, and the development of a bicultural climate appropriate to the National Capital and to the particular needs and objectives of the federal government;

(ii) reduction of inter-provincial disparities, with special attention to such measures as making all health services available to all Region residents, Region-wide acceptance of licensing of professional bodies or union certification by either province, and equalizing of pay levels, minimum wage standards, and sales tax;

(iii) improved coordination in municipal services that have inter-provincial implications such as planning, public transit, garbage disposal, and police and fire services.

III. Recommendation to NCR Municipalities

I recommend to municipalities in the National Capital Region that they:

29. *Consider* the analysis and recommendations contained in this Study, and discuss their conclusions with other local municipalities and with their provincial government.

IV. Recommendation to Residents of the National Capital Region

At the outset of this Study I said that a principal objective was to provide information for the public, as well as for the governments concerned, about the problems of governing the Capital. If the Study contributes to a much wider understanding of those problems by the people who live in the Capital, which they obtain from a reading of the Study or from the public discussions which I hope will follow, then I will be satisfied. I am convinced that such a public understanding of the problems will lead to correctional action by governments.

It is therefore to invite the help of residents in bringing about needed changes that my recommendation below is addressed. Among the major obstacles to establishing a new form of government for the Capital are institutional inertia and entrenched interests. Politicians understandably are reluctant to endorse structural changes in the institutions to which they have become accustomed, particularly if such changes are likely to diminish their own role or source of political power. But if the people who elect them want changes to occur, and want them badly enough to state their wishes loudly and insistently to their political leaders and to aspirants for office, then action will follow. In this sense then, the achievement of a new government for the Capital is very much in the hands of those who live in it.

I therefore recommend to the residents of the National Capital Region that individually, and collectively through community groups and other associations, they:

30. *Exert continuing pressure* on their political representatives to consider the issues raised in this Study, and, during every federal, provincial or municipal election campaign over the next few years, *demand* that those seeking office declare themselves on these issues, and on the conclusions and recommendations of this Study.

V. Recommendation to the Prime Minister and to His Successors

Anyone reading the history of this Capital cannot fail to note that new measures to bring about significant changes and improvements often stemmed from the particular interest in the Capital of the Prime Minister of the day. Naturally the extent of that interest has varied, but the progress recorded has been almost in direct proportion to each Prime Minister's commitment to and active involvement in the Capital's affairs. There is no doubt that Mackenzie King cared deeply, and many of the best things in the Capital to-day resulted from initiatives and decisions taken during this term of office. Yet almost every Prime Minister from Sir John A. MacDonald on down has done something at some stage in his career to make the Capital a better place and a worthier symbol of the country.

I suggest above that it is only with the active support of residents of the Capital that changes in its form of government will come about. I believe that change is almost equally dependent on the support of the head of the federal government. The demand from the people must find a response in leadership at the top. I therefore make this recommendation to the Prime Minister, and to those who follow him in office, that

31. he, and they, interest themselves actively in the Capital, in its form of government, in its beautification, and in its development as a unifying symbol for this country—a Capital to which all Canadians can feel drawn with affection and respect.

Index

Page references cover Study only, but some general reference is made to the Appendices.